broken broken broken broken broken broken
broken broken broken broken broken broken
broken broken broken broken broken broken
broken broken broken broken broken broken
broken broken broken broken broken broken
broken broken broken broken broken broken
broken broken broken broken broken broken
broken broken broken broken broken broken
broken broken broken broken broken broken
broken broken broken broken broken broken
broken broken broken broken broken broken
broken broken broken broken broken broken
broken broken broken broken broken broken
broken broken broken broken broken broken
broken broken broken broken broken broken
broken broken broken broken broken broken
broken broken broken broken broken broken
broken broken broken broken broken broken
broken broken broken broken broken **FIXED**

ROZ WESTON

A LITTLE BIT
BROKEN

A MEMOIR

ANCHOR CANADA

Anchor Canada paperback published 2023
Doubleday Canada hardcover published 2022

Library and Archives Canada Cataloguing in Publication

Title: A little bit broken / Roz Weston.
Names: Weston, Roz, author.
Identifiers: Canadiana 20220234310 | ISBN 9780385663304 (softcover)
Subjects: LCSH: Weston, Roz. | LCSH: Radio personalities—Canada—Biography. | LCSH: Television personalities—Canada—Biography. | LCSH: Weston, Roz—Health. | LCSH: Weston, Roz—Mental health. | LCGFT: Autobiographies.
Classification: LCC PN1991.4.W47 A3 2023 | DDC 791.44092—dc23

Cover design by Roz Weston
Cover photograph © Katherine Holland Photography

Printed in the United States of America

Published in Canada by Anchor Canada,
a division of Penguin Random House Canada Limited,
a Penguin Random House company

www.penguinrandomhouse.ca

10 9 8 7 6 5 4 3 2 1

Penguin
Random House
ANCHOR CANADA

For Katherine. Everything that matters. Everything that shines.

pg. three twenty one.

CONTENTS

INTRo
A BIC PEN
AND A ZIPPO 1

INTRO
A BIC PEN AND A ZIPPO

It never gets better, but it does get easier. That's the first thing I say to anyone who asks me for advice when they've lost someone. I say the same thing to anyone who's lost themselves. Anyone who's fighting like hell, or hanging on, or putting the pieces back together. It never gets *better*, but it *does* get easier. I should know.

Grief, self-doubt, crippling anxiety. Drowning the parts that hurt and burning the parts that don't. It gets easier. Managing shame, regret, and insecurity. It gets easier. All of it.

Broken and *fixed* aren't words we're supposed to use to describe people. When you deliberately stop counting time because you never want to know the exact day you've lived more life without someone than you did while they were alive—*that's* what broken feels like. When doctors lie and tell you there's no chance you can become addicted, but you do. When you're molested in a closet when you're nine, or when you almost destroy yourself with diet pills because one person said something shitty about your body so you try to prove them wrong. When your hands hurt like hell, but you still manage to fight through another day. When normal seems unattainable. On all these days, broken is all you feel.

When your marriage fails, you lose your job, and your dad is dying in front of your eyes, but you pretend he isn't. When you can't stop wondering if you fathered a child while you were still a child yourself. When you fail at therapy, and when every step you take comes with a decision: move forward or step back to avoid another cloud? When you're broken, *fixed* becomes an obsession.

It never gets better, but it does get easier.

Anyone who knows me knows two things to be true. The first: I'm pretty damn good at giving advice. The second: I'm absolute shit at taking it. That said, I want to be straight up here: this is *not* a how-to manual. This isn't a book about self-improvement, reflection, or *finding your light*. This is for anyone who isn't ready to give up, who still has a lot of fight left in them: it's about survival and overcoming bad choices.

Let's face it, the reason we make bad choices is because bad choices usually feel *really* good. And I've made them all. But this isn't a meme or another inspiring Instagram post. This isn't about speaking your truth; it's about *facing* the truth.

Every day, I stand on set of a TV show, as a face of one of the most recognizable brands in show business, while privately fighting and hiding Tourette syndrome, a disorder that causes involuntary tics all over my body. That's been my life for almost twenty years on *Entertainment Tonight Canada*.

Tourette's isn't the clucking and shouting profanities at strangers that you may have seen on TV, or heard someone use as the punchline to a joke. It's often much more subtle. I grew out of my very mild vocal tics when I was still a kid. I'd hum, or clear my throat or mimic sounds other people made around me. It was never a big deal or very noticeable. My tics have always been sudden, repetitive, and unwanted movements or "flinches." Mostly in my face, my neck, and my eyes. Especially in my eyes.

Tics lead to everything from minor discomfort to debilitating pain. For most of my adult life I've managed my tics publicly by masking them. I was a chain-smoker because taking a drag off a Marlboro Light 100 allowed me to contort my face in a social setting and release a tic while doing it. Sometimes I could get two or three out per haul. When I couldn't smoke, I'd chew gum. Inside, I'd wear sunglasses if I was having a particularly bad eye tic or eye roll.

I've figured out ways to hide tics in every social situation. But I'm on television. Most days I stand on set and I'm in hell. It's a fight, an actual battle between my mind, my body, and the teleprompter. My brain says go left, even though I know right is the only direction that doesn't lead off a cliff. That's what Tourette syndrome feels like—a cartoon devil on my shoulder whispering *Do it. Do it.* There's a red light on the camera, which in most cases means I'm on. That red light is the dream for a performer. That red light means I'm live, I'm on TV, I'm in your home, on your phone, and on your mind. But to me, that red light also means something else. It's danger. That's when I have to hide what's really going on.

Covering up my tics on television is one thing, but not being honest about them while hosting one of the most popular radio shows in the country is another. In 2009, with no clue what I was doing, I found the perfect partner and built that show. From scratch. We started at zero, and now *The Roz & Mocha Show* is syndicated across the country with a million listeners and downloads every month. It's a success story. But how we judge success is subjective, it's personal. In radio, when you do it right, fame isn't the goal. When you're truly successful and build an audience, you don't become famous. You become family.

I've built my fan base by splitting myself open every morning and pouring out all the good parts. But like with most families, there's some shit we just don't talk about.

Tourette's isn't even the half of it. Panic attacks, addiction, denial, jealousy, abandonment, terrifying feelings of worthlessness, and an overwhelming sense of my inevitable failure . . . I've struggled with it all. My best days were measured by how well I could fool people into thinking I was fine. But for years I thought I was ruined. I'd fight for incredible opportunities, knowing full well the only way they could fail is if I fucked it all up. Then I'd do my best to do just that—burn it all down. I was self-destructive and terrified. But I wasn't ruined. I was just a little bit broken.

So, this is it. A deeply personal, honest, and hopefully inspiring account of my life. From getting lost, drunk, and terrified in New York while interning for Howard Stern, to offering myself up to, and finding comfort in, the arms and beds of strangers while flunking out of college. It's about broken bones, broken hearts, and a broken marriage. It's about the opioid addiction that I didn't know I had after ending up in the hospital with two collapsed lungs.

All of it. From hitting rock bottom and finding purpose, to embracing vulnerability and healing. It's about betting on myself and falling in love. It's about Katherine, who never looked at me like a project. She never tried to change me; she just finished me. She's proud of me, which is something I lost and missed the most when my dad died. She's the pin that holds this entire grenade together. This is the complete rewrite of where I thought my life would take me. It's about becoming a dad and learning how to cry again.

This book is the whole story I've never shared before—everything you see and everything you've never seen. This is the shit we don't talk about.

Welcome to the family.

—

We don't fix things anymore. We replace them. I think about that a ton. I'm obsessed with it.

I was always rough on my toys. Hell, I'm still rough on my toys. When I was around eight, I broke the arm off Cobra Commander, the most badass G.I. Joe action figure there ever was. In my world, in the epic battles I created that took over our whole basement, he never lost. Action figures weren't something my parents got me on a regular basis. They were a Christmas, birthday, or good-report-card kind of gift. So that day, when I heard that snap and watched his arm fly off and land on the shag rug, I was devastated. I was disappointed in myself and worried my dad would be disappointed in me too. When I placed Cobra Commander, battle worn and in two pieces, in my dad's hand, I was at a loss.

My Pops had big, hard hands. They were rough and scarred, always smelled like cigarettes, and his fingernails were bitten down so low they looked like they were made of wood. He bit them until they bled. When they bled, he'd stop, but never before. But those hands could fix anything. Don't get me wrong—my old man wasn't a technical wizard or particularly artistic, and detail was never a priority. But he fixed things. No matter what you handed him, no matter what shape it was in, he'd fix it. It wouldn't be perfect, but it would work.

When I was finally old enough to carry a wallet, I remember loading it up with all my kid things: my library card, my mom's real estate business card, and my student card. But my birth certificate didn't fit. It was a bit bigger than a credit card and laminated with hard plastic that stuck off both sides. No matter how hard I tried to shimmy it into one of the little fake leather slots, it wasn't getting in there. As I struggled, my dad waved me over, put out one of those hands of his, and said, "Here."

I handed it to him, and in two smooth cuts he sliced the plastic sides right off with a pair of kitchen scissors, handed it back to me, and said, "There."

That's how he fixed things. He never thought twice about it, because he certainly wasn't about to throw away a whole wallet because *one* thing didn't fit. I carried that birth certificate around for years in that same wallet, like it was no big deal. Until the day I had to apply for a passport. They took one look at it, with the sides sliced off, and rejected it immediately because it looked tampered with. Of course it did. Because it was! I eventually got a new birth certificate that I now keep safe, but I still carry the old one around with me, in that same wallet where I also keep the last hospital bracelet my dad was wearing when he died.

That day when I handed Cobra Commander over, I remember saying, "It's ruined," to which he answered, "Nah, it's not ruined. It's just a little bit broken. Nothing we can't fix."

Ten minutes later he handed him back to me with *both* arms, and said, "There." The fixed arm was a little wonky now and sat a bit longer than the other one. It was melted back on with a piece of the cap off a blue Bic pen he torched with his Zippo. It wasn't perfect, it was never perfect, but it was fixed. That's what he did: he'd figure out what was broken and he'd find a way to make it work again. Nothing was ever ruined for him. Everything got a second chance. Even if that thing was me.

If I was stressed, worried, confused, frustrated, or afraid, he'd fix that too. Sometimes with compassion or the blunt truth, other times with a hug. My old man knew the healing power of a good hug. He also knew when to shut up just long enough for me to finally ask for help.

—

Every day on the radio, I throw out advice. In heaps. To people who are lost, or warring with their partner or with themselves. People who are rebuilding, starting over, or trying not to fail. People going through breakups, chemo, divorce, first love. One of the things I always tell people is to write it all down. Take every thought, memory, moment of pain, joy, or confusion and just write it all down. All of it. I've never done this myself. Until now.

I've never kept a journal. I've never wanted to chronicle my past, and the few poems, song lyrics, or unsent love letters I've written over the years were torn up, lost, or thrown out. Reliving emotion hasn't ever been something I'm comfortable with. Humour has always been my escape, and I always say the worst my day ever gets, I get to laugh. That's true. That's my life today. That's not bullshit.

But what if you love your life but you're terrified of your past?

What if you love your laugh but hate your body?

What if every day is a fight?

We *all* hide things; some of us are just better at it than others. I've become an expert in hiding things, but the thought of shame, judgment, or embarrassment doesn't bother me anymore.

This book is me trying to shine a light on the memories I've shut down or blacked out. The time I've lost. I'm filling those holes. My mother always told me: Never ask a question you don't want to hear the answer to. Well, this is me finally finding the answers to the questions I was too afraid to ask.

This is also for *you*. The late bloomers and the *others*. The self-doubters, and anyone who's still picking up the pieces. Anyone who thinks they're too far gone or beyond repair. Anyone who's ever felt broken or ruined. Anyone too ashamed to admit to or face the hurt because their current place in the world seems too goddamn good to complain about anything. That's us. We hide it or deny it and carry on. We're the same.

But it's nothing we can't fix.

WHAT
MATTERED
MOST

READ THIS WHEN I'M DEAD

What do you do when you're left with nothing? When my dad died, the house that my parents owned was not a house I'd ever lived in. It was in Acton, the small town I grew up in, which at the time had just shy of ten thousand people. This town is where most of my childhood happened. Two factories, an old flour mill, one stop light, and just enough of nothing to get you into trouble. That was Acton.

My parents had moved three or four times since I'd left, so I didn't have a lot of memories of my dad in that particular house. It was a small '70s-style three-bedroom townhouse that backed onto a graveyard. We'd had one or two Christmases together there, which was always Dad's favourite time of year, so that's what I remembered.

He loved turkey, and laughing, and having his boys home for the holidays. But there wasn't a lot of Pop in that space. He wasn't the sort of guy who owned a lot of sentimental things. He had a chessboard that he'd picked up in Mexico decades before, but other than that he didn't have anything he was overly emotional about.

Although I didn't know it at the time, on the day I went to that house that I barely knew, after my dad died, to help my mom clear out his stuff, I was looking for something, anything, to make me feel like he wasn't gone.

I don't remember a ton from that day, but I do remember it was hot as hell out when my brother and I got there. The air conditioning was on in the family room where my parents had spent most of their time in front of the TV, but it only cooled the one room. I remember looking around and thinking their tiny living room felt huge. There was this void now, an emptiness that Pops would normally occupy. My dad wasn't a big guy, but his laugh filled any room that was lucky enough to have him.

My mom said, "Why don't you and your brother go upstairs and see if there's anything there that you want?" It was painful to hear her say it, a sharp reminder that Dad wasn't coming back, but we nodded and headed up to their bedroom, even though the idea of going upstairs and spending even one minute in an airless room sorting through my dad's stuff sounded like a nightmare. My brother was quiet. I'm sure he felt the exact same way I did. We've still never talked about that day.

As I walked past the room my Pop had turned into a makeshift arcade, I was thinking to myself: *What if I find something amazing? What if my mom knows he's left something for us? Is that why she sent us up here?* He had been fighting cancer for a year, so it didn't seem totally unlikely.

In the room was a modest-size two-door closet full of clothes left in piles. There were old stereo cables and a couple of books that didn't look like he'd ever read them. There was car stuff, and a manual for a PlayStation. I started to dig through a box of old receipts, hoping to find a bag, a binder, or an envelope—anything that simply read: **Read This When I'm Dead**. Something where he would have written down all his thoughts and philosophies to carry over into my life. I wanted something that was from his past, something that was the truth. I wanted advice and answers to questions I hadn't even thought of yet.

I wanted *him*.

My dad was different from the other dads I knew. He was charming, charismatic, a recovering alcoholic. He was American, and he'd done two tours in Vietnam. He had scars and secrets. These stuck out in our small town, where everyone was all up in each other's business. Growing up in a small town, you get that kind of sameness, but my old man was different. He had an unrelatable history, and this unattainable cool that was tough as hell to figure out. Throughout my childhood Dad did have a few *close* friends, but aside from me and my brother, I don't remember him ever having a *best* friend. Not anyone he ever fully opened up to, anyway.

I don't know why, but my parents loved moving. They didn't want to settle, so we probably lived in seven or eight different houses in that little town, not including one horrid year they thought we'd be better off living in a sprawling suburb just outside of Toronto. My brother and I both had a hard time adjusting that year, so our parents bought us *waterbeds*? We still call that one the Waterbed House. But for our family, it was never about a house. It was always about us. Us against everything.

My mom worked, so my brother and I were typical '80s latch-key kids. My parents would get back into town around 6 p.m., they'd stop for coffee on the way, and then, as a family, we'd eat around eight. Dinner was pretty low maintenance, but always delicious. We'd crush hot hamburger sandwiches, which were toasted white bread with a hamburger patty and gravy, with mashed potatoes on the side, and we'd eat the whole thing with a fork and knife.

Or my mom would make spaghetti, and we'd eat the leftover sauce for days out of a giant pot that took up an entire shelf in the fridge.

We never ate alone; we always ate as a family. And we never ate and ran. It wasn't that we weren't allowed; we just didn't want to. This was always the best part of my day. Dinner lasted for hours, and it felt like a really safe space. There were no rules about swearing at the dinner table, and the dinner table is where I told my parents, while I was still in junior high, that I'd lost my virginity. The stories we shared over dinner were never talked about outside of that kitchen. Some things would carry over from one night to the next, but you never got grilled on a Saturday morning about something you'd said at dinner the night before. It was cool like that.

There was nothing my dad loved more than listening to his boys ramble on. He loved kid stories. He loved our drama, he answered our questions, he'd laugh when one of us would take a sip through a straw with our nose. My dad didn't have any of those moments when he was a kid. *His* stories were alarming and astonishing. He had a childhood so bad it barely sounded real to me.

His parents were drunks. They treated him with a mix of neglect and violence. Hell, he was so unwanted they left him at a gas station when he was a kid and just continued on with their road trip—just straight up left him there. That was normal. That was his childhood. At some point after he turned eighteen his best option in life was to join the Marines and escape. Vietnam was a better option than living at home.

He told us about the war, but like most vets who came back from Nam, Pop's stories were never full or complete. Instead, they'd evolve over the years as we got older. When he thought we could handle more, he'd tell us more. He never talked about PTSD— shell shock, as they called it then—and he never talked about Nam in any way that would come off as proud. My dad was the only person I've ever known who had killed someone. He'd always say, "Nobody likes war, but some people need to know how to fight." My dad was a fighter. I'm not sure where he put all the nightmares, but before my brother and I were born he dealt with them the way a lot of vets did. He drank. But at some point, he flipped the script, he made a commitment to be the first father in his family to not raise his kids with the back of a hand or the bottom of a bottle. My dad was the least violent person I've ever known. That was *not* the man my mom married. She got the other one.

The story of how my parents met and fell in love was told to me as a grand romantic tale. It shaped my view of romance; it was the first "true love" story I'd ever heard.

My dad served more than his fair share in Nam, and after two tours and facing a forced third, he went awol while on leave in California and took off to Montreal. The first thing my dad did when he landed was pack up his uniform, boots, hat, gloves, and anything else that identified him as a marine and send it to the Marine Corps Recruiting Station in Buffalo, New York, in a garbage bag. He kept his medals, but everything else went. To him, it was all garbage.

The second thing he did was find a place to live. This happened to be the same old Montreal duplex where my mom was living. At this point, in the late '60s, my mom was modelling part-time and singing in a mod band called Us and the Other Guys on weekends. She was also *very* much engaged. I don't know what my parents' first date was like, or how long their affair lasted, but I do know they fell incredibly hard for each other immediately. My dad always said, "First I fell in love with her chili, then I fell in love with her." Even then my mom cooked with her whole heart, and this was probably the first time my dad had ever eaten anything that was made with love.

My mom's fiancé was a guy named Cliff, and they all hung out. All three of them. Until they didn't. One dark, cold Montreal night my dad, Ralph Arnold Weston, took Cliff Something Something for a walk around the block where my dad calmly but bluntly said, "I'm going to be straight with you. You're with Diane, but I'm in love with her. I'm going to marry her. You have until we get to the front door to decide whether you want to do this the easy way or the hard way, but when we get to that apartment, you're going to take your ring back." Cliff knew what the hard way looked like. So, he walked right upstairs and took his ring back, and that was it.

For me, that was romance. That was my foundational understanding of how love could be found. Love over everything. Even if it had to be the hard way.

I don't tell that story anymore because, really, it hasn't aged well. It doesn't make you feel good, and frankly most people would find it horrifying. Most people would see it as toxic, chest-thumping bullshit, or they'd see my mom as some sort of victim or prize. The main reason I don't tell this story anymore is because I'd be heartbroken if anyone thought of my dad as anything other than gentle and kind. This version of him wasn't the guy who raised my brother and me. This was a young man whose entire life and place in the world had been shaped by violence. That was all he knew. Yet this story was told to me as romantic, because for them it *was*.

As we sat around the dinner table talking late into the nights, I'd look for that person, the man he used to be, that man who had no problem with the hard way, the man who proposed to my mom, the version of my dad who was confrontational, violent, and drunk.

I *never* saw him. During those years when my parents first met, he was a heavy, almost professional alcoholic, drinking hundreds of dollars a week in booze. One year, after my brother was born, for my mom's birthday my dad checked himself into rehab, and he never drank again. That was his gift. That was the sort of man my father was: committed, focused, present.

In my early childhood there was the dad of the stories, and there was the dad I saw every day, a gentle man—kind, wise, funny. My love of storytelling is rooted in those family dinners, forkloads of hot hamburger sandwiches, the truth evolving and shifting, and us all laughing until it hurt.

The year before junior high, I started hanging out with Andy, this kid who lived four doors down from us. Our parents were casual friends, but they always pushed for the two of us to hang out. Andy and I didn't have a ton in common, but his dad was a doctor, so he had way cooler toys than I did. They had a boat, and would vacation in Florida, but he'd still cry and complain about everything. For the most part Andy was a horrible friend. However, his dad did have the most incredible collection of nudie magazines I'd ever seen. Nothing domestic—these were all foreign, high-end, and hard to get. And there was a ton of them. Desperate for friends, and with a deep love for showing off, Andy created a club called The Bushmen: something he was in charge of. He had the porno; he had the power. The club started with the two of us before he recruited a third, a kid named Jake who had a leather jacket and a better moustache than kids twice our age.

Every day after school, Andy stuffed an Adidas bag full of the doctor's porno, always remembering the order they were stacked in so they could be put back into the sock drawer the same way, and we'd head out to Killer's Hill. Killer's Hill was this insanely steep drop-off at the end of a dead-end road made up of landfill, rocks, and old tree stumps. It was littered with broken beer bottles and scrap metal. Killer's Hill wasn't built for kids so *of course* this was where most dares took place, because, really, if you didn't almost die was it even fun? We'd throw ourselves down that thing on bikes, toboggans, or on each other—piggyback-style— screaming like maniacs as we raced barefoot to the bottom. Every single thing on the way down wanted to hurt you, and it often did. We'd hose off the mud and blood before heading home and then try like hell to convince our mothers we were fine. This rarely worked. Killer's Hill was responsible for more trips to the doctor than anywhere else in town, and we loved it. Andy was never interested in getting dirty or hurt, so when he was around, we'd sit on rocks, up at the top, and just flip through the pages of his dad's magazines. Very carefully. Although we were a group while we sat there, this was an individual exercise. Nobody got too close or made it (more) weird, and we barely spoke. To be honest, other than a shared love for doctor-grade pornography, none of us really had anything in common.

One day, Jake convinced Andy to leave the stack of mags at Killer's Hill while Andy and I went home for dinner. Andy, pathetic and, *again*, desperate to be liked, agreed. While I was at home and my mom was still cooking, I remember hearing this sound. It started small and then exploded. A torrential downpour! It rained more in those forty-five minutes than I've ever seen. I remember my mom looking out the window saying, "Roz, did you put your bike in the garage?"

"Yeah, Ma," I answered.

What she should have asked was: "Roz, do you trust that Jake kid enough to hide the doctor's smut rags to make sure they don't get ruined?"

"No," I would have answered. "Absolutely fuckin' not."

At some point after his dinner but before bed, Andy snuck out and went looking for the magazines. I'm sure he hoped they'd all be stacked back up in that Adidas bag and placed safely under a tree. They weren't. They were soaked to the point that the pages no longer existed. As a kid, and in a situation like this, you have very few options, but Andy panicked and snuck the wet stack back into the house while the doctor was in the bath. He piled them back up in the same way that he'd found them in the sock drawer and hoped for the best.

The best did *not* happen.

It took about a minute for Andy to rat me out to his dad and in the amount of time it took to walk past four houses the doctor was ringing our doorbell. Standing out of sight at the top of the stairs, I died a little as he stood there telling Pops what we'd done. It could have been the rain, but I swear the doctor had tears in his eyes. When Dad closed the door, he turned casually and walked up the stairs. He got about halfway up before he saw me. He stopped and looked me straight in my face to ask, "Were you guys into the doctor's things?"

"Yeah. I'm sorry, Pop," I said.

"Don't do it again."

That was the end of it. When I got to school the next day, I was the only kid who hadn't had the shit beat out of him by an angry father. Andy said that while his dad was kicking his ass, he kept telling him, "If you think this is bad, just imagine what Roz's dad is doing to him." As I stood there, feeling guilty as hell, Andy asked me how bad I got it.

"Brutal," I replied.

That day I missed gym and walked with a fake limp until the bus came. I don't carry a lot of regret with me, but selling my dad out like that still haunts me. It turns out that I was the pathetic one who just wanted to fit in. I hate that I did that to him.

I always knew my dad got shot. It was no secret. He had this round scar on his arm that didn't grow any hair. The skin was shiny and didn't look like it belonged there. When my brother and I were younger, he said it was an accident, that his gun went off when he was cleaning it. That was another one of the stories that changed over the years.

As a kid, my dad's war stories were cool. He'd go into detail about what snake tasted like, and how it would rain so hard in the jungle you could fill your helmet every five minutes if you turned it upside down. He taught us how to build fires, and how to camp, and to this day I still know that the key to surviving in the bush is to always keep your feet dry. *Always* keep your feet dry. As I got older, the stories changed. It wasn't an accident while cleaning his rifle; he was shot during combat. And that scar? The reason it looked so bad, he said, was because they took a small, round piece of skin off the very back of his hip, slapped it on top of the hole in his arm, loosely sewed the patch on, and pulled it tight like a change purse. Then they sliced off the skin that was sticking up off the top of it, wrapped it, and sent him back out there. He'd always say, "If you think *that* piece of skin is shiny, you should see the rest of my ass."

I remember walking through the dining room one evening, in my early high school years, on my way to the family room when I passed Dad sitting there, in his chair at the head of the table, with a handgun. He had two or three layers of newspaper spread out, and the gun was in pieces perfectly arranged in front of him, but I knew what I was looking at. I also knew he did *not* own a hand-gun. "Where'd you get the gun, Pops?" I asked him.

"From someone who shouldn't have had it." End of story.

My life with my dad was ever evolving. As I grew up, his stories constantly changed. It was one of the most fascinating things about him. It taught me just how important our stories are. They're foundational, and like our own DNA, our stories make us, us. Our stories create our world and carve out our place in it. Pops taught me always to tell the truth, but it didn't necessarily have to be the *whole* truth. At least not all at once.

Years later, on that hot, humid day in my parents' closet searching for something from my dad, the July heat just kept getting more brutal. My brother and I sat, each doing our own thing. Sweaty, sad, absorbed in our own heads, and lost in our memories. This is when I realized that what I was looking for didn't exist. There was no **Read This When I'm Dead**. No book or diary, no letter or card. No magical thing to bring my dad back. There was just a closet full of stuff, but not *enough* stuff to put him back together and take him with me. We loaded up a few boxes and helped my mom clean up. Everything else was garbage.

My brother took Dad's old pipe collection. It was a handcrafted, six-pipe wooden stand with a container off to one side that still smelled like Rum Raisin tobacco. He still has that on a shelf today.

I took one of Dad's old cardigans. It was generic. Light brown scratchy wool with faux suede trim and elbow patches. It wasn't his favourite, it wasn't a gift, and it had zero sentimental value. It wasn't special, but it *was* his. I asked Mom if I could have it. She said, "You can have anything you want."

"This is it," I told her. "This is all I want."

—

When you look through my world now, or my house, there isn't a lot of my dad in it. I have his cardigan in my closet, on the last hanger on the left, and it's never moved from that spot. There are hardly any pictures of him—good cameras were too expensive back then, and the cheap one we did have was always hidden away in his sock drawer. I have two framed shots of my dad: in one he's in his late teens or early twenties, in Nam. He's wearing his Marine-issue green combat pants and a Marine-issue thin white T-shirt, with Marine-issue bandages covering up the Marine-issue hole in his arm from a Vietnamese-issued bullet. He's smiling—looks happy. This was the kind of photo other soldiers took to send home to their families. My dad came home with his picture stuffed in the bottom of his own duffle bag. In the other one, he's a little kid wearing a suit and a tie, with his big ears sticking out. He had no idea.

My kid, Roxy, sees those pictures of him, but she never got to know him. Now I'm a dad myself, I don't have anyone to turn to. There's nothing my dad loved more than being a dad, and for the first time in the history of his side of the family, he was goddamn good at it. He died before I could ask how to do it—how *he* did it. I wish he had mapped it all out for me, from the heart and in whatever way he felt comfortable. It didn't have to be a book. Hell, it didn't even have to be typed or coherent. I would have taken his morphine-induced ramblings in his final days. I wanted him to tell me what I was supposed to do. I've never really planned for the future. I didn't have a vision board, and I didn't set goals or write checklists of things I wanted to accomplish at certain points in my life or career. I chased opportunity and made damn sure I was ready for it when it came. I lived for daily indulgences, quick deadlines, and fresh starts, with a willingness to walk away when things weren't going my way. To rip it up and start again.

—

Since we had Roxy, my focus has shifted from moving forward to looking back. Not obsessing about my past, but always keeping half an eye on what I left behind. To be honest, although I do leave a pretty huge footprint through the radio and TV show, thousands of minutes of YouTube vids, and months' worth of podcasts, so much of that's not me. Not who I really am. There's so much that I've never talked about, which is the reason I'm writing this book now. I'm leaving footprints for my kid, so she has a path to follow.

I'm writing the thing that I wish my dad wrote for me.

HOW
TO
FIGHT

My dad always used to say, "The best way to avoid getting punched in the mouth is to just never *do* or *say* anything that'll get you punched in the mouth." That was solid advice that I always followed, but some days I felt like an actual shit magnet. Trouble just followed me. No matter how much I kept to myself, minding my own business, not looking at anyone else's girlfriend, someone always wanted to kick my ass.

Acton was a tough town. Everyone fought. You'd fight your own friends, for no real reason at all. Hell, I even saw a fight at a wedding one time. Growing up, I knew exactly how hard every girl I went to school with hit. That's just the way it was: you'd say something shitty and you'd get hit. Sometimes in the back, or the chest, or the shoulder, or the side of the neck if they missed. The girls I grew up with hit fucking hard. They had to. It was a wild and violent place. But nobody ever held a grudge. None of it ever meant anything. By the time I was sixteen, I'd had my hand rebuilt twice. My baby finger on my right hand still has no knuckle, sits too much off to the side, and is about a half inch shorter than my left. It's hard to notice, but if anyone ever does and asks what happened, my answer is always the same: stupidity. That's all it was. Every broken bone and scar was the direct result of something stupid.

Fighting with my friends was never the problem. The real trouble happened any time I left town. Because I was so much taller than everyone else, and looking the way I did, people just wanted to hurt me. But these weren't ever kids. These were men. Grown men who, because I was six feet tall at thirteen years old, thought it would be a fair fight. It never was because I was a child. Junior high in the '80s was a different place than it is now. Fights were a weekly thing, sometimes planned out days in advance. Usually between two friends, just off school property, and always over something stupid.

In seventh grade I went to school with this one kid, Dale, who was so much smaller than everyone else. Word got out that there was going to be a fight after school, and that Todd, who was in grade eight, was really hot to kick Dale's ass. When these fights were about to happen, we all found out through whispers and rumours. There was no texting. Every now and then one of these fight rumours would make its way to a teacher and they'd handle it whatever way they could, which at the time was, at best, pathetic. That day, our homeroom teacher stopped me and my friend Jason in the hallway after third-period gym. Jason was tall too, but not nearly as skinny as I was, so he looked bigger. Our teacher backed us up against the lockers, got right in our faces, and asked, "What's going on with Dale?"

"Nothing," I said. Jason said the same. "Nothing. No idea." We were *not* narcs.

"Listen, I know that Todd wants to fight Dale," our teacher said. "That can't happen. I need you guys to make sure he doesn't get ahold of him." And that was that. Instead of calling a parent or getting the principal involved, that teacher just found the two biggest seventh graders he could find and deputized us. This was normal life in junior high.

Another hot afternoon right before the end of the school year, a massive crowd—kids from three different schools—gathered outside. In that part of town, just off Acton Boulevard, there was one corner that funnelled all the primary kids, the kids from my school, and everyone from the high school up the street. Everyone knew there was going to be a fight. My fight. That afternoon I stayed inside the school while most of the other kids left to join the crowd. I didn't want to go out to fight another friend over something stupid, and I certainly didn't want to lose a fight in front of high school girls. I remember standing inside the side doors by the gym when the woodshop teacher walked up to me, looked at the crowd outside, and asked, "Are you okay?"

"Yeah," I said.

He looked at me again, then out the window again, then put his hand on my shoulder, opened the door, and said, "Good luck," sending me out to fight in front of a hundred people. I was never great at asking for help, but that was one of many times in my life where I shouldn't have had to. He knew I was about to get hurt and he let it happen. In front of high school girls.

The fights never lasted long, and besides a broken hand, black eye, or split lip, there was no real permanent damage. The real damage, the stuff that actually hurts, never happens on a street corner at 3:30 p.m. It happens in a closet with someone you trust.

—

When I was about nine, my mom and I went over to our family friends' house. Their son was a little older than my brother, probably fifteen or sixteen at the time. Man, he was cool. I idolized him. He was never bothered if I wanted to hang out. We didn't have anything in common, but if you asked me then, I would have told you we were friends. Proudly. He was everything I wanted to be when I got to that age. He had girlfriends, guitars, and a pin-straight mullet.

That day when my mom and I were there, he and his family had just moved into a new place, so there wasn't much in it yet. There wasn't any art on the walls, the TV wasn't hooked up, and there was nothing for a kid my age to really do—so I hung out with him. At some point after running up and down their huge staircase chasing each other, and him giving me the grand tour, we wound up in his room, in his closet, out of breath and laughing. I don't remember exactly what he said to get me in there, but that didn't matter. I would never have said no. This was alone time with someone I idolized. Out of all the things he could have been doing that day, he wanted to spend time with me.

He was lying down and took his shirt off because, he said, he was hot. His closet wasn't big enough for both of us to lie down, so I sat beside him, running my fingers through the plush carpet. I had never felt carpet so soft before. It was freshly shampooed and still had the lines running back and forth across it from an industrial vacuum. He started talking about girls, and his girl-friends, and what women like. How to kiss them, what fingering felt like, what turns them on. I didn't know what any of it really meant, but I knew what sex was, and I was fascinated.

"If you want to make a girl horny, tickle her here," he said. "Like this." He put his hand around my small wrist and ran my middle and ring finger up from the top of his jeans to his nipple.

ROZ WESTON

He circled both, back and forth, and told me about how girls have bigger nipples, and that they love this. Then he slid my hand down so I was now tickling his stomach.

"Do it like that," he said, as he let my wrist go so I could do it all on my own. Then he opened his pants. I didn't know what was happening, but to be honest, I don't remember caring. He started playing with himself and then he took my hand and put it underneath where his was. Now we were both rubbing him. Together. I don't remember much after that. I don't remember if he finished or what we did next, but at some point we were both back downstairs like nothing happened.

At the time, I remembered it happening. I remember wondering if I was any good, and how I couldn't wait to try these techniques on girls for myself. I wondered if my dick would ever get as big as his. But I never thought about it as something that happened *to* me. It was always an experience, or more of a feeling. I distanced myself from it, like any other vague kid memory that you couldn't explain at the time. Over the years this felt more like a story that was told to me, rather than one in which I starred. I separated that story into two people: the person it happened to, and me. I was almost thirty when it hit me: I always remembered that day happening, but then, for the first time in my life, I realized it *shouldn't* have. I realized how closely that one day was tied to so many choices I'd made for the next twenty years. How that moment in a closet with someone who I thought was great affected so many things in my life. I thought about how I remembered things, blurring out pain and blacking out the rest. How I struggle to trust other people and why it's still hard as hell to trust even myself.

I learned to push feelings and fear deep inside. I learned to try to make myself smaller. Even today, I want an audience but, weirdly, I don't want to be noticed. I spent years hurting myself trying to do the opposite of being seen.

Not long after that day with him, I began a fight with my own body. A fight that continues to this day, a fight against the constant tics and tension that Tourette syndrome brings. My tics are all non-verbal—lots of eye-rolling, neck pulling, and forehead tensing. I wasn't diagnosed until I was older, and when I was, it all made sense. But I kept it a secret. I never wanted anyone to fuss over me. I still don't.

Most of my day is spent in front of cameras. Recorded, documented, and archived on YouTube, social media, video on demand, you name it. If I have a good day, there's really nothing like it. But if I have a bad day, I fail in front of a million people—over and over and forever. Whether you see me on a good day or a bad day, you probably have no clue how hard I'm fighting to control my shit, or what it's like to fight off tics. I've learned to mask them and make any excuse I can to turn my back to the camera or walk off set to my dressing room so I can let them out.

Tics themselves don't hurt—not mine anyway. But that doesn't mean I can't hurt myself *because* of tics. I've had tics that have left me with blurred vision and a driving headache after rolling my eyes deep into the back of my head a few hundred times in the span of an hour. I've had to massage my own leg back to life because of a severe calf tic where I spent a full day flexing that one muscle, as *hard* as I could, over and over until I couldn't walk. Tics are like an itch in a hard-to-reach place. You can feel it, it's not going to ruin your day, but it's there. When you scratch it, it feels wonderful—for a quick second, and then it's back again.

The best way I've heard what it's like to fight off tics is this: Hold your eyes open for as long as you can without blinking. While this is going on, that burn will be all you can think about.

As your eyes start to dry out, you'll start to get that feeling of incoming relief knowing all you have to do to make it stop is blink once—and when you finally do, the feeling is almost euphoric. Then do that same thing again. And again. That's what tics feel like. I've hidden, disguised, and managed my tics every day of my life until now. I've never talked about them publicly. Even writing these two or three paragraphs has taken longer than anything else I've written so far. As soon as I think about tics . . . I tic.

But that's me. That's how it's been for the last twenty years or so. Hide what's going on and try not to look too big. Even though I talk with my hands like a maniac, I still try to occupy as little space as I can. I hunch my shoulders forward and always tuck my feet in. I never want to put anyone off or make them uncomfortable. I'm still hyperaware of the physical space I take up.

In doing hundreds of interviews over the years, I've used a lot of my own life to shape the way I ask questions. The rule I use more than any other is to never ask someone what they *think* about something, I always ask how they *feel* about it. It triggers a different part of the brain. Because that's what it's like for me. If you went through my story and asked me what I *thought* about things, then asked how I *felt* about things, you'd get two very different answers.

WHAT DO YOU LISTEN TO AT CHRISTMAS?

In the late '70s my mom bought me my first record. I was around five, and we were out at the department store she worked at on weekends. She left me with the woman who ran the record section while she went up to the office to grab her paycheque.

I loved browsing and flipping through all the records. I didn't own any music, didn't have a favourite song, and couldn't name one band, but I loved album covers and the smell of the plastic wrapped around them.

As we were walking out Mom saw the Ace Frehley solo album and thought it looked cool. I didn't know what the hell I was looking at. I couldn't tell if that was a man, woman, or alien, but it didn't matter. It was the coolest fucking thing I had ever seen.

"You want this?" she asked very seriously, and then smiled. My eyes shot open. "Okay, I'll get this for you." And that was it. That was the beginning.

I'm going to ask you to Google two things in the next couple of minutes, and this is the first: look up the cover art for that album. This was the first time I saw what rock 'n' roll looked like. And I was hooked. All my musical tastes were born from that one record. From that one album I discovered KISS, and they were the first band I truly loved. Then, in 1981, Mötley Crüe dropped *Too Fast for Love* and I listened my way, very loudly, through Ozzy, Judas Priest, Van Halen, and Iron Maiden, then Hanoi Rocks, Guns N' Roses, Skid Row, Faster Pussycat, and Poison. Prince was cool, but Michael Jackson was *not*.

Those bands made me.

Sleazy '80s glam rock defined most of who I was at the time: those guys and these bands inspired everything about me. I bleached my hair and pierced my own ears in the bathroom using a safety pin and half a potato. I stuck the potato behind my earlobe so the needle had something firm to hit as I jammed it through. There was a weird rule back then when it came to guys and earrings, like an urban legend that was just accepted as fact. It went like this: if a guy had his *left* ear pierced it meant he was straight, while one in the *right* meant he was gay. I don't know who first said it, but *everyone* followed it. That first hole I punched into my own head, while standing over the sink in the basement bathroom, was in my right ear—because *fuck your rules*.

You couldn't buy rock-star clothes in my little town, so I got my mom to teach me how to use her sewing machine. I made every pair of jeans I owned tighter. In the '80s, jeans didn't have the same stretch they do now. They were thick—folding them was like trying to fold carpet. I'd take them in as far as I could from the hip to calf, then leave about three inches open at the bottom so I could get my foot through. Once the jeans were on, I'd grab a needle and thread and sew up the bottoms before school. I'd make the stitches tight enough to last the whole day, but just loose enough that I'd be able to rip them out by hand before I went to bed each night. I dyed my white shirts purple, and borrowed eyeliner and nail polish from girls in my class. This is going to sound crazy, but at that time and in *that* world, the more feminine you looked, the more masculine you became.

Now I want you to Google that second thing: look up the album cover for Poison's *Look What the Cat Dragged In*, and before you ask, yes, those are four men. *That's* the look I was going for.

After that album came out, I dove face-first into a world of pink nails and teased hair, of tighter clothes and pure, unapologetic gender-bending androgyny. This look wasn't "brave" in the way we look at it today, and you certainly didn't have the mainstream celebrity support you do now for letting your freak flag fly. To be honest, depending on where you were then, it was goddamn dangerous. It was the easiest way to an ass-kicking, and running from a fight wearing a Cuban heel and skin-tight jeans with zero give wasn't easy.

When I was growing up, the music you listened to defined you. It determined who you hung out with in high school—that was your tribe. There were the new wave kids who listened to the Cure and Morrissey, and the skinhead/punk crowd who wore pristine Doc Martens and bomber jackets. The artsy kids loved musical theatre; they lived for the yearly school trip to Toronto to see *Phantom of the Opera* or *Les Mis*. There were the rap fans, who did their best with what was available at the time, which wasn't much. The hippies hung around an older crowd and worshipped Grateful Dead, and the prep girls wore stirrup pants and Cotton Ginny sweatshirts and were into Madonna, Wham!, and New Kids.

The rest of us? Well, we were skids—the rocker kids who headbanged, were always bumming cigarettes, and carried guitar cases around school. Some skids were into classic rock, others leaned more metal, and then there were those of us who were raised on those acts that launched on L.A.'s Sunset Strip—the glam rock bands. As a guitar player I did really respect the metal bands. The licks they'd play were hard as hell, and I'd spend hours trying to learn them. I appreciated them, but they were just too dirty-looking. I never wanted to pay money to listen to someone who looked like they were wearing their own clothes. The metal skids were always the nicest and smartest kids in school, though. They were also the most welcoming. I still feel that metal is the only genre of music that is completely misunderstood when it comes to what it's doing. It's always had the most diverse fan base and it completely accepts whoever is willing to fight for their space in a mosh pit. If you were into metal, it didn't matter where you came from, what religion you were, or what your background was, because in that world, it was metal above everything.

In the summer of 1986, prep rock made its way into my life for the first time. I was almost twelve. Keep in mind, at that time I defined myself by music, I hated any and all music that wasn't glam rock or metal, I was so specific with my taste, and I would just rail against anything else, especially new wave.

That summer I had a "girlfriend" who moved from Acton to Georgetown, the next town over. After she moved, for three Saturdays in a row my dad drove me to Georgetown so we could hang out. She was a year older than me, and her sister was four years older than her. Girls with older sisters usually had the most eclectic taste in music. Older sisters were a gateway to shit nobody had ever heard before. These hangouts usually lasted the amount of time it took my dad to run a few errands around Georgetown. He'd drop me off, then hit Canadian Tire, Zellers, and a few other places they had in their strip mall we didn't have in Acton. While I was there, this girl and I would spend the hour or so watching music videos and dry lip kissing whenever her parents were out of the room. On that third Saturday, which would be the second-last time I'd ever see her, I went up to her room to find her.

When I walked in, she was playing U2's "Bad" off *The Unforgettable Fire*. I had heard *of* U2, but I had never really *heard* U2. I was instantly obsessed. I didn't know how to process what I was hearing, but I was in love. In the '80s, you couldn't go home and download any song—there was no Spotify or Internet—so I had to wait to go to her house to hear it again. Absolute madness when you think about it today.

When my Pop drove me up the following Saturday, I went in with a plan: I wasn't leaving without that U2 cassette. The first thing I did when I got there was ask her to put on "Bad," just so I could experience it again. Then we rewound and played it three more times. After the third spin I looked at her stack of cassettes and asked if we could listen to Thompson Twins. Now you have to understand, my requesting Thompson Twins was an absolute violation of everything I believed in. (Also, those three dudes were *not* twins and none of their last names were Thompson— just sayin'.) But I asked, and she pressed Play, and I pretended to love it. At some point during side A, she got up to either unplug her crimping iron or put her sticker books away, and as soon as she turned her back, I grabbed the U2 cassette out of its case and stuffed it in my pocket—which wasn't easy given how unforgivingly tight my jeans were.

Georgetown was one of three towns that surrounded Acton. Milton and Erin were the other two. I didn't know much then, but

I did know the rules, and rule one was that girls from Georgetown, Erin, and Milton did *not* date guys from Acton. It wasn't accepted or tolerated, so I knew our relationship was going to be short-lived. Besides, on the second Saturday when I'd arrived, she was still at the mall with her mom, and her older sister let me watch her change into her swimsuit in their pool house. One way or another, I was going to get dumped.

The first thing I did when I got home was use a Q-tip and nail polish remover to scrub the cassette of anything that identified it as U2 so none of my friends would see. I must have listened to that tape a thousand times. With headphones. Always with headphones.

My dad had zero interest in music. But he was a great dancer, which now that I think about it made no sense. I don't have one single memory of him willingly putting on a record or changing the radio to find a station playing a better song. Over the years I'd buy him box sets of songs from the '60s, Vietnam-era stuff. I'd spend hundreds on CDs I thought he would love. He'd unwrap them, thank me, give me a hug, and then add them to the stack beside the giant stereo system he'd put together. Which also made no sense.

My dad and I only ever really bonded over two songs, "The Gambler" by Kenny Rogers and "Hooked on a Feeling" by Blue Swede, the Ooga-Chaka song. These were the only two songs I remember us listening to together. I wonder if, for him, he felt that music was an indulgence. This was a guy who never got Christmas presents growing up; he never got anything at all like that. My mom gave him his first birthday party when he was in his thirties. Dad didn't need much, so for him, that meal at Christmas was it.

That was his *thing*, that's what gave him his most joy, and what he looked forward to the most.

On Christmas morning, Mom would fill the house with music, usually starting with Anne Murray. My dad would pretend to know who was playing and try to sing along, but mainly he'd use it as an excuse to change as many of Anne's lyrics to the word "fart" as he could. He found that hysterical, and so did I. Maybe it's nostalgia? Or sentimentality? But now I'm the same. Now I'm him. Those late afternoons on Christmas Day mean the world to me.

My mom hasn't cooked Christmas dinner for us in years. That's my job now. She put in her time. She spent enough years in the kitchen, exhausted in a housecoat, missing out on the fun while making sure that Christmas dinner was perfect. My love for food and cooking is directly linked to my mom, and the laugh-filled family dinners we do now are modelled off what she created for us. It's her blueprint. My mom would try to get me into the kitchen as often as she could, saying, "Little kid hands are good for doing the gross stuff," so on Christmas it was always my job to do the stuffing. She'd let me stand on a chair and really get in there with my hands. She'd load up our biggest bowl with toasted croutons, herbs, onion, and sausage, and let me go at it. The sausage was always cold, and every now and then the sharp corner of a hard piece of bread would stab me under a fingernail and hurt like hell as wet sausage squished though my fingers when I made little fists. It was gross and I loved it.

Now, when it comes to the headliner, the bird, let's get one thing straight. Turkey is a bland, dry, and unforgiving meat. For most of my career I've been fortunate to travel the world, stay in some of the best hotels, and eat in some of the best restaurants owned by some of the world's best chefs, and I've *never* seen turkey on a menu! If it was that good, they'd serve it. Believe me, I've tried everything to make turkey great. I've roasted a whole bird, I've roasted it in pieces and at different cooking times, I've done a twelve-hour brine and a twenty-four-hour brine. I've barbecued it, I've deep-fried it, and I've made my way through dozens of cookbooks and hundreds of YouTube videos trying to get it perfect. Keep in mind this isn't a how-to book, and I'm no chef, but here goes.

The first thing you need to know is, there is *no* perfect way to cook a turkey. That's why I'll usually flip back and forth depending on how much time I have or how showy-offy I want to be that year. But if that's what you want—the *show*—that perfect bird on display in the centre of the table, golden brown and ready to carve—then you have to spatchcock it (which is a super-gross name, by the way) and douse it with boiling water. Cut out the spine with a pair of hefty kitchen scissors, press it down flat—that's spatchcocking it—and put the whole spineless, raw bird flat in the sink, skin side up. Then pour an entire kettle of boiling water all over it. Get it everywhere and make sure it hits all the folds and crevasses. Boiling water tightens the skin and breaks down the collagen. This is the same process used for that ultra-crispy Peking duck you always see hanging in the windows of the best Chinese restaurants in any city. Pull it out, pat it dry, hit it with some salt, and leave it uncovered in the fridge overnight to fully dry out. The next morning, season it up again with salt, pepper, thyme, and more butter than you think you need and roast it up in an oven pan with a metal rack.

Other years, I buy all the turkey in pieces—two wings, two drums, two thighs, and three breasts (one for leftovers). The breasts are boneless and skinless, and the thighs are skin-on but no bone. I sous vide the breasts early in the afternoon and get them ready to be finished off and browned up in a blazing hot pan on the stove with oil, butter, and fresh herbs. This takes less than ten minutes, since the turkey is already cooked perfectly from the sous vide. I will say this: once you sous vide a turkey breast, it's very hard to go back to anything else. The French know what's up.

The drums and wings you can roast on a wire rack inside a pan at a high temp, like 450°. Flip them constantly, to make sure they brown and the skin comes out perfectly crisp all the way around. The thighs are cold-fried. Put them skin side down on a cold pan with *no* oil or butter, no nothing. Turn the pan to medium heat and leave them to do their thing. Don't flip them! That skin needs to stay down, and your pan will start to fill up with all that glorious fat. This takes longer than you think. When you see them cooked all the way up the sides, then turn them over. But *not* before.

If you're thinking my meat-to-skin ratio is off, that's because it is. But here's how you fix that. About a week before Christmas morning, I ask my butcher, or the guy behind the meat counter at my grocery store, to start saving me skin. They always have tons left over, and bag it up for me to pick up at the end of the week. I get pounds of skin, and they've never charged me a dollar for any of it. I line a baking sheet with parchment, season the skin (remember, thyme and turkey are best friends: let them play!), and lay the pieces out in a thin layer. Cover it all with another sheet of parchment and then cover *that* with another baking sheet the same size as the one on the bottom. Push down hard, and fire it in the oven at 350°. What comes out are these beautifully coloured, crispy long strips of skin that are perfect for dipping in gravy, mash, and just about anything else. I serve them in a big basket like flatbreads and watch my family fight over them.

The sous-vide breasts and cold-fried thighs will be the most tender, perfectly coloured, easy-to-carve, and best version of bland meat you could ever ask for. Turkey is a thing that I wish wasn't a thing. But my dad loved it. Katherine and Roxy love it. Next to my old man, Katherine may be the single biggest fan of Christmas dinner I've ever met.

They would have had a blast together.

I've interviewed Anne Murray several times over the years, and we always have the best time. Anne Murray and I getting along isn't something I ever thought I'd say, and certainly not during any of those Christmas mornings when my dad would add the word "fart" into as many of her classics as he could.

The first time I interviewed her, I ended it by asking, "When the rest of the world wakes up on Christmas morning and listens to Anne Murray, what do you listen to?"

She looked me straight in the eyes, smiled, and replied, "Anne Murray. Of course."

My dad would have loved that story.

ROZ'S BROTHER

My relationship with my brother, Richard, has always been a tough one to explain. People just don't get it, and watching someone wrap their head around it has always been, well, *fun*. With the exception of a year and a half when I went off to college and then moved to New York City, we've lived together. Even now, as full-on adults, we *still* live together. We've spent our entire lives together. We don't fight and we rarely disagree on anything, even though for the most part we're total opposites. I don't know a life where I couldn't sit on my couch, yell "Rich!" at the top of my lungs, and have him *not* answer. He's just always been there. He's never judged me or made me eat shit for any of my mistakes and has always been around to pick my ass up when I fall.

I'd like to say that he's the perfect older brother, the kind that you only read about in books, but the reality is nobody would ever find our relationship believable. I've never seen or read anything like it. He never resented only being referred to as "Roz's brother" when I was the popular one, and now he gets a total kick whenever someone finds out he's my brother and he's *the* Richard I tell stories about on the radio. "Yup, that's me. Roz's brother."

Our mom and dad put a lot on him when we were kids. When I was two and he was five, he was in charge of me. It was his hand I held when we walked across the street, and he was the one who'd slap mine if I tried to stick it into a light socket. Our parents gave him equal power when it came to making sure I didn't kill myself, and they gave him free rein to clobber me when I tried. When he was around, I was his responsibility. This was something that would either make him resent me for the rest of his life or make us form a bond that would, to this day, be hard for people to fathom. That was the chance our parents took. I'd like to think they knew what they were doing, but now that I'm a dad myself, I can confidently say they did *not*. There's no way they could have. All they did was remind us that we were brothers, and that meant something—it meant everything. It meant that we needed to be accountable to each other even more than we needed to be to them.

My brother was the first person to notice my tics, years before I'd be diagnosed with Tourette's. He called me Twitchy. We spent so much time together that we'd go on these long stretches where mine was the only non-parent face he saw. If I was having a particularly bad tic day, with lots of eye-rolling, blinking, and eyebrow raising, he'd ask me if I was "taking snapshots." There were times I'd really be in the zone playing the guitar, like in a deep fog, ticcing like crazy while trying to work through something like "Number of the Beast" by Iron Maiden, and he'd yell, "Hey, Twitchy," to break my concentration.

"Yeah?" I'd say as I snapped out it.

"You all right?"

"Yeah, why?"

"Nothing. Just checking."

And that was that. Neither of us knew what the twitching was, or if it was even a "thing," so for the most part we just ignored it.

Rich was the Artist; I was the Rock Star. That's who we were at home, those were our reputations at school—these were our dreams. I'd sit at one corner of the basement playing guitar, and he'd be at the other end drawing. Even as a kid, he was the best artist anyone had ever met. *I've* never met anyone like him. I've never met anyone who turned the thing they were best at when they were five years old into a career they've done for their entire life. You'd hear stories like this with guys who were great at hockey, or a young singer who crushed it on *Star Search* and went on to become famous, but this stuff wasn't an option for kids like us. Not in the town we grew up in, anyway.

For Rich there was one path, and one path only. From that first day, before I was even born, when he opened his first box of crayons, that was it for him. He travelled in a straight line from being the talented, and sometimes weird, "art kid" always covered in marker and paint, to being an incredible sculptor, character-artist, and animation director who's done Emmy-nominated stuff for PBS and shows for Netflix and just about every other platform that runs cartoons.

As far as I can remember, he's only had one job his entire life that didn't have him at a desk drawing—and of course we did that job together. We did everything together.

In our town, when you were a broke, underage kid who needed a little pocket money, your options for summer work were slim, so, just like Kevin Bacon in *Footloose*, we took jobs at the flour mill. "Pest Control and Maintenance" is what they called it, but really, what we were hired to do was kill rats and possibly each other. We weren't old enough to work legally, so this was a "cash at the end of the day" deal. The basement of the old mill was no place for a kid: dirt floors, low ceiling, mouldy piles of wet flour, and *rats*. Tons of rats. The rats were the problem, and we were the solution.

We were handed a shovel, a BB gun, and two pairs of old steel-toe boots that were about three sizes too big for each of us. Our boss explained that half the job was done already, and whoever was here before us had already nailed plywood sheets against the lower half of the dirt walls. He taught us how to mix a bucket of concrete and showed us where to pour it. "So, the holes in those walls are where the rats live, and you guys are going to pour new walls with that concrete," he instructed us. "One of you needs to dig out the holes, and the other one needs to pour the bucket into that gap. Once you start digging, and as soon as that shovel hits that wall, those rats are going to come screaming out of there. That's what the gun is for. If they're too big for the gun, that's what the boots are for." So that's what we did. We stomped, shot, and smashed rats with a shovel. For four bucks an hour.

Once all the rat work was done, which took about four days, we were allowed out of the basement and into the sunshine. The flour mill was right across the street from Fairy Lake, so there was always a breeze filled with that smell that all small-town lakes have—a combo of moss, fish, and goose shit—but we were excited to get outside and do some work wearing our own shoes that didn't involve killing things . . . with our feet.

Our boss took us up to the top of one of the huge silos out back. Getting there was a trip. A few flights of stairs and then a ride up the "man lift," which was a revolving vertical ladder that went up and down between floors that you would hop on and off of like a ski lift: grab a handle, hook your foot in a loop, and up you went. Once you were on the roof, there were three catwalks that led to each of the silos.

"These have already been primed. Now they need to be painted," our boss told us.

Rich and I stood near the edge and looked down. It was a long drop, with no railing. "Paint what?" my brother asked.

Our boss looked at us like we were idiots, like he always did, then looked down. *All* the way down. He didn't want us to paint the top of the silo. He was asking us to paint the side. We were sixty feet up, and there was no ladder.

"Grab that," he told Rich, and pointed to a pile of rope. "Bring it here."

As he instructed my brother on how to "safely" tie the rope off to the edge of the metal catwalk, I stood there trying not to shit myself, wishing we were back in the basement shooting rats. On the other end of the rope was a lawn chair. Not a fancy lawn chair, just a lawn chair, one of those white plastic stackable ones that you can pick up for under ten bucks just about anywhere. Across the seat of it was a five-foot piece of two-by-four, attached with more rope, with a can of paint hanging off each end.

"You'll probably want to stay up top," our boss told my brother. "Put your feet here, brace them against this, and lower *him* down." Him was me. "When he's done a little bit, unwind more of the rope and lower him down a bit more." He was now wrapping the rope around one of those things you use to wind up a garden hose on the side of your house. "Safety first," he told us. "*Safety third*," I mumbled back. "When he gets to the bottom, he can jump off and take the man lift back up and help you pull the chair back up here. You guys can switch off if you want, but I wouldn't. He doesn't look like he can hold you."

He told us where the extra paint was, and where to clean the brushes at the end of the day, and then he bailed. For the next thirty minutes we just stood there looking off the side and then back at the lawn chair. Rich picked up the rope a few times, then put it back down again. "We are *not* doing this," he finally said.

I was relieved, but to be honest, had he said, "All right, hop on," I would have. *That's* how much I trusted him. I never wanted to disappoint him.

"Follow me," he told me as he turned around and made his way across the catwalk. "We're going home."

"What are we going to say?"

"We're quitting," he shot back.

"Yeah, but what are we going to say?" Aside from soccer before the season even started, neither of us had ever quit anything before. We'd never stood up to an adult before or told someone to go fuck themselves. We hadn't ever made it clear that we would *not* stand for something, or that we deserved to be treated better than this. This was our moment, and I was excited.

"Don't worry about what we're going to say," he replied. And I didn't. I just trusted him.

We walked down, and out the side door, then made our way across the gravel parking lot. Our boss was alone, smoking a cigarette beside his truck. It was hot as hell that day, so his T-shirt was off and hanging out of the back pocket of his cut-off jean shorts. He looked pissed off and sweaty. As we got a little closer, he and my brother locked eyes, and Rich started walking faster. I thought, for sure, he was going to run up and drop-kick that guy's ass into the creek behind him. I'd never seen Rich like that before.

When we were finally all face-to-face, our boss went from looking annoyed to absolutely concerned. "What's the matter? What happened?" he said as he took his T-shirt out of his back pocket and handed it to my brother to wipe his tears with.

Wait. *What?*

I looked at Rich and he was bawling. Tears raging out of his eyes, snot out of his nose, and he was hyperventilating.

"What. Happened?" our boss asked again.

Catching his breath, and fighting to get the words out, Rich told him "the Story." "Before we started painting, we went back down into the office to get our drinks out of the fridge, and I called our mom to say we'd be a bit late today. She told me that one of our friends, in Georgetown, was riding his bike and got hit by a car."

I didn't know what I was watching, but I went along with it, nodding along while, unsuccessfully, trying to whip up a few fake tears of my own.

Rich was spinning a story with such incredible detail that *I* almost started to believe it. What our friend's injuries were, what the doctors were saying, how long this poor kid lay in a ditch for before someone finally found him. It was a hit-and-run! The cops were involved! The kid might die! We needed to leave!

Neither of us had *any* friends in Georgetown.

When Rich was coming up with this story in the short time we had before we reached our boss, I'm guessing he wanted to make sure there was no chance this guy would force us to stay. And there was certainly no way he was going to let that asshole call me a pussy for not wanting to get in that chair.

We were leaving, and we were leaving now. So that's the story my brother came up with. And it worked.

Rich is the smartest person I've ever met. It took me a lot of years to realize that I wasn't smart. Like not at all. I pretty much cruised through school riding on charm, charisma, and really great hair. Later in life I had a couple of wild awakenings where I understood just how *not* smart I was, when I realized all the things I didn't know—which was a shit ton. I did a lot of my education later in life. I was C-minus product of the public school system, and only made it out because teachers didn't want to fail me. I was a terrible student, but it didn't matter because I'd decided I was going to be famous. Actually, I *was* already famous back then, it's just that nobody knew it yet. I was raised on teen sex comedies, metal, and the glamorization of the American Shopping Mall. I was a Rock Star. I looked the part, acted the part, had the clothes, the big hair, the girls, and the attitude. The problem was, I was never good enough to even make a dent in music, and I was too terrified to ever step on a stage.

Rich was *not* a Rock Star. Rich was a nerd. And I say that respectfully with my whole heart, and if he were reading this, I'm sure he'd agree with me. He's *still* a nerd, and to a certain extent I guess I'm still that little Rock Star. We're both older versions of those two inseparable kids that were each other's best friend and biggest fan. The two kids that knew the only way we were ever going to make it was if we made it together.

In the mid-1980s, our parents made a catastrophic error. A mistake that almost tore our family apart. They wanted to be a bit closer to work, so they decided to move us out of our small town to the sprawling suburbs just outside of Toronto. A big city. *This* was the Waterbed House. I was in grade five and Rich was in eight. We'd have to go to two different schools, because they didn't have junior high out there. So I went to the primary school and he went to the high school.

I wasn't happy, but I adjusted fine enough and did what I normally did: found an older girlfriend and spent our afternoons dry-humping on the pull-out couch in her basement, then I'd go home and play guitar and watch wrestling videos alone in my room.

Her name was Chloe, she dressed like Madonna, wasn't a virgin, and her family was weird. She had two older brothers who used to eat her parents out of house and home, so every day before her parents left for work, they'd leave three pieces of white bread and a jar of Cheez Whiz on the kitchen table, then wrap a huge chain around the fridge and padlock it shut. Then they'd run wire cable through all the handles on every cupboard in the kitchen and lock them too. Nobody was getting into anything. I remember they had an old dog whose name was *also* Chloe. And the weird thing was, they had the dog *before* they had *her*! She was named after the dog.

Chloe and I were together for about six months, and then she cheated on me and dumped me for an older kid across the street named Carlos Ferrari. Let me just make something clear right now. Most of the names in this book have been changed. Some of them aren't even close to the real ones. But Carlos Ferrari was this dude's real name, and I'm using it on the off chance he reads this one day. I hope he reads this. I want him to know I still think he's a dick for doing what he did.

I have very few memories of actually being *in* the Waterbed House. It's one of the parts of my life filled with holes, questions, and blank spaces. I don't have one single memory of sitting down to eat as a family or watching a movie together. I don't remember laughing, where our kitchen was, or where we put up the Christmas tree. I *do* remember feeling isolated, though. Our parents knew Rich and I hated it there, so they got us waterbeds. Yup, that was their big solution. Like waterbeds would fix everything. Then they got us our own TVs, and when we got home from school we'd both disappear into separate rooms. We didn't have a finished basement to hang out in anymore, and I don't remember feeling anything other than detached. We weren't "us" in that house. The move was a mistake.

At first my brother and I looked at this move as an adventure. A fresh start. A chance to be someone new, and for him, a total reinvention. *Family Ties* was the biggest show on television, and Michael J. Fox as Alex P. Keaton was a legend. My brother loved that guy, so much so that on his first day of school he showed up in a dark blue three-piece suit, with his binders in a brown leather briefcase. This was his new look. This was the new Richard. He was the kid who showed up to a city school, with no friends, in a three-piece suit. But he wasn't Alex P. Keaton; he was a target. Students *and* teachers bullied him. It was merciless and never-ending. It was violent. Even when he ditched the suit and tried to disappear, it was still brutal.

I *do* have two very clear memories of that house. And only two. The first was watching the space shuttle *Challenger* explode on live television, and the second was the day Rich came home one afternoon and told me he was running away. I was in my room watching TV before our parents came home, and Rich walked in crying. These were real tears, not like in the parking lot at the flour mill, and as soon as I saw him upset, I started crying. I didn't know what was going on, but I could tell he hadn't been to school that day. He sat on my floor with me and opened his school bag. He was carrying a couple of changes of clothes, a little bit of allowance money, and a few family pictures that he'd pulled out of the albums from downstairs. Three of the photos were of me and him. I don't know all the details or what led him to want to run away, that's not my story to tell, but I did get the sense that he came back that day to say goodbye to *me*. I knew what was happening.

"What are you doing?" I remember asking.

"I just can't anymore," he answered without looking at me.

Now, over the years I've needed my big brother thousands of times. Too many to even count. This, I can truthfully say, was one

of the very few times he needed me. He's always been my protec-
tor, and the guy who never judged me. He picked me up when I
fell. But in that moment and for the first time, with the two of
us in tears on my bedroom floor with our backs up against that
goddamn waterbed, he needed me.

I remember pulling his bag away from him and tucking it
under my arm. Then I reached out and grabbed his hands. "No,"
I said, while bawling and shaking my head back and forth.
"Please no. Don't."

I don't know if what I said helped. Knowing Rich, I think
he stayed because he was the big brother, and he didn't want to
leave me.

I'm not sure when, or how much, he told my parents, but within
a few months they listed the house and we moved back to Acton.
My mom called the school principal back in Acton and asked if
my brother could attend their grade eight graduation, even though
he hadn't attended that school for a single day that year. Mom
knew that Rich needed a win, and so did his old school.

We moved back to town, Rich got to graduate with all his old
friends, and we all pretended that time away never happened. We
were home.

After that, my brother and I spent every second of every day
in our *new* basement, drawing and playing guitar while coming up
with the perfect plan to get the hell out of that stupid small town
again. Together.

THIRTEEN GOING ON FOURTEEN

I didn't really know much about cocaine when I was thirteen. Why would I? Sure, I'd seen coke plenty of times in movies, heard it referenced in the odd song, and knew it was on Nancy Reagan's list of shit she told us to "Just Say No" to, but I didn't really know what it did, or how you did it. And I *certainly* didn't know that if someone does too much of it their face can literally explode. That blood would come gushing out of their nose, fill their mouth, ruin their shirt, and fuck up the rug they were standing on. That, in a matter of seconds, someone's face can turn from beautiful, fun, and flirty with perfect lipstick on a gorgeous smile to looking like it just got hit with a bat. That's exactly what happened to Missy twenty minutes before we had sex for the first time, which was also twenty minutes before *I* had sex for the first time.

While my dad waited for me outside in the family car.

—

Going through my class pictures from about grade two through eight is almost comical. You never have to look too hard to find me because I'm in the same spot year after year: back row centre. That spot was always reserved for the tallest kid in the class. That was *my* spot. I was the tallest kid in the whole damn school. In grade eight, I was just over six feet—I towered over everyone and was taller than most of my teachers. Two weeks after school started that year, the principal of my junior high had to call the high school up the street, where my brother went, to get them to send over six high-school-sized desks and chairs so I'd have a place I could sit in all my classes.

"Here ya go! You're all set," I remember my homeroom teacher telling me as he smiled and pointed to my new desk. All my new desks were now in the very back row of all my classrooms. I didn't get to pick who I wanted to sit beside anymore because the priority, now, was making sure I wasn't blocking someone else's view. Sure, I was finally comfortable, but man, I felt like shit about it some days. I still do. I'm still hyperaware of blocking someone's view, getting in their space, or ruining their night. I haven't willingly sat in the middle of a row at a movie theatre in my entire life. I usually grab any available aisle seat and turn my body so my big head doesn't block the person behind me. I don't enjoy going to the movies, and I hate having anyone behind me.

Being that tall and looking so much older, people just assumed stuff about me. People either thought I *was* older or, because I looked older, they thought I'd be able to handle things that other kids couldn't. This was why guys double my age would think I was a fair fight, and why grown women would flirt with me or grab at me and say shit that you just shouldn't say to a kid who's thirteen going on fourteen. Men would see me as a threat, and women would sometimes look at me like lunch.

We don't ever really discuss sexualizing young men—and we sure as hell didn't then. Today, and when it comes to girls, we know what to do and how to shut it down. We know just how bloody damaging it is to sexualize young girls, even when we fail as a society to protect them. Courageous people with a lot of fight in them have battled for decades to change the dynamic for young girls. As a father, I am part of that battle now. But for boys, or at least for me, it was easier to just become the thing people thought I was than it was to fight back. So that's what I did. Most times I just became the person everyone expected.

But other times, every now and then, I'd use looking older to my advantage. Like to get into places I shouldn't be.

Midsummer, the year before grade eight, a friend of a friend named Ryan caught wind of a "teen bar" forty minutes out of town called Club 404, or 606 or Something-oh-Something, I don't remember. The legend was that this place was a headbangers' paradise. Loud music, a dance floor, cheap Pepsi, and tons of out-of-town girls, with a McDonald's in the *same* parking lot. Paradise. They didn't serve alcohol, but you still had to be sixteen to get in, which for me was never going to be a problem—I looked the part. I think on normal nights Club 404 or whatever was a regular bar for grown-ups, but one night a week they did this "teen night" between seven and ten. Putting the guest list together was a challenge because not everyone I knew would pass for sixteen, and if one of us got popped trying to sneak in, we were all going down and none of us were getting in.

The first time we went, Ryan and I roped in a third tall kid, convinced my dad that this was a place specifically for kids *our age*, and got him to drive us. While my old man sat in the car smoking cigarettes and reading the paper, we partied. Hard. We were *Rock Stars* in that place. Three skids who could clear the dance floor and headbang the hardest every time AC/DC played.

One night, we formed a circle with a dozen or so out-of-town skids when "You Shook Me All Night Long" came on. Out of the corner of my eye, I noticed a girl off to the side, by the tables, staring at me. After a few head whips and hair flips, I looked back to see if she was still there. She was, only now she was smiling. We locked eyes and stared at each other. I was paralyzed. I stood there, trying not to break eye contact while in the middle of teenage heavy metal mayhem. She started doing something with her hands, over and over, motioning towards me and then waving me over. I wasn't sure what she was doing, but she kept doing it as I made my way across the dance floor. When I got close enough, she reached out, grabbed me, and hugged me like we were best friends. I was so confused. I was convinced she thought I was someone else, but then she introduced herself.

"You're fucking tall," she said as she let her arms go from around my shoulders. "I'm Missy."

"I'm Roz. What *was* that?" I asked. "That thing with your hands?"

"It was sign language. I know sign language."

I didn't really know what to do with that, so I said, "Cool," dropped it, and moved on. "Are you from here? Do you live around here? Do you come here all the time? It's awesome, huh? How old are you?" I was burning through all my prime questions because I was nervous as hell. Missy didn't look like any girl who'd ever hugged me before. She felt different. She hugged different.

"I'm outta here in a few months," she said. "They won't let me back in after I'm nineteen. Soooo, too old for *this* place." She said that like I could relate. Then she grabbed my hand and pulled me in tight, and led me over to introduce me to her friends. One guy named Dude Rude who looked like a chubby David Lee Roth, and another guy named Vlad who was about six foot seven, hairy as hell, and told me he was the leader of a gang called The Law. I thought that sounded stupid and made-up, but I didn't say anything. I didn't want to blow it. Missy wrapped her arm around my waist and walked us away from the group.

"Don't you want to know what I was saying? When I was signing?" she asked.

Yeah, oh my god, for sure. "What?" I shot back quickly.

"I said 'I want you' . . ."

Jesus Christ.

"Then I said 'Come here,' and now you're here."

I was frozen.

"How old are you?" she asked, and without even taking a breath I leaned in and whispered the word "Seventeen" into her ear. A few minutes later we were alone in the back of the bar, in the dark, at one of the tables nobody ever sat at, making out. And that's what we'd do for the next two Fridays while my friends headbanged and my dad waited outside in the parking lot smoking cigarettes and reading the paper. I became the person she hoped I was. The person she expected.

Right around the time Missy was turning nineteen, I convinced my dad to drive me a half-hour out of town, to a "friend's" place. I don't remember exactly who I said she was, or how I said I knew her, but I was a trustworthy and convincing kid. Plus, I said her parents would be home, so it wasn't really a problem. I got the address, gave it to my dad, and scheduled a time for him to pick me up. I knew he wasn't going far, so there was no way he was going to be late getting me.

I had *two* hours.

Missy answered the door. This wasn't her house, she told me, "But sometimes I stay here." She was wearing the same white blazer and black stretch pants she was wearing at the bar the week before. I think her T-shirt was different, but her socks were definitely the same. Thick, green, and wool. The kind you'd find if you went digging around an Army Surplus store. Missy introduced me to her friend and said that this was her place, which I already knew because her living room was covered in framed family photos. It was clear that the friend's parents were *not* home.

We spent the next hour or so sitting in their living room listening to music. Those two were on a completely different level from me. They were fucking loud and all over the place! There was no making out, and when Missy *did* sit beside me, she would just squeeze my hand, close her eyes, and sway back and forth. I didn't really know what I was doing there, or why I was invited. Missy seemed like she really didn't give a shit, but she looked beautiful doing it. As the two girls danced around the living room and made their way into the attached dining room, singing Bon Jovi at the top of their lungs, I sat on the couch mouthing along to "Wanted Dead or Alive," trying to fit in. Then the singing stopped, and all I heard was "Fuck, fuck, fuck, fuck! Missy! Too much blow. Fuck!"

I shot up out of the couch. They'd been in the other room for maybe two minutes, but when I ran in Missy had her T-shirt pulled up over the front of her face while her friend had her hands cupped under Missy's chin trying to catch the blood. Missy saw me standing there and just said, "I'm sorry."

Her friend pointed her bloody hand at me, and then at the couch, and shouted, "Sit! Don't move."

Fifteen minutes later Missy came back into the living room wearing only a towel. Her hair was soaking wet and brushed back. Her makeup was washed off, and she was out of breath. Exhausted.

"I'm so sorry," she said again as she put out her hand and pulled me up off the couch.

I said nothing. I had nothing *to* say.

She led me upstairs to her friend's bedroom, closed the door behind us, and walked me over to the bed.

Fifteen minutes later I was in the car with my dad.

"All right, you all set, dude?" my dad asked as I slid into the passenger seat.

"Yeah, Pop. All set," I blurted out, trying to seem enthusiastic and normal as I attempted to put the pieces together and process what the hell had just happened in there.

"Hey! What. Did. You. Guys. Do?" he asked as he gave me two fist bumps on my knee to get my attention, which was probably the second or third time he'd asked that same question without getting an answer from me.

"Yeah. It was fun. Listened to music. Hung out. Played Ping-Pong in the basement. Stuff like that. Cool parents."

The ride home was awful. I could tell my dad knew something was up. He didn't know what, but he sure as hell knew something. I knew that *most* of what had just happened was, eventually, going to come out over the dinner table with him, my mom, and my brother. I couldn't remember all of it, but what I did remember was going to come out. It's what our family did.

During that time, I was pretty much living a double life. Half of me was juggling the lies and cover-ups of my relationship with Missy, while the rest of the time I was just kickin' it doing normal kid stuff. I played with wrestling dolls, rode bikes, listened to metal, and hung out in Ethan's basement playing darts and watching his older brother's porno. Normal kid stuff. Ethan and I started hanging out just before the end of grade seven, right before summer. He lived down the street and had one of those basements that mothers of young boys never went down to. The most you'd get was yelled at from the top of the stairs when dinner was ready, or she needed you to flip the laundry. Moms knew better.

Ethan made me laugh like no other kid ever did. He's still one of the funniest people I've ever met, and the only friend I told the truth to about my relationship with Missy. And he knew *everything*!

On September 24, 1988, Ethan and I were in his basement getting ready to watch the men's 100 metre finals at the Seoul Olympics. Like everyone else in the country, we were glued. This was the Ben Johnson versus Carl Lewis showdown that we had been waiting weeks for. Up to that point Ethan and I would bet on the events as they were happening live. Neither of us had any money, so we'd wager things like a charley horse punch to the thigh, pouring an entire glass of water into the other guy's ear-hole, or having a tennis ball whipped at your nuts if you lost. Stuff like that. Totally normal. For the 100 metre finals we both agreed that this last bet had to be the biggest. High risk, high reward. After picking our favourites to win—I had Ben Johnson, he took Carl Lewis—we both agreed that the loser would have to eat a fart. If you lost, you'd lie down on your back, open your mouth, and let the winner squat over your face and fart right in your mouth. Then you'd have to chew. It wouldn't count if you didn't chew.

Ben Johnson won that night, in record time, and Ethan made good on our bet. He ate my fart.

As I was leaving his place he asked if I wanted to hang out the next night. "Sorry, man, I can't." Sunday nights were Missy Nights.

On Sundays after six you could make long-distance phone calls for half the price, so my mom would let me call Missy for an hour after dinner. On Sundays I lived that *other* life.

In the next few weeks Ben Johnson would be stripped of his medal for doping and they handed it to Carl Lewis. It was the biggest scandal in sports history. And my bet with Ethan became the biggest scandal in friend history.

Later that month Ethan's dad died of a heart attack. Suddenly. I remember Ethan took about a month off from school, came back for a week or two, and then he was gone. His mum packed them up and moved to the West Coast, and he just disappeared. We saw each other briefly one other time, but other than that we never talked again.

The time came, and I sat down with my family at one of our spectacular dinners to tell them everything. That I'd met a new girl, that the club was *actually* for older kids, and I lied to get in. That I was in love with Missy, that her friends wanted me to join their gang, that we had sex, *and* that she was eighteen going on nineteen. I somehow thought that if I said she wasn't quite nineteen yet that this would lessen the blow a bit. It didn't.

"I want you to meet her. I want her to come over," I said.

"How old does she think *you* are?" my mom asked.

"Seventeen," I replied.

"Does she know about me?" my brother asked.

"Yeah, of course. I didn't lie about that."

"So how old am I supposed to be, then?"

"You're still sixteen."

"Wait! So now I'm your *little* brother?"

"Yeah. That would be cool if we could go with that," I replied.

As a parent, and I'm saying this now as one myself, you play out scenarios in your head all the time. You have conversations, make plans, and try to have all the answers and solutions ready to go when your kids come to you looking for advice, or ask you to expand your boundaries with trust and freedom. Sleepover camp, a cell phone, or those first relationships—the innocent ones. We prepare for those, and I'm sure my parents had too. But *I* had just told my folks that I had been to the moon, on a stolen ticket, and I wasn't coming home. They were *not* prepared for this.

"Okay. We'll meet her," my dad said, clearly trying to process all that while still keeping his cool. "Bring her over. But no more going there, understood?"

"Yeah, Pop. No problem."

I knew that what I was asking my family to do was huge. I was asking them all to lie for me, switch our entire family dynamic so my big brother became my little brother, talk to me like I was a senior in high school, and allow me, who just turned fourteen, to have my much older girlfriend come to the house for sleepovers. And my family did. All of them.

For years I thought it was cool that my parents and my brother went along with it, but as I got older, I realized that they were all just terrified. They did their best, right or wrong, not to lose me. There was no going back for me. There was no way to rewind time and pretend none of that was happening. They were afraid I'd leave, or run away, take off with Missy and my new *much* older friends. That I'd join a stupid gang called The Law, get into trouble, and fuck my future. My family did what they always did. They tried to keep me safe. Keep me close. Keep me home.

For the rest of that fall, through the winter, and into spring, I kept things going with Missy, while my parents, and my *little* brother, played right along. We'd talk on the phone for an hour on Sundays and once, maybe twice a month she'd come and spend the night when she could borrow a car. The rules were pretty simple in my house: I'd sleep in my room, and she'd get the pull-out in the basement. But that never stopped us. We *always* found time.

Missy never really talked about her family, and when she did, she'd flip back and forth between referring to her parents as Mom and Dad and using their real names. She always looked like she was catching herself in a lie, and she'd correct it right after. It was confusing, but I never asked.

She always seemed to over-pack when she'd come to my place for the night. She had an old white canvas bag with a broken zipper that everything was always spilling out of. For one night at my place, she always packed the same things—two or three pairs of stretch pants, a few T-shirts, her white blazer, an extra pair of shoes, her makeup bag, and an old pencil case with all her jewellery. This seemed a lot for just one night, but, again, I never asked.

As the weather started to get warmer, I went through a period of well over a month without seeing her. We'd still talk on the phone on Sundays, but it wasn't the same, or enough. Missy couldn't get a car and there was no cheap or direct bus that would get her to my place. I begged my dad to go pick her up, which after a long conversation with my mother, he agreed to. What choice did they have? I was going to see her one way or another.

While my dad waited in the driveway, I walked up to Missy's front door and rang the bell. I had never been to her place before, and other than her parents' first names, I knew nothing about her family.

When I walked in, the house was absolute mayhem. There were kids everywhere—all different ages, and all different races.

No two looked even remotely like brother and sister, and her parents were old! Like *grandparent* old.

I didn't know anything about group homes or foster care, but Missy did her best to quickly explain it all to me as she led me down the basement stairs to her room. She said this was the fifth place she'd lived and because she was over eighteen, she'd "aged out," but she was good with the kids, knew sign language, and helped out with expenses, so her "parents" were letting her stay a little longer.

Missy's bedroom was at the far corner of their unfinished basement. She'd built herself her own space by hanging bedsheets with thumbtacks onto the wood stud walls. She whipped open one of the sheets and led me in, then told me to grab a seat while she packed up. Missy's bedroom was a cot and a sleeping bag on a concrete floor. There was an exposed light bulb up above with a shoelace dangling from it.

"Cool," I said, not knowing what else to say. "I love it."

Missy didn't reply as she frantically gathered up her things and threw them into her white canvas duffle bag with the broken zipper. She wasn't over-packing for one night, she was packing up *everything* she owned, which I then realized was what she did every time she left. She was on the clock, and this family was temporary, and it was going to be her last. Missy was living a life that I didn't understand, but I didn't ask too many questions or open up. I'd told too many lies, and if we started talking, like actually telling each other things, I would have blown it and it would be over.

By this time, I was a couple of months away from graduating grade eight. Those were my last few months in junior high, which sucked because our house was *right* beside my school. On our street it went: my house, a small parking lot, then my school. I could go home to pee if I wanted to. One afternoon in woodshop my teacher walked up behind me and told me they were calling me to the office. I left my goggles and gloves on the bench, brushed off the sawdust, and walked out.

"Your mom called and wants you to come home," the secretary told me. Mom was working in real estate at that time, so her being home in between showings wasn't unusual. But pulling me out of school early *was*.

"Like, right now?" I asked.

"Yeah, she said to grab your things for the day and head home. She needs you home."

The only other time my parents pulled me out of school was when my mom's brother, my uncle Mac, died years earlier and we had to drive to Montreal for his funeral. I was terrified. Who'd died?

As I headed across the small parking lot, I saw a car parked in our driveway. It was *Missy's* car. The one she sometimes borrowed to drive to see me. This wasn't a planned weekend visit—this was a Wednesday afternoon. I was *dead*. I knew that in less than a hundred steps I was going to walk through that front door to my own funeral.

Missy and my mom were sitting at the kitchen table.

"Sit down," my mom said without looking at me. "Missy, what do you want to say?"

I sat down, right where my mom said to, looked at Missy, caught my breath, and looked away. I never looked back. Her face was covered in tears. "I came to take you for lunch. To surprise you. I went to your school, the high school, and asked the receptionist if she could page you to the office. She told me they didn't have a Roz Weston at the school, but that they *did* have a Richard Weston. She said you were his little brother who went to the junior high down the street." I don't actually remember Missy saying any of this. I don't remember anything after I sat down right where my mom told me to. My only memory of this conversation, how it all went down, was listening to my mom retell it to my brother when he got home from school, and then *again* to my dad when he got home from work.

I also don't remember what I said, or how we decided what we decided next, but after all that—after there were no more lies and the truth was out—Missy and I didn't break up.

Reading that probably doesn't make you feel good. It shouldn't. But for me, this was about guilt and survival. Any hurt caused was caused by me. This was *all* on me. These were my lies, this was my mess, and this was all my fault. I felt incredibly bad that I put my mom through that situation, that now she was a liar too. I was devastated that I just ruined what was most likely the closest thing to an actual family that Missy had ever known. I didn't have the maturity or skills to fix *any* of it—so I just carried on like none of it ever happened.

Grade eight graduation was coming up and there was no way I'd be able to take Missy as my date, so I asked a girl in my class named Kathy if she'd go with me. Missy still went to my grad, but she drove there herself, and sat in the audience with my parents. Nobody asked who she was.

One of the last times I saw Missy, we spent the entire time talking. We'd never really talked before, not without lying, anyway. I have tons of holes in my memory of my past, but especially from that year. I don't remember the details of a single one of our Sunday-night-after-six phone calls, or how we'd spend our time when she came for those weekends. Even writing this was a fight to try to put the pieces together. It's a blur. So I'm not sure how or why we started talking about it, but the question of what we would do if she ever got pregnant came up. This wasn't something I'd ever really thought about, but it was obvious Missy had.

"You'd never know if I got pregnant," she told me seriously. "I'd just disappear. I'd never ask you to be a part of that. You don't have to worry about that. Ever. Okay?" *That* I do remember, because she said that to me looking straight into my eyes, with one hand on the side of my face. Then she pulled me in and kissed me on the forehead, and that was the end.

Missy only spent the night that one last time, and then, just like that, she was gone. I don't remember the last conversation we had, but I certainly know we never said goodbye or officially broke up. She was just gone. I called the house a few times and spoke to her foster parents, left a couple of messages, but I never heard from her ever again.

In the years after, while I was still in high school, Missy's name would come up every now and then among friends, and to be honest, I didn't have enough hands for all the high-fives I was giving. I was an absolute Legend, but I'd *always* end the story right before the part about what we'd do if she ever got pregnant. Nobody ever got the whole truth. Nobody ever got the part that hollowed me out. This is a story I stopped telling when I came to realize how out of their depths my parents were. How they just tried to manage a complicated, and terrifying, situation as best they could without losing me. I wonder now how many nights they must have stayed up talking about whether they were doing the right thing or not. I wonder how awful they must have felt.

Do I think my parents failed me? No, and I hope you don't either, because there's a real good chance that if they didn't handle that year the exact way they did, *I* wouldn't be here. They did their best. But like everyone else in my life back then, they probably thought I could handle much more than a kid my age should be able to.

As an adult, I can truthfully admit that that year fucked me up. But it was years—decades—before I realized it. Did Missy vanish because she was pregnant? I don't know. Is it something I think about all the time, even today? Absolutely.

I never wanted Missy to fall in love with me, but I did want to be the person she thought she fell in love with. And that right there is the thing I would repeat—the mistake I would make—for most of my life.

Every relationship after Missy, I would become the person that the other person saw. I would become the thing that they wanted me to be. When someone would describe me to somebody else, they would be so off, and so wrong, but I didn't know how to be with people my own age or build an honest relationship. Even when I was married, I wasn't really me. I was this person who adapted to be who my then wife and her friends thought I was.

Once social media became a thing, and I got on television, just about everyone from my past who I was ever friends with reached out in one way or another. Hundreds of people I went to high school with, old teachers, people I used to headbang with, and just about every girl I ever dated connected and said hi.

There are, however, two people I've *never* heard from. Missy is one of them. At least once a year, even now, I'll do a search for her, but her real name is very common, which makes things tough. I just keep replaying that conversation we had over and over. I probably always will.

I wish I could tell you that Missy was the last woman that I terrified my parents with, but she wasn't. I spent a lot of my high school years bringing home strippers, more girls who did more drugs, and more women years older than me. Again and again my mom and dad would just do their best, manage the risk, and try to keep me close.

I've grown to hate not getting closure, and I absolutely can't stand the feeling of owing anybody anything. I always have to close things out. Debts, favours, relationships—I hate loose ends.

The second person who never reached out on social media was Ethan, that friend from grade eight who I made that bet with. All I know is that even now, with me being a level-headed and totally respectable dad with a big fancy job, if Ethan ever came calling looking for payback, I'd happily close out that debt. I'd eat a fart.

THE NAKED GUITARISTA

I never burned myself because I felt worthless. It certainly wasn't because of neglect, and I definitely wasn't trying to punish myself. I wasn't taught to suppress emotion—the exact opposite, actually. My dad led with his whole heart and *embraced* emotions. He was all about clarity and closeness.

My parents built a home that was safe, a family who could tell each other anything—and, for the *most* part, we did. My friends loved my parents too, and it wasn't at all unusual for me to come home and see one of my buddies sitting in our kitchen with my mom and dad smoking cigarettes and just shooting the shit. *All* my friends called my parents Mom and Dad, while some, the ones who got close, just called my dad "D" for short.

It was a safe house, and nothing any of my friends ever told my parents ever escaped those walls. They'd show up with coffee and they always knew exactly how my parents took it. My friends could talk to my parents about anything, and they did—girl problems, school problems, or trouble at home. My mom and dad were so dialled in to what was happening in all their lives that they knew exactly who needed advice, who could use a good kick in the ass or an ego check, and who just needed a place that felt safe to hang for a few hours. Sometimes my friends needed somewhere that felt like home, and that's what our house was for them—a second home. It was nothing for us to have another kid at the dinner table three or four nights a week. But after so many of those nights around the dining room table, the nights my dad loved, full of those kid stories and uncontrollable laughter, I'd disappear to my room and pull out the cigarette lighter and a small purple box full of my mother's sewing needles that I kept hidden in the back of my guitar amp.

Nobody who hurts themselves ever does it because they're in a good place. Nobody thinks it's cool to self-harm. Nobody cuts, burns, screams, fucks, or drinks the pain away for the attention. But for me, it was more *reward* than punishment. It was ritualistic and routine. It became the thing I looked most forward to, even though I knew I'd often hate myself afterwards. It was a compulsion. An addiction. A purpose. Burning myself gave me everything and asked nothing in return. The snap of flint off the lighter, watching the end of a needle go from silver, to black, to red, then white. The feeling of my skin popping up in tiny lines and dots when I'd drag the tip of it across my body was like meditation. It was a recharge.

I never hurt myself out of anger, and I never slid the end of a hot needle under my toenail because I thought I was a bad person. I did it because the pieces inside me that never felt like they fit together suddenly did.

I know this now, but I didn't then. I couldn't articulate it; I didn't have the tools. I couldn't ask for help because I didn't know what I needed help *with*. I'd go from feeling overwhelmed to feeling nothing. There was never much in between. I was popular but never felt close enough to anyone to really care one way or another if they walked out of my life and never came back. Some pieces just didn't fit. Burning was never a way to cope with emotions. It was a way to *feel* them.

I had no point of reference for why burning worked, but it did. I wasn't trying to accomplish anything, and there was no nihilistic endgame. To be honest, I didn't know if I was different or completely normal. But I knew that in those moments, I'd feel normal. Whatever that was.

Having spent so much time with my brother setting up the Cub Scouts hall for the weekly AA meeting my dad would host, and hearing so many stories, I learned two things about addicts. The first was that distractions work. That's why so many people in AA smoke—one cigarette right after another. It's a distraction.

My brother and I would get there early with my Pop on Saturday nights, put the industrial-size pot of coffee on, set up four or five rows of chairs, and place an ashtray on every other seat. I'd usually fall asleep within the first half-hour or so, face-down on a folding card table off to the side. I'd wake up two or three times— when everyone clapped at the end of a speech, when someone got emotional and needed support from the room, or when the entire group would say "Hi!" followed by some stranger's name right after a not-so-anonymous drunk just courageously announced to the room that they, too, were an alcoholic. Those Saturdays were never easy, but I never regretted being there.

The second thing I learned was the one universal truth that binds all addicts together—they lie. All addicts lie. I was a *great* liar, although I always tried my best not to. I never wanted to have to lie about my burns, so I hid them. Bottoms of my feet, backs of my arms, behind my knees, but mostly the tops of my thighs and the one place nobody would be able to see unless the lights were on. In those rare moments when someone did notice, I'd say my scars were from chickenpox when I was a kid, or mosquito bites, or I'd cop to having an STD that I didn't have. That was the tradeoff. I was far more comfortable with someone spreading the lie that I had herpes than I was with telling the truth. All addicts lie.

Playing guitar was my distraction. That's what worked for me. Like all those guys in AA who chain-smoked to keep their hands busy long enough to not drink, I'd play guitar long enough to try to feel something. I don't really remember ever crying, but I do remember every single time I *should* have cried and didn't. I wasn't "anti emotions" or anything like that. I was the exact opposite, actually—I wanted my feelings to all come out in music; I wanted to write love songs, heartbreaking ballads that people would listen to when they got dumped or that kids would slow dance to for the first time in junior high. And to try to get those emotions down in words, I did everything I could—I'd strip myself down to nothing. Literally. I'd get naked, light a candle, and sit in the middle of my room in the dark with my cold guitar across my lap, listening and playing along to the saddest music I had—which at the time was Sinéad O'Connor and my brother's Enya tape. I sat there for hours in my own head, listening to New Age emo shopping-mall music, trying to cry.

And when that didn't work, I'd turn my amp around and grab that little purple box of needles and my cigarette lighter.

For me and the guys I hung out with, most of our teen years were spent fighting off boredom. We didn't have a ton of options in Acton. There was no mall or movie theatre, and going to McDonald's on a Saturday was a plan you made on a Wednesday because it took two or three days to find someone who was able to borrow their parents' car to make the trip to Georgetown. Avoiding boredom was just what we did. No matter how much it hurt.

The first time I burned myself it was on a dare. I was showing off.

That night, one brutally humid July evening in about 1990, there was a house party down the street from our place. And believe me when I say that "house" is a major overstatement. Imagine handing a seventeen-year-old the keys to a converted garage and saying, "This is yours now, go nuts." That was Scott's place. There was a mattress on the floor, a half-dozen stolen lawn chairs, a hot plate, and a mini fridge. The walls were six different shades of plaster and primer, and covered in holes from fists, heads, and beer bottles being thrown at a red target that was spray-painted just beside the back door.

Scott was a big, tough, sometimes violent, and very misunderstood town heavy. He was a fighter. His mom lived in the main part of the house and didn't give a fuck what he did. I didn't know what happened to Scott's dad, why his half-brother was in prison, or why his mom didn't care what he got up to. Nobody knew. I always found it strange that none of this was ever acknowledged. Nobody bothered to ask. They all just got drunk at his place and threw shit through his walls.

It was weird. We really shouldn't have been friends, but we just developed this thing. He was obsessed with the military and knew my dad was a marine—he respected that, and I suppose he respected me *because* of that. Scott was hard inside and out, but when you needed him, like when someone was going to kick your ass, he was a pretty good friend to have around.

We never had any deep moments, never talked about feelings or secrets, and when he'd ask me to go with him to the emergency room because he'd sliced his own arm open with a hunting knife or broke his hand on a wall, I never asked, "*Why?*" I never needed a reason, and he'd never volunteer one. He didn't have to let me in, and I was fine with that. That's why I'd always get the call to go with him. On nights like that we'd drive to the hospital with all the windows down because Scott was usually a little too drunk to be behind the wheel, so the fresh air would keep him sharp enough to get us there, and the two hours in the emergency room and a dozen stiches always sobered him up *just* enough to get us back home.

Nobody ever discussed mental health back then. To be honest, it was probably *years* later when I even heard those two words put together like that. Back then, you were just weird, odd, or fucked. That was it. Most times it wasn't because of anything that anyone could help, but if someone asked, the easiest answer was always just "Yeah, that guy's fucked up." It's not that people weren't compassionate, but anytime anyone offered help it was *only* because they thought you were fucked.

I was drawn to people like that. I didn't know why, but I always gravitated to people who seemed hard. People who I could tell were made of rock. People with secrets and scars. The broken and the fucked. That's probably why I fell so in love with Missy and became such good friends with Scott. We gave each other everything and asked for nothing in return.

That night at Scott's place the party was the same as it always was—a total skid fest. Older drunk guys kicking around, Lynyrd Skynyrd and Steve Miller Band on repeat, shit beer, and all of us just trying to escape boredom or impress a girl, and maybe win a bit of money along the way.

Pass the Penny might have been the worst idea of all bad ideas. This wasn't a competition that took place in one night, and the only way to win the cash would be if you showed up the following weekend with proof of your victory.

Here's how the game was played. Four or five guys all threw five bucks into a hat and the group chose a treasurer to hang on to the cash until one of us eventually won. *With* proof. Everyone was handed a two-inch nail, a penny, and a beer. Each of us had to come up with a very distinct way of marking our penny with the end of our nail. This wasn't easy, especially when you were drinking. Mainly we'd just try to carve a straight line or an *X* into it—at least that's what I did. When we all had our pennies marked up, it was up to *you* to remember what you had scratched across the Queen's face. Once all the coins had been appropriately vandalized, you'd close-hand pass it to the guy on your left, and without looking at it, you'd pop it in your mouth, like a children's vitamin, and wash it down with a beer. You'd swallow. The fucking. Penny.

Now comes the gross part.

In order to win, you had to show back up next week with your penny, and get it validated by the guy who'd handed it to you. Once I swallowed mine, I knew there was no way I was going to spend a week looking through my own shit for twenty-five bucks. I was never going to see that penny, *or* my five bucks, ever again, and I was totally good with that. At this point I was just hoping I wasn't going to die—or worse, that I'd have to explain to my dad that I swallowed a penny for a chance to win less than thirty dollars in a stupid game that *I* invented.

Horseshoes was different. It wasn't so much a game as it was a test of strength, or courage or stupidity. The trick was this: If you took your cigarette lighter, lit it, and turned it upside down, the flame would heat up the oval-shaped metal cap that covered the flint and housed the little wheel that you had to roll forward every time you used it. If you held it there for a few seconds the metal would heat up, then you'd blow out the flame and touch the metal cap to your arm. Just a super-quick dab, like a stamp.

The hot end of the lighter would leave a little burn on your arm in the shape of a horseshoe, and that was that. No big deal. The burns were nothing more than you'd get accidentally touching your hand against the side of a hot frying pan. It would blister for about a week and disappear shortly thereafter. This was a game I could win.

At the party that night, I took a cigarette out, lit it, and smoked about a third of it with my left hand while I held my neon pink lighter upside down with my right. Both the tip of my thumb and the knuckle on my index finger burned and turned black as the metal started to smoke, but I held it. When the wheel burned free and popped right off, I held it. When the cap went from silver to black to red to white, I held it. When I lifted the sleeve of my T-shirt and sank the metal end of it into my shoulder, I held it. When the bottom of the lighter exploded in my hand . . . I held it.

This wasn't a burn that was going to go away in a week or two. I knew I'd just permanently scarred myself. I knew this was something I was going to have to lie to my mother, and everyone else, about. Probably forever. And I did.

But I didn't care.

In that moment everything made sense. The reason I was able to slide the hot end of a lighter into myself so easily was because *I wasn't afraid*. I was never afraid of pain. My whole life I had a pretty indifferent relationship with physical pain without realizing how directly tied it was to my inability to deal with what was happening on the inside.

That was the *second*-last time I ever burned myself in front of anyone else.

Oh, and yes, there *was* a Pass the Penny winner that following week. One of the older skids showed up with his penny and collected his twenty-five bucks. Nobody cared.

THE PARKING LOT

I always took the long way home after school so I could smoke two cigarettes. I'd light the second smoke with the butt of the first, and slowly scuff and stroll home enjoying the headrush. So there I was, looking the way I did with the hair, the tight jeans, narrow hips—the whole deal. My brother *loves* telling this story, by the way. I was about three or four houses from our place when Rich and his friend Brad drove up behind me before turning in to our driveway. As they got a little closer, and only seeing me from behind, Brad tapped my brother on the leg so he wouldn't miss out and said, "Nice ass! Wonder what her face looks like."

"Dude, that's my *brother*," Rich said.

My dad never really gave a shit about how I looked. I mean, I'm sure there were times he wished I'd dial it down just a bit, but mostly he just got a kick out of it. I'd walk out of my room with a fresh piercing, full-length spandex, cowboy boots with a bandana tied around my thigh, and a T-shirt I had just taken apart and sewn back together. The most I'd get was a "*Nahhhhhh*, come on. Really?"

followed by one of his famous laughs. To which I'd always answer something like, "*Ohhhhh yes*, Pop! Really!" This drove people nuts. People had such a hard time believing I was the son of a marine, which only made me realize how all those people got my dad so very wrong.

In those years when I was trying my goddamn hardest to become a teenage glam rock nightmare, I didn't dye my hair a *little* blonde—I went full platinum. I always made sure my jeans were tight enough to throw people off. You'd know right away these weren't anything you could buy at a regular store. Somehow going over the top made me *less* insecure. There was a power to it, but a power I ate a lot of shit for. I've been beat up, had knives pulled on me, got kicked out of more places than you could count, had fathers dump me on *behalf* of their daughters, been refused service and ripped off—all because of how I looked.

Which was fabulous, by the way. The times I heard the word "fag" followed by a sharp pain to some part of my body while walking through a crowd were more than I'd like to remember. Even years later, when I'd get lost, alone on the middle of a dance floor or high up on a speaker while people threw stuff at me and bouncers grabbed at my feet to pull me off, I never went a *little*. I was always extra. Over the top. I never left the house with *some* makeup on, it was never subtle. I'd cake on eyeliner and rub it in with my pinky, so it looked like it had been there for days. I never wanted anyone to ever ask, "Are you wearing makeup?" That's what I feared most. Talking about it or having to justify it. That's what made me nervous. I never wanted to be the topic of conversation, so I never gave people a place to even start.

Even today, I'm never *really* what anyone would call "appropriate." If I had to, I'd describe my current personal style as someone who's doing a pretty good job at handling a *very* bad day. I'll never fully fit in. When I started working on TV, I'd get all these crazy invites to these glossy, strict-dress-code-only parties and I'd show up wearing actual garbage. I looked like I had just come from a bachelor party—but one that started two days earlier. I'd wear the weirdest, most destroyed and wrinkled outfit I could put together, just to see if they'd let me in. And when they did, once inside, drinking their free booze, I'd cheers to sixteen-year-old me.

Being over the top—or flamboyant, for lack of a better word—and making myself a target gave me something to fight against. Gave me an enemy. Dealing with judgey strangers allowed me to push my own shit deeper and deeper. It was a perfect distraction.

Managing ego with crazy insecurity is a contradiction most of us live with. For me, it's every day. Every minute. Always has been.

Growing up in a small town, you quickly realize that how you treat people matters. No one was anonymous—you couldn't be an asshole to someone and get away with it. If I was a dick to the guy who ran the corner store, when my dad stopped there to buy smokes on his way home after work he'd hear *all* about it. How you treat people matters. That's the lesson.

So there I was, polite, pretty, and clueless. Desperate to be famous and desperate to fit in. You need to know all of this so you understand why what happened next happened. This is the story of when I was definitely *almost* molested by Sebastian Bach's manager.

It was around 1989, and my friend drove us out of town to go to the record store: Sunrise Records at Stone Road Mall. I always knew what I wanted to get before we even left the house, but I'd still spend hours in there, just flipping through cassettes and listening to whatever the clerk decided to spin, while fantasizing what it would be like to have my own album in a place like this while some other kid, just like me, came in to spend their allowance on something I made. I was cruising the aisles with a Skid Row tape in my hand when this guy walks up to me and asks, "Are you a fan?"

In my head I was like "Obviously, you dumb shit—LOOK at me!" Sebastian Bach, the singer for Skid Row, was my style icon. "Uh," I mumbled.

This guy was older, like my father's age. Short-sleeve dress shirt tucked in, dad jeans, thick glasses. He looked like he could have been a pen salesman or a Radio Shack model.

"You like Skid Row? You a fan?" he said. "I'm asking because I manage him. Sebastian Bach."

There was a part of me that wanted to call bullshit right away, but I knew Sebastian was from a small town not that far from where I grew up, so I gave this guy two seconds of my attention. Just as I was about to shoot back with "*Oh yeah, how long you . . .*" he jumped in with "You know he's gay, right?"

I was stunned. Not surprised but *stunned*. As someone who lived off every piece of information I could get my hands on about my favourite bands, I was enthralled and intoxicated by the fact I had dirt that nobody knew. Secrets. So I responded with a very polite, "Fuck off, man."

To which he immediately replied, "You look like him." He paused, then added, "You have great hair. He'd love that. He's really into that."

That was it. That's all it took. Up to this point no adult had ever acknowledged the way I looked with anything other than "Cut your hair" or "No" or "Not with my daughter." This guy was into it. *And* he was Sebastian Bach's manager. And now I believed him.

At this point I was losing my shit over the idea that Sebastian Bach might be into me—even though I was pretty sure he wasn't gay, and even *more* than sure that *I* wasn't. But for some reason the idea that I might be his type was blowing my fucking mind! What do you even do with that?

The guy introduced himself. "I'm Mick Nickle, 'keeper of the case.'" He laughed and waited for me to pick up the bait. I must have taken a beat too long, because he said, "I'm closer to him than anyone in the world, and I'm in charge of his case."

I took it. "His case?"

"Every time he's with a guy, Sebastian cuts a piece of their hair off, wraps one end with an elastic, and puts it in a briefcase. He takes this case around the world with him. With us."

In my head I was like *Wait. What? You're fucking with me. Gross.* But for some reason, maybe because I didn't want the gossip to stop, or maybe I was enjoying feeling like I fit into this story and this world, flattered that this dude, who knew Sebastian Bach, was into the way that *I* looked, I replied with "Cool."

The next five minutes were a blur. Mick went into this long, involved story about how he'd discovered Sebastian Bach, how he got him hooked up with the right people, and how he landed Skid Row their first record deal. He knew everything. Dates, places, names, and every detail I'd read, and already memorized, from the metal magazines I devoured.

I started to think I'd just got discovered! The '80s were full of stories of young women being discovered in American malls who went on to become supermodels. Their discoveries couldn't have been any less weird than this one!

Mick asked if I had a demo tape—which I did. I always carried it with me on cassette in the top left pocket of my purple jean jacket. He then asked if I wanted to head out to the parking lot, to his truck, to hear the new Skid Row album before anyone else. He said I'd love it, and afterwards we could listen to my demo.

This was one of the first times my insecurity did battle with my ego. I wanted him to like me, but I knew as soon as he heard my demo I'd be done. It wasn't *that* good. I told Mick that I couldn't head out to the parking lot but that I would call him. He said that he was right out front, and he could tell within minutes if I had what it took. He pushed harder. "Just come on out, follow me. Let's go. No big deal."

"No. I really need more time." I was nervous. If this was my one shot, I wanted to make it count. I wanted time to work on it. I also knew my buddy had to get the car home in an hour because his dad worked nights.

Mick took a long pause, then said, "Too bad. I bet you're perfect. Okay, call me tomorrow night at nine. Play it for me over the phone." In that moment I sort of remember hearing "play *with* me over the phone," but I knew what he meant. We shook hands, he handed me his card, and he walked out.

I was so unbelievably pissed off with myself. Why hadn't I gone to his truck? I'd blown my one chance!

I worked all night on my demo. I woke up the next morning and headed to school armed with the story of a lifetime. At first it started as a whisper, which eventually became a scream. I was the guy who told anyone who'd listen that Sebastian Bach was a perv who cut chunks of guys' hair off after sex *and* that he had a guy on the payroll whose job it was to travel the world with him, taking care of his briefcase of gross souvenirs. This never made me think any other way about Sebastian Bach. It was rock 'n' roll. And in some weird way, it gave me a connection to him. I was in on a secret that maybe only a few dozen other people were in on . . . Okay, probably hundreds.

At nine that night, I called Mick the manager from the home phone. I had everything set up, the perfect demo, the perfect speaker to play it through at the perfect distance from the receiver. I knew this because earlier that day I called two friends and did a distance test with them over the phone. I'd sat there moving the receiver back and forth, close then farther from the speaker, until they yelled, "Good! Right there!"

I was set.

The phone rang once before a woman picked up and yelled, "Hello? It's late! Who's this?" The other end of the line sounded like chaos. There was yelling and a TV was blaring so loudly that I could barely make out what she was saying.

"Hi, my name's Roz. I was supposed to call Mick at nine."

"Who?" she yelled back.

"Roz."

"No, who?" she yelled even louder.

"Mick!" I shouted.

There was a super-long pause, then I heard her mumble, "I don't know, maybe it's for you . . ."

Another voice jumped on the line. "Yeah. Who's this?"

"Roz," I said. "We met at Sunrise. You said to call. My demo."

"Yeah," he said. "What?"

This was a disaster. He was clearly not at the office, and I could hear ice tapping the side of a glass as he took sips of a drink.

"It's Roz," I repeated. "You said you wanted to hear my demo. I'm good to go, man."

"Yeah, call me right back in five minutes," he said. Then click. Dial tone.

I waited five and called back. When Mick picked up there was silence. No TV, no yelling, no ice hitting the side of a glass.

"Thanks for this," I said. "You ready?"

"I'm alone now. But I need to hear you. Press Play on the tape, sure, but I need to hear you live. Sing for me."

Singing live was something I'd never done. I'd never had an audience of anyone, let alone a big-time manager.

I hit Play, put the phone down, and just went for it. I sang the whole thing—a song *I* wrote. When I was done, my hands were shaking. I was sweating. I reached down with both hands to pick up the receiver. As I put it back up to my ear, I could tell the line was dead. Mick was gone. No dial tone, no nothing. I called back, and nothing. I called again and nobody picked up.

I was pissed. Fucking livid. Devastated. I had definitely and totally blown my one chance.

Why didn't I just go out to his fucking truck at the mall?!?

I left my room and went in to talk to my dad. Told him the *whole* story. Everything. The only question Pops had was, "Did you go out to this guy's car?"

"No, Pops," I told him again.

"Okay," he said. "Gimme his card." At that time, we didn't have call logs or redial. So that card was the only place Mick's number existed.

I never told this story to anyone. I was too embarrassed. I blew my over-the-phone audition with a guy who carries hunks of men's hair for a living.

But for years I *did* tell people what I'd heard about Sebastian Bach. I retold *that* part of the story to anyone who would listen. Given how fast gossip travelled before Google, I'd say there's probably a few thousand people in this world who still believe that Sebastian Bach cuts his young male lovers' hair and keeps it in his luggage. Even when I saw a picture of his wife years later, I thought it was all bullshit. Of course he'd have a beautiful wife!

She was the perfect cover. I felt bad for the guy that he couldn't be the freak that he wanted to be.

I felt worse that I blew my audition and would probably never get the chance to tell Sebastian that.

In my head, Mick hung up because I wasn't good enough. I'm sure my dad felt different. I never really thought about what actually happened in those twenty-four hours. I never tried to analyze it. It was a painful memory of inadequacy that I filed away. Once I realized that I wasn't good enough, along with my growing stage fright, I abandoned the idea of being a performer altogether. I still loved playing and writing songs, but I was never going to stand on a stage. I think that's what drew me to TV and radio: you can have a massive audience, but you'll never have to see a single one of them. For most of my twenties I kept behind the scenes. I was a writer and a producer, far away from the spotlight. I didn't take my first on-air job until I was thirty.

The cool thing about interviewing celebs for a living is that I've talked to most of the people I had posters of up on my wall when I was a kid. A lot of them let you down, but sometimes they surprise you. If you told me at fifteen that when I was thirty-something I'd get to sit in front of Sebastian Bach and ask him anything I wanted, everything I've always wanted to, I would have *died*. But that's what happened.

Sebastian Bach was in town promoting a new album, tour, or book. I don't remember. I hadn't thought about my run-in with his manager in a long time. I hadn't told the story about the briefcase in even longer.

The interview was wonderful. Sebastian Bach was charming and honest and humble. I brought my high school yearbook to show him how much I looked like him when I was a kid. To show him how much of a fan I've always been.

As we were wrapping up and the crew were taking down the lights and unhooking us, I asked if he still worked with Mick Nickle.

"Who?" Sebastian asked.

"Mick Nickle? He was your manager from twenty years ago."

"No, man. Not me. Not mine. Never heard of him."

I was sort of pissed because I was really looking forward to telling him the hilarious story of blowing my over-the-phone audition. How could he *not* remember? Surely he'd remember the guy he paid to be in charge of his . . .

Fuck. That was one of the most devastating realizations I had ever had.

It wasn't until *that* moment that I realized how dangerous the situation had been. I sat there, in front of Sebastian Bach while he flipped his hair around and held my high school yearbook, frantically putting all the pieces together like Chazz Palminteri at the end of *The Usual Suspects. Fuck,* I thought again. And *fuck* was right.

I don't know what my dad did with Mick's business card, but I never called the guy again and my dad never brought it up again. I regretted for years not going out to that guy's truck because I thought it would have been my big break. But most likely it would have been something very different. And it definitely *almost* was.

I'm still not 100 percent sure that my dad didn't kill that guy. And I'm not even joking.

SHOCK
AND
AWE

January 17, 1991, two days after my brother's nineteenth birthday, my family, like every other family, sat in front of the TV and watched Operation Desert Storm unfold live on CNN. For anyone my age who grew up in this part of the world, this was our first real experience with war and what it looked like. It looked like MTV. It was a show. I remember all the excitement and pageantry really pissing my dad off. At the time, nobody knew anything. Nobody knew the entire thing was only going to last a month or so. This was the first time I ever turned on the television and saw the word "war" flash across the screen. It was scary and confusing, and I remember firing questions at my dad like he was some sort of expert. I was trying to make sense of it. "What happens now? How do they win? What are they fighting over?"

My Pops did his best to answer, the best he could, while trying to mask his absolute rage. He knew what he was watching. He'd seen this all before. He'd lived it.

"What happens if there's a draft?" I asked.

That was the last question of the night and the easiest one for him to answer.

"You won't have to worry about that," he said, shaking his head, clenching his fists, without taking his eyes off the TV. "They won't do that again. Not here anyway. But if they *did*, there's no way. There's no way you're going off to fight someone else's war. You're not going to die for whatever lies started *this* shit show. I'd take a baseball bat to your knee. Both of you—you *and* your brother. Your left knee. You'd still be able to drive a car, maybe not a standard, but you'd never make it through the physical, let alone bootcamp. I'd make sure of that."

I'd always had a pretty good idea of what my dad was willing to do to keep me safe, but this was the first time I realized what he was willing to do to keep me alive.

My parents never hit us. I never got spanked, slapped, or anything else. They were never into violence, but they sure as fuck *were* into fear. Right around this time, I was like every other teenage boy who pushed the limits and boundaries while carving out a little independence. My dad was always cool. He understood young men and gave me every inch I fought for with a casual combo of compassion and terror.

I was leaving one night, heading out with some friends a little later than I normally would. There was no lecture about curfews, rules, or respect. Pops didn't know what me and my shithead friends were going to get up to, and he didn't care, because it was never going to happen. "Let me tell you something," he said to me right before I left. "Let me tell you what happens if I ever get a call to pick you up from the police station. First off, make sure you call me. Don't ever be afraid to call me.

I'll come down, stand at the desk with all the other dads picking up their sons, and I'll be the nicest of them all. Cooler than cool. The other dads will think I'm crazy. When they walk you out, I'll give you the biggest hug you've ever had, like we haven't seen each other in *years*. I'll pay your fine and walk out of the cop shop with my arm around you, tell you I love you, all that stuff. But as soon as we clear those doors, be prepared to defend yourself. Okay?"

I was never afraid of being hit by my dad, but I was terrified that one day I'd have to *fight* my dad. And that's a whole world of difference.

My mom was the same—she was terrifying in her own wonderful way. When I was old enough to start using public bathrooms by myself, maybe five or six, she tried to "street proof" me. Before I went in alone that very first time, I don't remember what I was thinking, but I was probably a little nervous and maybe a little proud. I was a kid. *Most* moms would have said something like "Go in, do your business, and come right out. I'll be right here." What *my* mom said was "Don't talk to anyone and *never* fully face the wall. There was a little boy, on the other side of Montreal, last year who went in to go pee and a man walked *right* up behind him, reached around, and cut his pecker off with a pair of scissors. Then he left with it, too. He put it right in his pocket and walked out. They never found the man *or* that poor boy's penis. Okay, honey?" She kissed me on the top of my head, spun me around by my shoulders, and pointed me towards the door. "Go ahead, I'll be right here when you get out."

That's fucked up, right? Like why would you tell a kid that story? I'm not sure it was even true. I'm actually pretty positive it's *not*. But how do you fact-check that? I've often thought about looking it up, to finally call her out on it, but there's just no way I'm typing *any* of the key words from that story into Google.

Even into my late teens, I was still leaning so far into a urinal, creating a perfect sealed barrier between my body and the porcelain, that I'd have to stand with my shirt under the hand dryer for five minutes to dry out the spots from condensation and other guys' piss before I could leave.

But I always made it out with my penis.

SMELLS
LIKE
TEAM
SPIRIT

I'm pretty sure I'm the only kid to be kicked off a high school basketball team for wearing too much jewellery.

Basketball was another one of those times where people just assumed things about me, thought I was someone I wasn't, put me in a position to fail, then blamed *me* when I did. I didn't try out for the team, never showed interest in the team, but wound up *on* the team. As its star player.

Other than gym class, I had never touched a basketball in any sort of competitive way, let alone played in an actual game. I didn't know the positions or the rules. I was awkward and skinny, I didn't own a pair of running shoes that fit, and none of the girls I went to school with had *ever* seen me in shorts. The tops of my thighs were covered in burn marks, and I hated my legs. This was a problem. But there I was.

—

In my last year of high school, I had late-period lunch, around two, so the cafeteria was usually empty. In the nicer months I'd always go home for lunch, barbecue a couple burgers, smoke a few of my parents' cigarettes, and suntan on the roof of the house. I'd climb up the side of the deck, put down a towel right there on the shingles, cover my chest and face in vegetable oil from the pantry, and get a little colour. I wouldn't even pour it into my hand—I'd lie back and drizzle a line of it from the top of my jeans to my neck, then I'd rub it in with both hands, from my bellybutton to my forehead. I'd bake myself. And I could do all that in less than an hour.

At this point I still had my long hair but was much less glam than I had been years before. The world was changing, fast. Everything that I thought was cool was suddenly a joke. My idols were now clowns, and my taste in music was outdated and laughable. That was the year grunge happened, and I was *not* ready. For everything Nirvana stood for at the time, the rage, the passion, and the genius, I don't think Kurt Cobain's influence on *fashion* gets enough credit. I think we should talk more about that. Not only did Nirvana show up and destroy everything I loved musically, but overnight preppy prom queens who smelled like cotton candy, who'd spend *hours* on their hair and makeup before class, with bra straps showing and skirts short enough to get them a letter sent home to their parents, were showing up in baggy jeans and their fathers' old flannel shirts, with unwashed, uncombed hair. It was incredible to see. I've *still* never seen anything like it. Never before has one indi-vidual, who never wanted to be an example of anything, let alone fashion, had such an impact on the way teenagers saw themselves. Within a month my high school looked like Project Grungeway and Cobain was their God. I hated Nirvana.

I was *not* grungy. Far from it. My whole life I was shy, pretty, and constantly mistaken for a girl. And I could *always* tell when it was about to happen. I remember as a kid being at the mall and fighting for space at the perfume counter while Christmas shopping for my mom, when a man cut in front of me. He was a bit of a dick and shoved me to the side. The woman behind the counter watched this all go down and put her hand out, waving it back and forth in that mom way with one finger extended right up in that guy's face. "No, no, no. This young lady was ahead of you, sir. Sorry."

This happened often, and I never corrected anyone. It would have been easy to just say "Thanks, but 'boy,'" but I never did. It was easier to just go with it. It was less embarrassing. I was *far* cooler with people thinking I *was* a girl than I was with them wondering why I'd choose to look so much like one. So I never set them straight. Even on the phone, I was one of those boys whose voice changed *way* late. I'd answer a call and the person on the other end would say something like "Oh hi, miss. Is your mom or dad home?"

I'd say nothing and just hand the phone over to my mom. All the time.

Grunge did *one* thing, though. It normalized facial hair. Back then, facial hair wasn't cool. We were young men raised by fathers who peaked in the late '60s or mid '70s. Our dads had moustaches, big thick gnarly ones. The kind you'd see in porno. The kind we'd make fun of. Nobody *ever* wanted to look like their dad, and my old man had a legendary moustache. But suddenly, in the early '90s, goatees, soul patches, and beards were the shit, and the girly makeup-covered, smooth glam rock faces were out. Facial hair was cool, and *this* was a way for me to finally look like a guy. The first day I could grow something on my face, I did.

It was a flag, a badge, a way for me to end the confusion about what exactly I was.

I've had some sort of facial hair ever since then. I haven't been fully clean-shaven in over thirty years. I never had that moment with my Pops where he taught me how to shave. Never stood in the bathroom, both of us lathering up in front of the mirror.

By the end of high school, the only two holdovers from my glam years were that my toenails were always painted. *Always* something fun and bright, and *never* black. Goth kids painted their shit black, and I was not goth. The other thing, that last little bit of that glam rock kid I used to be, was jewellery. Just before I started grade nine, years before, I started collecting bracelets. Most of them were cheap metal bangles from headshops or were given to me by girls I dated who'd add to my collection. I never took them off. Ever. And because I'd had them on for years, while I was still growing, I wouldn't have been able to take them off even if I wanted to. My hands grew too big, so these were permanent. These were *my* thing. My wrist underneath was always some shade of green, and if I ever raised my hand to ask a question in class, I sounded like sleigh bells.

So one afternoon in grade twelve I was walking back though the empty caf coming in from the smoking pit. Back then, schools let kids smoke cigarettes in a designated area. This was *on* school property, and close enough to the side doors that you could dip out for a quick one while on a bathroom break from class if you needed to. I was walking one way, smelling like cigarettes and vegetable oil, and our gym coach was coming at me. We didn't really know each other, but he stopped me. Coach was a cool yet crusty younger teacher, but we hadn't ever talked after grade ten when I didn't have to take gym anymore.

ROZ WESTON

"How tall *are* you?" he asked as we passed each other.

"Six three-ish. Why?" I answered.

"You know we could use you, right?"

"For what?" I asked.

"On the team. Basketball."

"To do what?" I was so confused.

"Basketball," he explained, while sounding just as confused as I did.

This is the moment I should have politely said no. Thanked him and moved on. This is when I should have told him I knew absolutely nothing about basketball. But I didn't.

"Do you have gym clothes here?"

"I have track pants, yeah," I said.

"Swing by for practice in an hour. We'll get you out there."

Being that tall, at that age, I got mistaken for a basketball player almost as much as I got mistaken for a girl. This was constant and almost comical. But like those other times, I'd never correct anyone. I'd actually avoid anything that had to do with basketball, just to avoid the embarrassment of having no clue what I was doing.

I'm not going to lie: that first practice felt great. I mean, I was the only kid in sweatpants, and I wore my socks on the court because I didn't have runners in my locker, but I did all the things. The coach told me to stand under the net and for forty-five minutes I just stuffed guys. Anytime anyone would come in for a layup, I'd stand on my tiptoes, put that big jangly, bracelet-covered arm up, and shut them down. Basketball was easy.

I'd never been on a school team before, and this whole thing felt really good. I should have kept it to myself, but I went home and told Pop that I was on the squad. My dad was just as much of a sports fan as he was music fan, which wasn't much. He'd watch the odd hockey game with me but didn't know who the players were or who had the best shot at winning. It was just a way for us to hang out. Hockey wasn't fun for him, but time together was.

He was pumped for me, and we high-fived when I told him how I spent all practice shutting guys down, and how the coach said the other teams were going to shit themselves when they saw me walk onto the court. I may or may not have told my dad that Coach said I was their "secret weapon," even though I'm 100 percent sure Coach *never* used those words while talking to me.

Once again, this was ego doing battle with insecurity.

My high school was small, so when it came to sports, music, or drama, everyone just sort of did everything. We didn't really have "jocks"—everyone got to play. Two days after that first practice, I played my first game. I had my uniform, tied up all my hair into a giant ponytail, wrapped two bandanas around my left wrist to hide all my bracelets, and walked out with the team.

It was an away game, and other schools always made us eat shit. For everything. People just hated Acton. We were the trashy skids who all the other schools agreed to hate, and I looked like their mascot. When we walked onto the court the gym went silent. There I was, six foot three-ish, and beside me was James. James was born with dwarfism; he was a little person. He was a kid we'd always gone to school with. I stayed far away from sports so I hadn't really thought about how other people would react to seeing him on a basketball court. And now he was standing beside me, a giant with a high ponytail in a pink scrunchie. The other team and their fans had no clue what to even do with this, so they whispered and laughed. Which is something I was very used to, and I'm more than sure James was too. Neither of us let on like we cared. I'm not sure James even *did* care.

The first five minutes of that game were a disaster. I didn't know where to stand, what the plan was, who to pass the ball to, or what a foul was. I knew *nothing* about basketball. In those first few minutes I was double- and triple-teamed by their defence. They assumed I was a killer, and tried to shut me down, but soon realized I was a *huge* waste of resources. James was ten times the basketball player I was, so for the rest of the first quarter the other team just let me awkwardly run up and down the court like a baby giraffe. I wasn't a threat. I was an embarrassment to the game.

I remember the coach saying, "What are you doing, man?" to which I just answered, "I. Don't. Know!"

He seemed as pissed as he was confused.

Before the end of the half, one of my bandanas came loose and my bracelets started to show. The ref blew his whistle and walked me over to the bench. "Those have to go," he told my coach. "They're dangerous. Someone is going to get hurt with those. Take them off," he said to me.

"They don't come off," I told them.

Coach grabbed my wrist and started digging his finger under the other bandana to loosen it up. "Get rid of these. Now," he told me.

"No. I can't. They don't come off," I repeated.

"Cut them off," he snapped.

Those bracelets, and my hot pink toenails, were the last two things that made me, me. Everything was changing so fast, and here I was trying to be someone I wasn't. Again.

"Get that shit off or you're gone," the coach told me.

Okay, I thought, and I started to walk over to the bench to take a seat when he grabbed my shoulder and spun me around.

"No!" he said. "Get your shit and go. You're done."

I knew he wasn't really mad about the bracelets; this wasn't about jewellery. He was pissed at himself. He'd been wrong about me. I never wanted to be the *star* anything. I'd never been on a team, didn't want to be singled out, and hated taking orders. Sure, I had one good practice, but I was shit at basketball. I was tall, and that's *all* I was. He'd thought I was something that I wasn't, and I made him look like a fool, even though it was *me* who just got kicked out of a high school basketball game for excessive jewellery wearing.

In my school, being chosen valedictorian was more of a popularity contest than something you earned. It wasn't based on grades or your volunteer work or how many awards you had won. It was an open vote, democratic to a fault, and anyone could get nominated. Anyone could win. The election was student-run but teacher-supervised. If enough people wrote your name down on a piece of paper on vote day, you'd be the kid who'd get to send off the senior class with words of wisdom and encouragement and the confidence to chase their dreams and crush their goals. Just like in the movies.

On nomination day, I was as shocked as anyone to see my name on the shortlist. It was me and three girls. Three really smart girls who were all going off to high-end universities. Three girls who had spent their entire high school careers preparing for a moment like this. Me, I was just popular. I think people wrote my name down hoping I'd get up there, shotgun a beer, yell, "Acton High School seniors rule," throw my fist in the air, crush the can on my head, and walk off to thunderous applause. That's what guys like me did in the movies. I could do that. I had never, comfortably, been on a stage in front of people, and I certainly wasn't equipped to be anything close to inspiring. But I *could* make a fool of myself. I could make people laugh.

Election Day was an absolute scandal. A shit show. A screw job to end all screw jobs.

When all the ballots had been counted and recounted, I was chosen by my peers to be their valedictorian. By *four* votes. I won because four more people in that school wanted to see me get up there and say some crazy shit than the ones who wanted to be inspired.

Kerry-Anne deserved it. And we all knew it.

Three anonymous teachers were in charge of overseeing and validating the vote. Apparently four votes were just "too close to call," so they hit a hard pause on the entire thing. I hadn't even celebrated yet. I didn't get a chance to tell my parents, but before the end of the day there was going to be a revote. I don't know what exactly they were hoping for, but I assumed it was any result that wasn't *me*.

In the two or three hours between votes I started to take things seriously. It really hit me. I wasn't sure I wanted to be the guy who flashed the crowd, did a shot, and walked off. I didn't want to *do* the thing they all hoped I would. I didn't want to just be funny, and I certainly didn't want to let anyone down. I skipped two periods and sat in the smoking pit just outside the cafeteria and played this out in my head. Over and over. I barely passed grade eleven English, didn't take any poetry or creative writing classes, and hadn't got a grade above 60 percent on a book report in my whole life.

How do you write a speech when you have nothing to say?

I sat there, chain-smoking, feeling the exact same way I did when I'd sit naked with my guitar in my bedroom trying to force myself to cry, looking for something inside of me I knew I'd never find. I wanted to write a great speech the same way I wanted to write a great ballad. I wanted to be heartbreaking, thoughtful, inspiring, and motivating. I wanted it to be the thing people would remember. The kind of speech you see go viral on YouTube today. I needed this. I needed to go out this way. I wanted to surprise people. I wanted to stand there on a stage, with an audience, validated and vulnerable.

The recount happened and I lost. By *two* votes, and it was official this time. There was no way they were ever going to give this to me, and nothing anyone said was going to turn this around no matter how unfair it seemed. This was a screw job. It was *never* going to be me.

The second vote, by the way, would have been even closer had I not voted for Kerry-Anne. She deserved it, and I had nothing to say anyway.

These were people who thought I was something that I wasn't, and there was no way I was going to make a fool of myself to prove them right. I didn't want to be put into *another* position to fail and then get blamed for it, again, when I did.

I'm still not sure who those three anonymous teachers were who were in charge of the whole thing, but I bloody well guarantee you *one* of them was the basketball coach.

2

BRIDGES
AND
TUNNELS

EIGHTEEN GOING ON NINETEEN

College was going to be fucking awesome! It was 1993, and I spent a good chunk of that last year of high school sending off letters to UCLA, USC, University of Miami, Boston College, and anywhere else that had a media program, requesting admission forms. This would be my total reinvention. I didn't have big dreams of good grades and graduating with honours, but I knew damn well I could be a legendary student. I wanted to be Rob Lowe in *St. Elmo's Fire*, tortured and lost, sitting on the roof of a frat house with a saxophone, a cigarette, and knock-off Ray-Bans. Partying half-naked with girls who were *also* half-naked, while chugging beer and dancing around to Def Leppard. I wanted football games and pep rallies. Drunk, popular, and falling in love. Having my goddamn heart broken. I could be that guy. I *was* that guy.

None of that happened.

My high school grades left me with very few college options. Actually, they left me with just one option: the radio broadcasting program at Humber College, about a forty-minute drive from the town I grew up in. I applied to exactly one school. I never wanted to be a DJ. I only ever wanted to be an entertainer—I wanted an audience. Humber had a decent, well-respected radio program, and more importantly they had dorms, which meant I wouldn't have to live at home with my mom and dad and commute in every day. A school with a dorm was my top priority, and these were single rooms—no roommate. They had cable TV, you got your own phone, and you could smoke.

I certainly didn't get accepted because of my grades, or my in-person audition, which involved me reading an old traffic report along with a made-up commercial script for chicken tenders in front of the entire admissions team. My voice was a little deeper at this point, but even still, two weeks before my audition I remember chain-smoking cigarette after cigarette and screaming into my pillow at night trying to destroy my vocal cords *just* enough to give me a great voice. None of that helped.

I got accepted because I was the only person in that room who had real-life experience inside an actual radio station.

Every Saturday night during my last year of high school I'd sit on a bus for two hours to go and work in Toronto, for free, at a rock radio station—the biggest one in the country. I'd run the mixing board for the DJ, load up the CDs, organize the commercial carts, and press Play on the reel-to-reel machine if we were running something on tape. The studios were incredible—state of the art—and there was a punching bag and a grand piano in the lobby. The piano was just for show, but the punching bag was set up because the general manager got tired of the hotheaded sports reporter punching holes in the walls every time he got into an argument with the boss, or at least that's the story they told. The halls were lined with autographed gold and platinum records from every band I loved.

There was a kick-ass Jock Lounge with a purple felt pool table and a wraparound balcony on the twenty-fifth floor. Before that, I'd never met an actual DJ, and these dudes were gnarly. Old-school "jocks" with big voices, big egos, making big money. But here's the crazy part: they all really seemed to hate what they did. Don't get me wrong—they *loved* their own voices, and getting paid to sit around listening to Led Zeppelin was cool too, but my god did they hate the audience. If you called into a radio station, to them, you were a loser. A fucking idiot. They'd call you a "prize pig" or a "loogan," whatever *that* meant. If you were a kid who called in to request a song? Forget about it—those assholes would keep you on hold for twenty minutes and then just dump all the lines, all at once, hanging up on you and everyone else. To them, this was hilarious. To me, it was heartbreaking, because I used to be one of those kids.

The day my dad helped me move into my college dorm was very much like the movies. That weekend, I remember, my mom stepped back a bit and let Pops have these moments with me. Nobody on my dad's side of the family had ever gone to college before. My brother started the year before I did, but he was still living at home, so I was the first Weston to ever *go off* to college. My parents sold our house and moved into a rental to make sure we could afford it.

After Pops set up my room and hooked up my TV, I laid out the sheet set my mom got me for the single bed that I was way too tall for. My dad grabbed me and pulled me in. He didn't say much, but he gave me one of those hugs of his—the best kind. "This is an incredible opportunity," he whispered to me. "I'm proud of you. You got this."

"Yeah, Pop. I got this."

He was right. This *was* an incredible opportunity. So I did my absolute best to fuck it all up.

I didn't know much about college. Hell, I didn't know much about anything, but I certainly didn't know that you had to take English courses in order to pass. Like actual English classes with book reports where spelling counts. I honestly thought I'd walk into radio school and spend all my time learning how to make pro-level prank phone calls while coming up with a killer radio name like Tarzan Dan or Brother Jake. For two weeks I tried to make Roz Bozwood happen, or Roz Boz for short. That did *not* happen. Because it was stupid.

I wanted classes on humour, improv, storytelling, and contract negotiations. I wanted to spend my days writing jokes and my evenings screaming into my pillow trying to perfectly destroy my voice. *This* was *not* that. There was no course called How to Be Howard Stern 101.

On the first day of class, our English teacher assigned a huge project right out of the gate. This was less of a test and more of a challenge. She knew nobody wanted to take the class, so she made it simple: "Anybody who gets above ninety-five on this essay doesn't have to take this course and you'll never have to see me again." That was it. It was that easy.

I worked my ass off on that essay. For five days I spent every minute in the library, skipped meals, and watched zero TV. I crushed it. It was a literal masterpiece. I had never felt so confident about anything in my entire life.

The following Wednesday, I walked back into that English class and yelled "You ready for this?" as I one-arm-slammed that thing down on the teacher's desk. "I look forward to never seeing *you* again," I said with full snark and a half wink.

"Same," she replied.

I got 21 percent.

I'd never seen anything like that before. My essay was so marked up, crossed out, and pulled apart it looked like redacted FBI testimony.

That was, however, the last time I ever saw that teacher again. I never went back. Everyone just assumed I aced it and I never said otherwise.

I was a kid who had incredible confidence but pretty low self-esteem. I've always believed that when you're young, those two things are built in two very different ways. Confidence comes from people *telling* you you're great. Self-esteem is built by *doing* things that are great. Accomplishments. I'd never done any great things. I had all the confidence in the world but would always lower the expectations I had for myself just to avoid failure. Nobody ever saw me fail. At anything. I couldn't handle that.

Those first few months of college were different, though. I was now nineteen and could already feel the shine rubbing off me. My confidence took hit after hit, and my self-esteem was non-existent. I was irrelevant and invisible. It's not that people started to expect less of me, it's just that nobody cared. I wasn't ready for any of this, emotionally or otherwise. I felt lost, I missed my brother, and even doing my best in the classes that I did like I was never going be good enough.

For the first little while I really did try hard to take part, to make the best of it. I made a few good friends, talked a lot of shit, did the Thursday pub crawls, and discovered that Jack Daniel's and I do *not* mix. The thought, though, of having to stand out or impress anyone was killing me. I didn't have that *thing*, that spark, that other people in my class had. I still had nothing to say.

—

It was cheaper for us to eat lunch at the strip club up the street than it was to eat in the dorm cafeteria. Giant bowl of spaghetti, garlic bread, and a large Coke for six bucks. You just couldn't beat those prices, so that's what we did. A couple of days a week, a few of us would hop the bus for two stops to hit up the Manhattan Strip.

This was always mid-afternoon, so transitioning from the blazing fall sun to a super-dark, neon- and smoke-filled club always felt weird. Oddly, a suburban strip club in an industrial area at two in the afternoon is *not* the happiest place on earth. The girls were all day-shift dancers who never expected much from anyone—certainly not from a gang of poor college kids who were only there for the garlic bread—but we were always respectful. We'd clap after each one of their understandably uninspired routines, and we'd all tip the bartender a buck each on our way out even though none of us were drinking. Every other customer was there alone. Solo tables. They'd smoke a few cigarettes and nurse the same beer for an hour while making small talk with the dancers. Nobody who walks into a strip club alone in the middle of a Monday does so because they're looking for a good time. It's where people go to hide. Where lonely people go to feel a little *less* lonely. Even if they have to pay for it.

On Thursdays, a stack of *NOW* magazines would be dropped off at the lobby of our dorm. *NOW* was very much like *The Village Voice* in New York, a free weekly paper with snarky editorials, ultra-liberal politics, in-depth artist interviews, and all the movie and concert listings for the entire week. *NOW* was our bible. We lived and planned our lives by that thing. The last few pages were all the same classifieds that most indie papers use to fund their operations. Buy & Sell, Missed Connections, local business ads, and hundreds and hundreds of listings for escorts, strip clubs, and chat lines. I'd

ROZ WESTON

never used a chat line before, but the ads were very provocative and over the top, and they had names like Quest and the Night Exchange. Sexy anonymous fun for sexy anonymous strangers.

The chat lines were always free for women, but men had to buy a thirty-dollar monthly membership. To get guys hooked, they *did* have a few free spots assigned to a separate phone number, and if you called and called and got lucky, you got in and were given five free minutes to chat. I didn't have a credit card, so I'd spend hours getting a busy signal before getting through. Those free five minutes would expire, I'd get kicked off, and I'd start all over again. And again.

Once you got through, you'd have to record your name and a quick personal greeting. That was all that the women online would hear. You'd hit 3 on your phone to skip through the messages, you could press 2 to send a voice message, and pressing 1 would request a "live one-on-one private conversation." Building enough of a connection and rapport, while getting kicked off every five minutes, made private conversations almost impossible. I'd get close, exchange a few flirty messages, say something personal but not in any way true, and hope for the best. I'd only hear their names; the rest was up to me. The ultimate goal was to eventually talk live, exchange numbers, and call each other *off* the chat line. For free. This would take hours of work, every single day. Absolute dedication.

I spent months waking up at six in the morning, trying the chat lines until my first radio lab class. Then I'd head out for spaghetti lunch at the strip club right after that, skip the rest of the day, and lie on my bed in my dorm room trying to connect with someone. Anyone. Most nights I'd fall asleep with the phone still jammed between my ear and the pillow, with my hand on the keypad after hitting redial a few hundred times.

I was rarely myself on those things. It was always easier to be someone else. A fake name, with a fake story and a fake life. I was used to that, and always assumed the women were all doing the same thing, so I never felt too bad about lying. On the chat lines, in *that* world, my name was Jack, and after much trial and error I'd come up with the perfect five-second greeting that almost guaranteed me private messages within seconds. I've never told anyone this before, and my god is it embarrassing. Mortifying. So let's all agree that you'll read this one time and one time only and never repeat it ever again—because it's absolute cringe—but here it goes:

"Hey, this is Jack. Just looking for a nice warm voice to rub up against for a while."

That was it. Fucking kill me.

Eventually, and inevitably, things escalated. I'd exchanged numbers with dozens of—maybe even fifty or sixty—women, and I'd spend almost every hour of the day missing class, locked in my room talking to strangers. We'd have these incredible conversations that became less and less about sex. Little bits of truth would break through the characters we'd created. I'd hear about their jobs, their horrible husbands, their broken marriages. We'd talk about our bodies, insecurities, and fantasies. We'd also laugh—we'd laugh a lot.

This whole thing became an escape and I became the thing they needed me to be. This was a connection, the thing I looked most forward to in most of my days. In some weird backwards way, it felt like an audience. I was performing. These anonymous women saw something in me that I didn't know existed, and I could be whatever it was they needed. And none of the women could see me; they couldn't see me tic or see anything else I wanted

to hide. I'd just turned nineteen and these were the closest relationships I'd ever had.

Once I started meeting women off the line, there was no going
back. I'd sneak out of the dorm, way past curfew, and take the
bus into the city to meet up with someone my mother's age at a
bougie downtown hotel, or I'd head to a parking lot out near the
airport and spend a few hours with someone else in the back of
her minivan. I'd never felt more valued as a person than I did when
I was there.

Before your head starts spinning, *no*, I wasn't a teenage college
gigolo, and *no*, I never took money—but everything was up for
grabs. They saw something in me that was great, even if it wasn't
true. It didn't have to be. I was whatever they needed, and I was
goddamn good at it. For the most part, these were women who
were alone or broken, who needed an escape from trying to hold
it all together. And for me? It gave me purpose.

I bought a second-hand suit in a vintage store for when I
needed to be a bit fancy, and I picked up a bag of my old glam
rock clothes from my parents' house for when I needed to be a
bit more, well, *that*. Some dates lasted minutes, others the whole
night. One woman found out I'd never been to the Olive Garden
and took me there for dinner every night for an entire week.
Another, who I was meeting for coffee at noon, showed up drunk
off her ass in an American-flag bikini, took one look at me, and
started throwing glass saltshakers at my head that she'd grabbed
off the hostess stand on her way in. I don't know what I did, but
I sure as hell did something. But most nights, these meetings were
exactly what you think they were—sexy anonymous fun for sexy
anonymous strangers.

If that year taught me anything it was that having a one-night stand can be awesome but *being* a one-night stand feels pretty fucking awful.

I was building a life around short-term, frivolous pleasure, torching the idea of any kind of long-term growth. And yet most nights I'd come home feeling great about myself. Whether I was a shoulder to cry on or a body to climb on, if I felt like I helped or made any kind of difference, I was good. The other nights, though, the ones where I let them down, when I wasn't the exact *thing* they were expecting, or when I'd get dropped off in the middle of nowhere with no way home, on those nights I'd head back to my dorm, flop on my tiny bed, and hit redial.

In 2014, Humber College inducted me into their Radio Alumni Hall of Fame.

NEW YORK SPEED

I wound up in New York City out of a combination of desperation, white lies, and jealousy.

In the spring of '94, during my last few months of that first year of college, I started working on this plan, this hustle, to get my ass to New York City. In order to graduate from the radio program, you needed to complete two years plus an internship. The internship had to be approved and always came after your second year, never before. The other kids in my class hadn't even started thinking about an internship yet, but some of them were already getting job offers and leaving early. Which enraged me. I was so jealous it caused anxiety, and I couldn't be happy for anyone. I'd avoid their goodbye parties at the pub, and I never offered up even a simple "congrats" or "good job." Everyone was moving forward, evolving, and making shit happen. All their dreams were coming true, and I was fading. Being left behind.

I'd almost given up on the idea of stardom. This was now about survival. I knew, at this point, that if I was going to become anything, I'd have to learn from the best. I needed to surround myself with the smartest people who worked for the biggest shows.

I needed to work for Howard Stern.

I was still working for that rock station in Toronto on Saturday nights. The woman I was working for had been around forever, and she didn't give a fuck. She was pretty good at her job, but she'd smoke in the studio, take home records from the library and never return them, and spend hours of her shift talking to her boyfriends on the studio phone. She was messy, but we got along great. While the songs were playing, we'd have tons of time to just talk—and when you're sitting alone, for *that* long, together in a soundproof booth, you just start saying shit. Opening up. Sometimes the conversations would get flirty, and would usually end with her saying something like, "You should meet this friend of mine," or, "I have the perfect woman for you." These quickly went from fun suggestions to blind dates I felt I couldn't get out of.

The first one she set up was on a night when I should have been in there working with her. She didn't so much ask as instruct me on the when and where. I couldn't tell her I was too busy because she knew exactly what I did every single Saturday night. These women were all ten or fifteen years older than me, which was fine—I was used to that from the chat lines. But these dates were different. I had to be *me*; I wasn't a made-up character. I don't really remember much from those nights, except one started in a bar and quickly ended up at her place, and another woman openly referred to me as "young bone" while flirting across the table at a restaurant that I couldn't afford but still paid for anyway. I was insecure and I didn't want to piss anyone off or let anyone down, so I went along with it. All of it. I'm sure my boss thought I was having the time of my life.

To apply for an internship on *The Howard Stern Show* you needed a resumé, cover letter, proof of college credit, and a signed recommendation from an industry professional. The cover letter

ROZ WESTON

and resumé were a snap. My mom worked on those with me. Actually she worked on my entire package with me. She was meticulous. She'd been working in an office for years by now and had seen hundreds of resumés come across her desk. Mine looked high-end and professional. She didn't even call it a resumé: she wrote "Curriculum Vitae" up at the top, which looked fancy as hell.

The letter of recommendation was another story. The only person I could ask was the DJ I worked with on Saturday nights, who, when I asked, said, "Should I add 'good in bed'? Because that's what I hear." If there's one thing I learned about that generation of DJs, and that I've avoided becoming my entire career, it's that no matter what, everything is *all* about them, and my letter was no different. She knew this was going off to *The Stern Show*, so she filled it with horribly unfunny jokes, puns, and one-liners. She was *auditioning*. She called me poor, talked about my hair, and described me as someone she "scooped up out of the gutter" and said I "only show up to work for the free food." It was an embarrassing disaster.

I handed my mom the letter to look over. This was the first time I ever heard my mother call another woman a bitch. She was livid, and immediately started going to work on it. My mom was crafty as hell and had access to a laser printer. The first thing she did was cut out the station logo and signature with a razor blade. She saved those bits for later. Then she started firing questions at me, one right after another, as she sat at the family computer hammering out all my answers into my new letter.

"What did you do there? Like actually do?" she asked.

"Played the CDs, turned on the mics . . ."

"What else?"

"Put stuff away, cleaned up. Stuff like that." I certainly couldn't tell her I'd spent the last few weeks sleeping with my boss's friends.

"Okay, what did *other* people do?" she shot back at me, waving her hand in front of my face like my two previous answers didn't count. "What are the other jobs? What did the *other* people do?"

"I don't know. Like the music director?"

"What's that job? What do they do? The music director?"

"He's the one who picks and schedules all the music."

"Okay, you were the assistant to the music director," she insisted.

"But I wasn't . . ."

"Just because you *didn't* do that job, doesn't mean you *couldn't* do that job. What else? Who else did what?" She kept asking, so I kept answering. "You've given up every Saturday night for two years for what? For this piece of shit?" She grabbed what was left of that original letter and swiped it off the side of the desk. "No. Absolutely not. You're not getting screwed because some broad thinks she's funny."

My mom took my new letter to work the next day and copied it all back together with the station logo and signature attached. It was perfect. A perfect forgery.

And that's what got me my interview with *The Howard Stern Show*.

My uncle Gary, who wasn't really my uncle, was cool as hell, had a killer moustache, and was one of my dad's oldest and closest friends. More importantly, Uncle Gary drove for Greyhound and managed to score me a free bus ticket to New York for my interview. My parents sent me off with a little spending money and enough cash for a hotel room for one night—and anybody who knows anything about New York in the early '90s knows exactly what kind of hotel took cash without a credit card deposit. The shared-bathroom-and-no-pillow kind.

The first time I walked through those doors of the Port Authority Bus Terminal and out onto Eighth Avenue, I was hit with everything New York had to offer. I felt huge and anonymous all at the same time. It felt like home.

At this point, Howard was still on K-Rock at 600 Madison Avenue. This was the same building *Seinfeld* used when Elaine worked for Pendant Publishing, and I recognized it right away. I was ten minutes early for my interview, and I put my hair up in a ponytail before walking onto the elevator. As a fan of radio, walking into the studios where Howard did his show was shit-your-pants crazy. The show was on vacation that week, though, so the place was pretty dead. I met with a woman named Carol, who ran the intern program. She talked like a sassy New Yorker, and she reminded me of every great teacher I'd ever had. I loved her right away. Carol didn't want to know anything about my years of experience as an assistant to the music director, or what my college grades were like. She just wanted to know what the hell I was doing there. *The Stern Show* wasn't even on in Canada, and she was blown away that a kid from Toronto would want to intern on the show. I had read Howard's book, seen all his appearances on Letterman, and knew that this was the biggest show in the world. Even though I'd never heard a minute if it.

She offered me the job on the spot, and I accepted on the spot. I was about to be Howard Stern's first Canadian intern. The only thing she needed was proof that I'd be getting college credit for it. I had zero intention of doing a second year of college, and I knew this opportunity probably wouldn't be available then anyway, so I had to convince my teachers this was a once-in-a-lifetime chance. I promised that they could hold all credit until after second year. If they hadn't agreed, I'm sure my mom would have forged that letter too, but they did, reluctantly, and signed off on everything.

That was the last I ever saw of that school.

You never forget your first time in New York City. It's the most infectious place on earth. You don't ever visit New York; you try New York on. And it *always* fits perfectly. You know when a co-worker comes back from one of those all-inclusive beach vacations with their hair still braided, a fresh tan, wearing a "Don't Hassle Me I'm On Island Time" T-shirt? New York is like that too. It rubs off on you and you want to take it home. But instead of turning up at the office in January still wearing your sandals and a shell necklace, New York makes you want to just start telling people to fuck off. There's not a single person who's ever visited New York that didn't take a little of that back home with them.

That June, I packed up just about everything I owned, which wasn't much, and moved to Manhattan. A friend from college, Alex, managed to score himself an internship in New York too, so his dad offered to drive us both. Alex was a good guy and had been to New York tons of times with his family, so he knew what was up. Me? I hadn't been anywhere—especially America. We were never that family that did weekend trips to Buffalo to hit up the outlet malls, and I was the only kid I knew whose parents never took them to Disney World. America was different in our house: it was always off the table. After my dad went awol following his second tour in Vietnam and came to Canada, he never went back. He was terrified. Even though they had long given amnesty to the draft dodgers, the guys who did serve but went awol were still subject to military disciplinary action. My dad was convinced that if he ever crossed the border, he'd be arrested.

Alex and I moved into an apartment in the Village, right at Union Square and 14th. It was a one-bedroom that we shared with two other guys we'd never met and who, until they moved in, hadn't met each other either. Two beds in the living room, two in the bedroom, and the smallest kitchen I'd ever seen. The apartment was run by NYU Housing, so hundreds of nineteen-year-olds had lived there before us. There were no curtains, no air conditioning, and the whole joint smelled like fresh piss. It was perfect.

That June the Rangers and the Knicks were both in the playoffs, the World Cup was happening, and the Gay Games were getting started all at the same time. The city was bonkers. It was a hundred degrees every day, and it felt like a fight was about to break out on every street corner. We hadn't even hit July yet and New Yorkers were already fucking sick of it. They were done.

I'd convinced myself that New York was the answer to everything because I had the freedom to reinvent myself into anything I wanted to be. Over and over again. Every morning before work, I'd sit and have a coffee on the same stoop, at the same time, and watch the same guy run up and down Broadway wearing only a pair of women's pantyhose, pulled up past his bellybutton, with no underpants. Everything was all mashed up and deformed under there, and you could see it all. People would say hi, and he'd tell them to fuck off. This was his routine. This was New York. You could be anything you wanted to be.

Me? I wanted to be smart. I wanted to have something to offer. And I wanted to matter. I didn't want to be a dumb skid anymore.

To put things into context for the hardcore Stern fans, I started my internship the same day Gay Rich did. Gay Rich went on to become a legend on that show. Sure, I was Howard's first Canadian intern, but Rich was Howard's first gay intern. There was no way I could compete with that. Not on *that* show.

Howard mentioned me once on air, not by name or anything, but he said he had "a Canadian intern now." Of course, Howard used this as an opportunity to show how awesome *he* was, how international he'd become, though, for me, it was still one of the greatest moments of my life. The goal for every single person who ever walked through the doors of that show was to get airtime, to be invited in, to become a character, to shine. About two weeks in, Carol handed me a blank sheet of printer paper and a Sharpie and asked me to write Howard's promo for the end of the show. These were all plugs for what was coming up the next day, promoting what the guys on the show were up to that night. One of them, Stuttering John, was doing an appearance at Tower Records that evening. I wrote it all up, handed it to Carol, and she walked down the hall and handed it to Howard's producer. I sat in the corner of the office with my ear pressed up against the speaker of the tiny radio on Carol's desk.

"And tonight at nine, Stuttering John will be at the Times Square Tower Records singing . . . John, are you singing tonight?" Howard asked.

"No," John stuttered. "It's a signing. An autograph signing." He stuttered harder.

Howard read the words I wrote, one time and one time only, and it was clear I didn't know the difference between "singing" and "signing." Now, you can chalk this up to nerves, or a simple mistake, or whatever, but I didn't. I could have looked at the promo for a hundred hours and still wouldn't have been able to find my mistake. This killed me. This ruined me. This was the closest I ever got to being on with Howard and I blew it. In front of fifteen million people. "Who wrote this?" was the last thing I heard Howard say before I shut the radio off.

I spent the next couple of months keeping my head down, obsessively and quietly observing. I made notes about everything. I watched how people did things, figured out who did what, and got a handle on how they ran the office, how they produced the show. Sure, *The Stern Show* was wild, and the office was fun, but it wasn't the frat house environment you might imagine. There *were* days when the guys in the studio would be painting strippers' boobs because it was someone's birthday or some shit, but the office, just on the other side of those doors, might as well have been a bank or an H&R Block. It was all business, and people took it very seriously. I spent most of my internship working on the paperback version of *Private Parts*, Howard's first book. Most days, I worked alone.

Being broke in New York is different from being broke in other places. If you're broke in L.A., you can always go to the beach. But New York has a way of reminding you, over and over, how broke you are. Everything you can't afford is right in front of your face. All the time. I couldn't afford shit, so I walked. I'd take the subway to SoHo and walk up to Central Park, grab a beer, smoke a few cigarettes, then walk back down to Union Square. I'd go for drinks in the East Village at Coney Island High or the No Tell Motel, then stumble back up to Times Square to wander around for a bit before hitting up a peep show. Times Square was still sleazy then. It was beautiful. I had long since figured out that if you showed up at a peep show looking like you were going to throw up in the booth, they wouldn't let you in, so you always had to sober up a bit first.

One of those nights, while sitting alone on Broadway, hoping I'd be able to walk straight enough to spend my last ten bucks on peep show tokens trying to connect with a naked stranger on the other side of a filthy plexiglass wall, I had one of the most devastatingly beautiful moments of my life. It was like someone flipped a switch and shut the city down. I remember looking down at the toes of my shoes as I smashed a cigarette butt out under my Converse, then all of a sudden—nothing. Absolute silence. I looked up and for thirty seconds I was alone. I caught the perfect New York wave. I don't know if it was the way the streetlights cycled, or where all the people went, but for that quick moment it was empty. It was just me. There wasn't one other person or car in sight, and everything just went quiet. For half a minute, I was the only human being in one of the busiest places on earth. I'd never felt so small and alone before. Then, in the time it took me to light another smoke, everything changed. Everything went back to normal. Except me. I was done.

That next morning, I called home to talk to my Pops. I didn't really have anything to say, but I needed a laugh and a pep talk. I couldn't tell him I was failing, or how sad I was. I just felt so bloody heavy. My heart hurt every day. When I wasn't being the most invisible intern in the history of *The Howard Stern Show*, or sitting alone in an East Village dive bar, I'd lock myself in our tiny bathroom back at the apartment and hurt myself. I burned myself more in those few months than I had in years.

Dad wasn't home when I called, but my brother was, and he had big news. Huge. He told me he just got a loft in Toronto with a co-worker. A big industrial joint, right downtown, that had one of those cool old elevators that went right up into your place. I asked if there was any space for me. "Of course," he said. "Always."

"Cool. I'm coming home."

MICKEY ROONEY WAS AN ASSHOLE

Kill at least ten roaches before bed, and the last one to turn out the lights had to reset the mousetraps. Those was the only rules in the loft. A few weeks before I moved in, while I was still in New York, my dad showed up in Toronto with a truckload of lumber and tools and built out three bedrooms for me, Rich, and our roommate Parker.

It all looked a bit wonky and homemade, but we all had our own rooms now, with a ladder and space up on top for a couch and the TV. It wasn't perfect—none of my dad's projects ever were—but it worked. We had twelve hundred square feet, a bar fridge, a hot plate—and roaches. We had a *big* cockroach problem. The space sure wasn't pretty, or well maintained at all, and technically we weren't even allowed to live there—the guy my brother swung this deal with was happy to take our money, but it wasn't legal, so we had nobody we could complain to or ask to fix things when they broke or fell apart. Every pair of socks I owned was soon covered in holes because the floors had nails popping up everywhere, and we were missing so many windows that in the winter you could stick your arm right out and catch snow if you wanted to.

We rented out half the space on Tuesday and Thursday nights to an art school for nude life drawing classes, and shortly after I moved in Parker started making extra cash by running an "erotic massage for women" business out of his room. The life drawing classes offset our rent by a few hundred dollars a month, so walking in a few nights a week to an impressively cocked naked male-model standing on a stage in our living room quickly became normal. There was very little in the way of privacy, which meant that when Parker had a "client" over, the faint hum and muffled buzz of vibrator mixed with unmuffled shrieks and orgasms also became normal. This was *not* an easy place to bring a date.

The only thing I knew about cockroaches was that they were punishingly hard to kill, and they gravitated to dark, moist places. I slept in underpants every single night in that place. But for $333 a month each, what did I really have to complain about?

I quickly realized that an internship on *The Howard Stern Show* opened more doors for me than a second year of college ever could. I got an in-person interview for *every single* job I applied for—even ones I had zero chance of getting. *The Stern Show* was at the very top of my resumé for years because people would bring me in for interviews just to get the dirt. I was never fully truthful or forthcoming. I'd entertain them, make shit up, tell them what they wanted to hear. I kept everything I *actually* learned to myself.

Within a week of landing in Toronto, I found a student-run salon to chop all my hair off for twelve bucks plus tip, and I did my best to reinvent myself. I wanted to try to be as New York as I could. I'd spend whatever cash I had at Black Market Vintage on

Queen West, buying up old T-shirts, leather jackets, and as many pointy-toed shoes as I could afford. I had thrown out all my old jeans, all the ones left over from my high school days, and started exclusively wearing women's jeans. They were tighter in the ass and the thighs and usually had a little flare on the bottom. Other times I'd leave the house in pyjama bottoms, cowboy boots, and an undershirt. I did my best to look cool with what I had. I was a fashion-backwards work in progress. In the loft, we all kept all our clothes in garbage bags—nothing ever got hung up or folded away in drawers. Everything I owned went from the dryer straight into a garbage bag with a double knot tied at the top. That gave me the best shot at walking out of the house roach-free after I got dressed every morning.

The three of us lived in the loft for just over a year, but I don't remember cooking one single meal in that place. I don't ever remember bringing groceries in, or even using the fridge. Everything Rich and I ate was takeout or delivery. When we were growing up in Acton we didn't have delivery. Nobody delivered anything. I had never once picked up a phone and had food show up at the door thirty minutes later. This was all new for us. On weekends, we'd split a large pizza, six pieces of fried chicken, and a box of fries from this joint called Double Double. We'd order at ten in the morning, right when they opened, eat half for breakfast and save the rest for a late lunch. It was eighteen dollars for everything. Then, at around eight, we'd order the exact same thing for dinner. We did the math, and three meals for two people at thirty-six dollars was a deal too good to pass up. Sometimes we'd get the same delivery guy for round two. He'd see all the empty boxes on the counter from the first round of the day, grab them for us, and throw them down the chute on his way out. My brother and I were finally together again. We were happy—and bloated.

My first job—as in actual paying job—in radio was chase pro-ducing for a news and public affairs show, making $18,900 a year. I remember the exact number only because of how happy I was after my first raise, which bumped me up to an even $20,000. A chase producer's job is to book the show. I'd be handed stacks of articles, newspaper clippings, and press releases all cut up and highlighted with the names of the people they wanted booked for interviews. Then I'd go to work on the phone. I'd track people down all over the world—celebs, authors, academics, criminals, politicians—and book them all. I made it look easy. I was great on the phone. I don't know if it was all those anonymous nights on the chat lines in college, but I could convince anyone to cancel whatever they were doing and come on our show. I was comfortable on the phone, and it was the only time I really felt like I fit in, when I looked like I knew what I was doing. Every other interaction I faked and fumbled my way through.

Anytime I booked a big star, I'd always call my dad to tell him. He thought it was just the greatest. The idea that his boy would be hanging with all these legends, and doing a great job, really made him proud, and there was nothing like that feeling. I never shattered his bubble, though. I never told him when someone was an asshole. At least, not until I met Mickey Rooney. I'm normally not one to talk shit about the dead, but Mickey Rooney was an asshole. I didn't really know much about him, other than my dad telling me he was a huge fan when I told him I'd booked Mickey on the show.

Mickey was in town and came in to promote his one-man show, or play, or something else totally forgettable. My job was to get the guests comfortable in the green room down the hall from the studio and go over the rundown of the show with them. It was a speech I'd given a hundred times, but I was always nervous doing it. I wasn't great when I had to do face-to-face. Mickey was flopped in the corner of the couch, feet dangling off the side, with his head back and his eyes closed. I got about halfway through telling him how things were going to go down when I started to think he legit just fell asleep while I was talking. I didn't know whether to walk out, poke him, or keep going and just say it all. I was just about to tell him I'd be back in ten minutes to bring him into the studio when his head shot forward, his eyes wide open staring a hole through me. He was pissed off.

"How. Old. Are. You?" he asked, with a long pause between each word.

"Uh, I'm twenty," I answered.

"Yeah," he said. "It shows." I'd never seen someone so disgusted to be in the same room with me before. "Out," he said, pointing to the door with one of his little feet, before closing his eyes again.

Now, what I *should* have said was, "Get bent, you old little crotch." What I *did* say was, "Yeah. I know. No problem." I was crushed.

I walked back into the office to tell my supervisor what the hell just happened. I was shook, but Paul, who'd hired me for this job, was always great in these situations.

"Fuck that guy," he said.

"Yeah, I know. But that dude's a legend. He's been in like three hundred movies. One of the most famous actors ever."

"First off all that guy is barely famous anymore. You want to be famous? I'll tell you what, in thirty seconds you could easily become just as famous as that asshole. All you have to do is take this pencil, walk back into the green room, and jam it into Mickey Rooney's eye. You'll be one of the most famous people in the world by dinner, you'll be on *Larry King* tomorrow night. Fame doesn't mean you can just be a dick to whoever you want, and if you are, then don't be surprised when every now and then you get a pencil in the eye." Paul said all of this in one single breath and without even looking up from his typewriter. Which is how most of our conversations happened.

Paul saw something in me all those years ago that most people, especially me, didn't: potential. This job was the absolute definition of starting from the bottom. I was the hardest-working, and lowest-paid, person in the company, and I ate a ton of shit. The rest of the staff on the show could be diabolically cruel. Humiliating and abusive. But I wasn't going to quit, no matter what. This was an opportunity I wasn't going to fuck up. I was preparing for whatever was coming next. No matter how awful I felt at the end of each day.

I did not stab Mickey Rooney that afternoon. But I did tell my dad what happened, and for me, knowing that my Pops spent the rest of his life telling anyone who would ever listen that Mickey Rooney was a huge asshole was good enough.

I've worked two jobs at the same time since I was twenty. Even today, I work two full-time jobs, sixty-five hours a week, for two massive and competing companies. I was never the smartest person in the room, but I sure as hell could out-work anyone. Working long hours got me out of my own head, reduced my anxiety, and became the perfect distraction from anything or anyone that could hurt me. Especially myself. In 1994 minimum wage was eight dollars and ninety-five cents, so working seventeen hours a day was also the only way I could survive and keep working at the radio show. I was desperate and driven, and I found myself a second job for every night *and* weekend so I wouldn't have to quit the industry.

That's how I became, without question, one of the most successful telemarketers Toronto has ever seen.

I answered an ad in the back of the *Toronto Sun* for a job with the Toronto Symphony Orchestra subscription department. It was evenings, the office was right around the corner from the loft, and it was all on the phone. I could do this. I could sell symphony subscriptions and raffle tickets to old people.

Now, I don't care how wonderful your organization is or how well you think your business is run, I can guarantee you that your telemarketing department is one of the saddest and sleaziest rooms in your building. This one was no different. I sat beside a woman with thick glasses and thick hair, big home-perm curls, who spent most of her time complaining that we didn't have hands-free headsets, so before every shift, she'd reach into her purse, pull out a granny-style knee-high beige stocking, tie it around her head, pulling half down almost to her cheek, and jam the ear end of the phone receiver up under it. This was her way of problem solving while *also* protesting.

Our boss was a whole other story. He'd spend his time power-tripping, barking orders, and pretending to look natural and inconspicuous as he rubbed his dick on things. I don't know if it was a nervous tic or if he was dealing with something serious down there, but he couldn't stop pinching, squeezing, and pressing it up against anything he could reach with it. All the pants of his cheap grey suits had started to wear thin around there, and by the end of our shift each night, that little spot on the front would be wrinkled and covered in stains from the grease and dirt off his fingers.

It was the weirdest thing. If he was standing in front of us for any long period of time, say giving instructions or a pep talk, he'd eventually try to incorporate something like the photocopier or the filing cabinet into what he was saying just so he could walk over and mash his crotch up against the corner of it. There was a bell at the front of the office that if you made a sale you'd have to walk up and ring. Anytime *that* happened, he'd run up to celebrate with you, and after a few high-fives he'd turn around and casually slide his penis across the bottom ledge of the whiteboard we wrote our sales numbers on. I was the *only* one in that room who noticed, and anytime I did try to point it out to anyone, like the guy who sat across from me who made all his calls in a fake English accent and wore a cape to work every night, no one had any clue what I was talking about.

I made almost double my radio salary in that room that year.

One morning in the loft, around six, I got up to go pee. I walked into the bathroom, like I did every morning, and stood in front of the toilet, groggy and a bit hungover. As I pulled the front of my underpants out, I watched a cockroach fall from the inside of my waistband right into the toilet. I'm not sure how long it was in there, trapped between the thin strip of elastic and my stomach while I slept, but it was long enough to *almost* kill it.

"Rich!" I yelled, loud enough to wake him up on my first try.

"Yeah?"

"Can we move?" I shouted.

"Okay."

PAINKILLER

I worked an entire half a day with a collapsed lung because I was too afraid to let anyone know I needed help. I didn't want to be someone else's problem. I didn't want to let anyone down. I didn't want to get yelled at, and I certainly didn't want to get fired. I'd never taken a sick day, or vacation. No matter what I had done to my body the night before, how sick I was, or what kind of shape I was in when I woke up, I always made it in to work. My body could take an incredible amount of punishment. I knew this about myself, and nobody ever saw anything I didn't want them to see.

This was 1995 or '96, and I was now producing two radio shows and working at a video store in the evenings, living roach-free with my brother in a condo we were now renting in the financial district. My friend Alex, who I'd met in college and had moved to New York with, was having a rough time finding a radio job after graduation, so his father bought him a video store to run. His parents were loaded. Alex hired me right away, which meant I could quit telemarketing and instead spend my evenings watching movies and bullshitting with customers. Because of Kevin Smith's *Clerks*, video store jobs were now the shit. Everybody wanted one.

My days always started at 5.30 a.m. I'd leave the condo and walk two blocks to pick up the daily newspapers for the show and coffee for everyone who started the same time I did. Even though I was the lowest-paid person on staff, I was the one who did the coffee run every day. And I'd still eat shit if I got an order wrong, even on the mornings when I paid. I'd work a full day, until about five, then hop a subway and a bus uptown to be at the video store for six. I'd work there until closing, which was usually around eleven, then head back downtown and drink hard until last call, which at this point was still 1 a.m. I'd find my way home, do my best to not throw up when I got in, pass out in my clothes, and wake up at 4:46 to start the entire cycle all over again. I'd pound back as much water as my body could handle and take whatever pills I thought would help—vitamin C, extra-strength Tylenol or Advil, and two or three Daytime Cold and Flu capsules, which always kept me from falling asleep at my desk. I'd spend the first hour in the office piecing together the night before. Every day.

I think, for the most part, we take breathing for granted. Like *actually* breathing. We just do it. It just happens. But if I think about breathing, it's almost like I forget how. If I sit and try to concentrate on my breathing, my heart starts racing, my face gets flush, and I'll have to throw my head back to force air down my throat just to catch a breath. Even today, after I got heavy into Transcendental Meditation, if I focus on my breathing, I immediately panic. It's irrational, I know, but I can't help it.

One unusually warm but rainy mid-September morning, it was still dark when I left the condo to go grab the papers. I was more than used to feeling like absolute death on this walk, but this day was different. Every step I took came with crushing pain. It felt like I'd been shot or harpooned. My chest was heavy, I was out of breath, and I started to black out.

There was a small park near the St. Lawrence Market that I'd sometimes cut through so I could sit on one of the benches and watch the sun come up before walking to the station. It was my favourite spot, but I didn't make it to my bench that day—I couldn't. So I sat on the curb of the road, my shoes in a puddle and my head between my knees, trying to force myself to get it together.

I didn't know what to do, so I did what I always did—lit a cigarette and tried to calm the fuck down. I was convinced this was just a side effect of one bad night. One bad night that followed a hundred other bad nights. I thought I'd finally done too much.

I thought I was dying.

I managed to pick myself up, grab the coffee and the papers, and make it to the office. I sat through two meetings, produced an entire show, and made it to lunch without anyone knowing what I was going through. I had an hour for lunch, which I rarely used, but I figured I could make it to the emergency room, see a doctor, get fixed up, and make it back to the station without anyone asking questions. That was the plan, anyway.

"Hi, how can we help?" the ER nurse asked me.

"I can't breathe," I replied.

Everything after that is a blur. I was rushed though processing, X-rayed, and wound up on my side on a bed in a hallway while a doctor tried to explain to me what a chest tube was, how it worked, and why I needed one—immediately. She sliced a little hole in between two of my ribs on my right side and pushed what seemed like two feet of clear hose into my body. Quickly feeding it, hand over hand, all the way in.

I remember the popping sound it made, followed by incredible relief when my lungs drained into a clear plastic container hooked to the end of the bed. The doctors told me later that all but 10 percent of my right lung had collapsed. A nurse put me in a wheelchair, took me over to a bank of phones, and asked if I wanted to call anyone to let them know that I needed surgery.

The first call I made was to work. The second was to my mom.

Piece of advice, here. If you're ever in the hospital, *not* dead, and have to call your mother, the first words out of your mouth should always be "Mom, everything is okay. I'm going to be fine." *Then* tell her what happened. *Never* start the story at the very beginning. Don't make your mom wait.

I never did make it back to work that day. In fact, I never made it back to work that fall.

The doctors explained I had something called spontaneous pneumothorax and that my lungs were filled with these tiny little air blisters that all decided to burst at the exact same time. Two days later I went in for surgery to fix my right lung, and five hours after that, while still in recovery, my left lung collapsed. All the way.

My parents were with me, at my bedside, as much as they could be. My mom was great with everything, but this was really tough on my dad. Even being as out of my mind on morphine as I was, I could still tell he'd just stopped crying every single time he walked into my room. I felt guilty. Like I'd somehow let him down. I'd never made my dad cry before—I don't think I'd ever *seen* my dad cry—but here we were.

When he was in the room with me, he was great. He told me jokes and sneaked in food I wasn't allowed to have. He held my hand, slid his chair in, and rested his head on the side of the bed until he fell asleep watching TV with me. My mom was pretty much living with my brother at this point, sleeping in my bed, so she could visit me most days. I didn't have a ton of friends, so besides my family, the only other visitors I had were when Alex showed up with two strippers from the Zanzibar we'd met the week before I went in. He thought this was hilarious and would cheer me up. He wasn't wrong.

—

The doctors took me off morphine and started me on what became a long run of Percocet. In the '90s nobody ever talked about opioid addiction. These were miracle pills. Nobody really thought about addiction at all. And if you did bring it up, because of course my mother did, what you were told was, "As long as you're dealing with pain, there's no chance of addiction, dependency, or side effects." But as we all know now, and they knew then, this was total and complete bullshit.

I was drugged for months. My body was in horrid shape, and I wasn't healing nearly as fast as the doctors had hoped. I lost thirty pounds and I didn't even look like me anymore. For months I didn't know what day it was.

My life was built around the small windows of time between pills. I didn't know if it was morning or late afternoon, but I sure as hell knew when I was three minutes late for my next Perc. I also knew that I had fallen totally and completely in love with the night nurse. It was nothing she did—she wasn't flirty or anything—she was just kind, great at her job, and had this way about her that made me think everything was going to be okay. She was beautiful, funny, and always called me by my first name when everyone else used "Mr. Weston." She was also the only nurse who was never late with my pills. I remember being so high and telling my mom that I wanted to marry that nurse. I asked my mom—sorry, *insisted*—she go to the gift shop to get me flowers that I could give to the nurse. She did, and I gave them to her. I'm not sure what my nurse did with them, but she never made me feel like a loser for shooting my shot.

About a week before I was discharged, that same nurse came into my room. It was late, so she woke me up. She explained that there was a virus ripping through the hospital, and they needed to make sure I didn't have it. "Okay," I said. "Do whatever you have to do." At this point I'd had so many needles, tubes, and hands stuffed in me, nothing mattered anymore.

"Can you roll over for me?" she asked while pulling my blankets down to my ankles. "Yeah, just roll over *real* quick for me."

I rolled over onto my side and she opened up the back of my hospital gown. I'd never felt more exposed, or unattractive. Ever. I was in love with this woman, and up to this point I'd always tried to look my best with what I had going on—which wasn't much. And here she was about to swab the inside of my ass. An ass that had been lying in a bed for two months. An ass that hadn't seen the sun in even longer. The ass of her future husband.

The whole process took about three seconds, then she covered me up, rolled me back over, pulled up my blankets, and said, "All right, all set. I'll have someone come up tomorrow and take a look at that hemorrhoid for you. It's a big one."

Fucking kill me.

The only word to describe what it's like having a chest tube removed, *two* chest tubes actually, is "violent." It's a brutal process that can't be done gently. A nurse stands beside your bed with all their weight on their back foot like they're about to throw a punch, then they put one hand on your ribs to hold you still and with the other hand they *rip*. They yank that thing out of you like they're starting a chainsaw. You can feel every inch of it leaving your body. It's almost demonic. Like an exorcism.

It was snowing when I finally got home from the hospital. That's how long I'd been there.

I was home. In my own bed. But at that point, I was still dealing with a slight infection, which quickly became a severe infection. My mom sat with me all night with a cold cloth on my forehead as I begged her not to take me back to the hospital. To get me through the worst of it, they sent me home with antibiotics and enough Percocet to start a business. I'd never seen a pill bottle that big before, and I still haven't. It was about an inch shorter than a beer can, but just as wide. Hundreds of them. But now there was no nurse to make sure I took them on time, or with any sort of regularity. There were no rules.

I walked with a cane for a few weeks and started back at work mid-November. I'd also figured out how to get the most out of the pills I had left. Which was a shit ton. I knew the times of day I was at my best, and when I felt my worst. I managed the actual pain naturally, fought through it, and saved the pills for when I wasn't in agony—almost like a reward for going through so much shit. I always felt as good as I was going to get in the morning, right after a shower, so that's when I'd take two. By three in the afternoon, I'd be in actual hell, sweating and dizzy, and I'd ride it out with nothing. I had built a routine, a system, that kept me high for most of the day. Nothing mattered. I was in an impenetrable fog. Work stress became non-existent.

But I wasn't addicted. That was impossible.

The pills ran out after about a month and a half, but I wasn't pissed. They were a way to get me through the day. Nothing more than that, really. I looked at them like a gift, or a fun ride that was now over. I really didn't think too much about it. But when the pills ran out, I got sick. Really fucking sick. I had dealt with so much that year, and it had been months since I actually felt normal, so being sick was something that I was used to. But this was a different kind of sick. And I was a different kind of person now. I took another two weeks off work and called my doctor to get more antibiotics because I was sure the infection was back.

None of that was true. I was kicking an opioid addiction I didn't know I had. Alone in my room with Gravol and fucking Gatorade. It was years before I understood what had actually happened.

Early that spring, I had an appointment with a specialist who wanted to test me for Marfan syndrome. A doctor had recommended this, months before, because I was a tall young male and "skeletal." Apparently, I was the poster child for Marfan's. I didn't know much about Marfan's, which was fine, because I didn't have Marfan's, but after three appointments with three different doctors, I was diagnosed with Tourette syndrome.

The diagnosis explained everything, especially all those years my brother called me Twitchy. But the *thing* I never thought was a *thing* was now a *thing*, and I hated that. I took the diagnosis and walked out of that room and never talked about it again. I never even went back for my follow-up appointment, and I certainly wasn't interested in being medicated.

When I was sick, alone, and high in that hospital bed, thinking I was going to die, I spent a lot of time in my own head. In the brief moments of clarity in between pills, I made the decision to chase opportunity. Money became secondary. From that point on, I promised myself I would become an opportunity hunter, and I was going to make damn sure I was ready when it came. I needed to educate myself, and I needed to learn from the best no matter what. No matter how I was treated, no matter how much shit I ate, no matter how much it killed me inside. Learn from the smartest people. That was my rule.

I ATE WITH
THAT FORK

The first time you look in the mirror and don't recognize the person staring back at you is going to be the worst day of your life. That's the good news. The bad news is that likely won't be the last time it happens. I got very used to days like that. Too used to them. I was twenty-two, and I'd placed my whole self-worth in the hands of someone else. My identity and future were entirely dictated by my new boss, and I let it happen.

I walked away from the radio show and took a gig booking and producing a new network TV talk show. Think *Larry King* but with zero budget and shitty lighting. This was a senior position, on a small team. The kind of job that normally would, and *should*, go to someone with far more experience than I had.

This was a fantastic opportunity. I'd never been more unhappy.

When you're young and insecure, unsure and racked with self-doubt, you tend to lean into loyalty. You offer it up to anyone who'll take it, even if they don't deserve it. *Especially* if they don't deserve it. It's a way to make a mark and get ahead when you have little else to offer. And this new relationship, with my executive producer, was the most codependent, manipulative, and unhealthy relationship I've ever had, but I was loyal as fuck. I was responsible for managing her career and her mental state. Her personal drama became *my* personal drama. I built her show and her confidence. I protected her. She hired me for a job I wasn't even close to being qualified for, and I felt I owed her. So I gave her everything.

People couldn't stand her, which meant they couldn't stand me either. Half our co-workers looked at me like I was her pet, the other half thought we were sleeping together, and I didn't blame them one bit for thinking any of it. That all said, she *was* incredibly smart—fucking brilliant actually, an unbelievable producer, and one of the best writers I'd ever met. I followed her around and hung off her every word. I studied her.

She saw us as something different, though. This was personal to her. She was convinced, and would tell anyone who'd listen, that we were "so much alike." We were "the same person." Truth is, she had no idea who I was, because she never bothered to look.

If we went out for drinks after work—which was often mandatory—she'd always order for the two of us and use me as an excuse to get an entire bottle of wine instead of just a single glass for herself. I hated wine, but she never asked. She'd order the foie gras appetizer and push half of it onto my plate. Then she'd eat all the little pieces of bread that came with it, so I had to down all mine by the spoonful, gagging with every bite.

Everything she ate she ate with her hands, scooping up whatever was left on her plate with the underside of her fingernail. Everything she loved I hated, and she'd always order enough for the both of us—then we'd split the bill and I'd pay the tip. I could never say anything, of course, because I knew just what would happen if I did. The same thing that always happened. She'd ignore me for a few days, make me redo all my work, cancel entire shows I'd worked my ass off to book, and call me drunk and crying at three in the morning to scream, "Why are you trying to ruin my life?" before I even had a chance to say "Hello."

Over these couple of years, I quietly but relentlessly tried to re-invent myself to make up for lost time and wasted years in high school and college. I don't think I'd ever read an entire book. I still haven't. Don't get me wrong—I've *almost* or *pretty much* read dozens of books. But have I ever read an entire book cover to cover without skipping a few words or paragraphs, skimmed lines I thought were boring, spaced out for a minute and forgot where I was, or put it down and failed to pick it up *exactly* where I left off? No. Not ever.

So I read through as much as I could of every single book that came through the office. I had stacks of them all over my desk at work and boxes full of books in my closet at home. I'd take the entire week to get through the Sunday *New York Times*. *TIME*, *Newsweek*, the *Economist*, and *Vanity Fair*, all of them, cover to cover. I'd go to academic lectures at the library and sit through boring political debates when they hosted those too. On days we didn't have a show, I'd watch CNN, *Jerry Springer* (without shame), and PBS, then sometimes head to the city courthouse and sit through a random trial just so I could hear how smart people argued and made a point. I had Christopher Hitchens's direct office number and would call him and do these monster, *extra-long* pre-interviews when I booked him as a guest. This was my education. I quizzed and talked the ear off any intelligent guest we ever had on the show, then followed up on my own on everything they said.

I never knew if I was actually good at this job or if I was just excellent at doing exactly what my boss told me to do. Most days I felt like a total fraud and was convinced it was only a matter of time before everyone figured it all out. Even on the days I did my best work, I still felt I was faking my way through it. Like it was all one big hustle. I was convinced that without this job, without her, I was nothing.

She had nicknames for people we worked with, like Fat Ass Francis, and if I didn't use them, she wouldn't hear me until I did.

"Hey," I'd say, "Fran said we couldn't run late in the studio today."

"Who?" she'd ask, without even looking up.

"Francis," I'd say.

"Who?" she'd ask again, *still* not looking up but raising both eyebrows and cocking her head to one side.

"Fat Ass Francis," I'd finally answer.

"What does she want now?"

Francis was *not* fat, and I never really noticed her ass, but from what I remember, it wasn't anything other than perfectly normal-sized. But this is what my boss did, she hammered stuff like that into your head, made it normal, hoping it would one day escape the lab and I'd be the one to slip up and say something out loud close enough for Francis to hear it. That way *she* could hurt her, or whoever else, without taking any of the blame.

Every day was a demoralizing indoctrination. Fully comply or you were dead to her. I sat with her for hours at the hairdresser three days a week, just to keep her company because her stylist had long gotten sick of her shit and no longer talked to her. She'd go on about how everyone was out to get her, how everyone was out to get *us*. How "the world was Walmart" and she was sick of having to "dumb things down for the masses." Each week, she told me who I needed to hate, and how we were in this together because everybody was coming for our heads. It was us against the world. She was paranoid and irrational.

"Two little elves" is what she used to call us. And whether I thought I deserved it or not, I was now twenty-four years old and making $75,000 a year—a salary that she negotiated for me, and *never* let me forget it.

Most mornings I arrived at work a little after six. At this point, we worked out of two small, connected offices. Mine had a desk and a large round heavy wood coffee table in the middle of it stacked two feet high with her old newspapers, books, lipstick-stained napkins, and last week's takeout containers. The building staff had long since stopped cleaning the room because every time they did, my boss would swear something went missing and accuse them of stealing.

When I'd get in, I'd drop a stack of newspapers on my desk, then walk directly into her office and crank up the heat. All the way. Every day. I got that room humming. It got to ninety degrees in under an hour, uncomfortably and unbearably hot. My boss was a lot of things, but late was the one you could always bet on.

I always heard her coming. She burst through that last door in the hallway like a high-heeled tank. A devil in pleather.

When I heard her, I'd jump up, sprint in, turn her thermostat back down to something normal, and race back out to my desk. Every single morning, she stormed in, threw her purse on the chair from across the room, dropped whatever else was in her hands on my desk, grabbed a piece of whatever I was eating with her fingers, and marched directly into her blazing hot office.

For the first thirty minutes of her day, every day, she was in hell. Agitated, angry, and sweaty. While she sat on the phone with building maintenance, shrieking "The thermostat! The thermo-stat!" at some poor soul who didn't deserve any of it, I'd casually walk in to fiddle around with the little dial, using bullshit precision. Sometimes I'd even put my ear to it like I was cracking a safe. "There!" I'd say. "I think I heard it kick in. There was *definitely* a click." Of course, I did absolutely nothing, and the room would cool down fifteen minutes later all on its own, but I was the hero. I had the magic touch. These were the best thirty minutes of my day. Every day.

I never really talked about work when I got home, or if I was ever out for drinks with friends. And if I did ever mentioned anything, I'd only give them a fraction of what my days were actually like. Even then, they'd be horrified. But I didn't want anyone's opinion, advice, or judgment, so for the most part I just shut up about it. I added everything to the stack—that place inside us where we keep all these things. All the shit we don't talk about.

Rich and I moved up the street and rented a proper two-bedroom condo, which meant I didn't have to sleep on a futon in the solarium anymore, and we got our own bathrooms. That's where I spent most of my days after work. I'd grab an ashtray, and a beer from the fridge, and sit naked, sideways on the toilet so I couldn't see myself in the mirror, and go at my thighs, and everything else, with a lighter and the end of a hot pin.

I'd be in there long enough to finish off a King Can and smoke three cigarettes back to back. Then I'd stand up in front of the mirror, staring into the bottom of the sink, while trying to push my fists through the top of the counter. I'd let up when I couldn't feel my hands anymore, take a few deep breaths, get dressed, and rejoin the world like none of it ever happened.

My boss had this incredible talent for framing every critique, compliment, or opinion in the exact same way. The first words out of her mouth were always, "You know what *your* problem is . . . ?" What followed could be anything from "you're just *too* good-looking" to "you just don't fucking listen." No matter what it was,

ROZ WESTON

though, I'd always get one of her long, unkempt acrylic nails waving two inches from my face as she went on and on. She was convinced she knew more about everybody than they knew about themselves. She was *that* type.

One night, we went out for oysters. Her idea, not mine. I knew this night was coming because she'd informed me two days before. I'd never had oysters before, but she assumed I loved them because *she* loved them. This was a new spot that she was dying to try, and if I didn't go, she'd have to eat alone in public, which of course would be all my fault and would absolutely ruin my next two weeks. I was terrified I was going to gag and make a whole scene.

The night before we went out, I went to a restaurant around the corner from our condo, sat at the bar, and ordered three shots of vodka and one lonely oyster. I needed to know what I was getting myself into. I quickly realized that I'd need to be way more drunk than I was to ever do *that* again.

So there we were, drunk, and on our tenth round of "You know what your problem is . . ." as she tried to analyze and fix my life, like somehow telling me "You just need all new friends" was in any way constructive. I was more than used to this. Her never-ending self-pity-filled rants could go on for hours. I sat quietly in the oyster bar, nodding and agreeing while throwing out things like "Yeah. No, you're absolutely right. Thank you," whenever I could get a word in.

I didn't have the tools or the self-esteem to argue, fight back, or stand up for myself. So I took it.

When she leaned forward, slurring while schooling me on how much harder I needed to work for her, I took it and said nothing.

When she casually reached across the table, grabbed my little oyster fork, and used it to clean under her fingernails before sliding it back beside my plate like nothing happened, I took it and said nothing.

When the oysters finally arrived, *I ate with that fork.*

And I said nothing.

I never really had a good handle on what it meant to be successful, and I certainly hadn't ever felt successful. I didn't know what I wanted to become, but I sure as fuck knew how I wanted to feel. The bar was now set. At that moment, gagging on the food and every word I should have said but didn't, I knew I never wanted to feel this ever again: powerless.

I never wanted to feel like I had to eat with a fork that someone just dug bits of shit out from under their nail with, because saying something would somehow embarrass *them.*

I kept my head down, planned my escape, and prepped for the next opportunity. I knew that capitalizing on opportunity, outside of my comfort zone, was the only way I was going to get out. I knew I had to separate myself from my boss and learn new shit. New skills. New skills would lead to more opportunity, and then eventual freedom. I didn't know *how* to get there, but I knew I had to try. I had no choice.

To me, freedom is simple. It's two things: the ability to confidently tell someone "No" and have it be respected, and the willingness to walk away from anything without hesitation or fear. No regrets.

The people I'd work for needed to know this. They'd need to know where they stood in *my* world, not the other way around.

I worked another four years with my boss on that show.

LA LA LEXI

In late 1999, I spent $25,000 of my company's money to fly an entire television crew to California just to meet a girl who left me stranded, alone at 2 a.m. at a dildo store on Sunset Boulevard. This was the calm before the millennium, and my first trip to Los Angeles. I had no intention of ever going home. Of course, none of that worked out, but I did meet O. J. Simpson at the hotel bar, woke up to an earthquake, and spent two days at the Playboy Mansion. Also, dildo store.

That's how my year ended. Now let me tell you how I got there.

In the few years leading up to this, the TV show had grown, so we now had more staff, which took some of the heat off me, but I was still somewhat ostracized and definitely not trusted by my co-workers. I did my best to bond and be cool with everyone else, but I always got the sense that people were holding back, as if anything they said to me was going to get back to our boss. People *still* thought we were sleeping together.

The show was now produced out of a small corner of a much larger area of the newsroom, with six desks, a TV, and one computer with the Internet. The desk in the far back was empty and semi-private. It was surrounded on three sides with cubicle wall, and nobody ever went back there. This was the Cry Corner. At least a few times a month, one of the people on the show—a producer, intern, or researcher—would wind up back there to just let it out. My boss had carefully crafted and expertly curated *the* most toxic work environment any of these people had ever experienced. It was a work of art—it was, and still is, legendary—and the few years leading up to 1999 were a revolving door. New people would be hired from outside, others transferred to our show from other departments at the station. *None* of them lasted.

One woman I worked with, a wicked talented producer with more than a decade of experience, pulled me aside on her last day. "Get away from her," she told me. "*Far* away from her."

I did not listen.

Every now and then someone on staff would ask me how I managed to do it: how I hadn't killed her or myself after all the years I'd been there. What I wanted to say was, "Well, that's because I'm dead inside," but what I always replied, without fail, was "You get used to it." This never went over well because it was never enough. It was a bullshit answer, and they all knew it.

Truth was, I had no identity. So much of my self-worth was tied up in what I did for the show, what I did for my boss. That job was my life, and I measured my days based on how much abuse and manipulation I could handle while still moving forward. How I felt didn't matter, and I considered any day that I could actually stomach food as a huge win. I'd convinced myself that happiness at work was a luxury for the weak.

But I never wanted anyone to feel the way I did. I'd always try to help the other staff through the rough parts, and when our boss left the building, which was always within sixty seconds of the show wrapping, I'd let everyone know she was gone, and watch a collective sigh wash over our small crew.

Every day, after work, I took two buses, a subway, then a streetcar back downtown. The whole trip took just over ninety minutes. I never read or listened to music or made small talk with other commuters. I always sat alone, but never liked being alone. I was always more comfortable on a bus rammed with people than one that was empty. Most nights, I stopped for a beer at a bar, then headed home to mess around on the Internet before leaving for a club. Everything was new then. There was no Instagram, Amazon, or iTunes and everything online took forever. If you did a Yahoo search for "boobs" but forgot an *o* you'd wait a full five minutes for a page of famous Bobs to show up before you could fix your mistake. I quickly became a Bob expert.

I remember watching CNN when they were doing a story about virtual chat rooms, and I was hooked. According to them, these were either the future of human connection or a predator's playground. Turns out, they were both. The best was CU-SeeMe, developed in the early '90s by Cornell University. By today's standards, it was laughable and archaic. Absolute shit. Black-and-white, pixelated, and choppy as hell. Imagine a Zoom call with twenty strangers who looked like eight-bit *Mario* characters with a forty-five-second refresh rate—*if* you were lucky. I used these, off and on, from about 1997, talking to strangers and flirting.

Doing anything sexual was always an embarrassing disaster, so for the most part, we kept our clothes on. I never used a fake name, like I had on the telephone chat lines in college, but otherwise the experience was very much the same. I was always more comfortable talking to people I knew nothing about, who knew nothing about me. Some of my closest relationships were entirely based on typing four or five words at a time and holding up hand-drawn pictures to a web-cam sketched-out on a Post-it.

I chatted, off and on, with a woman named Alexis: LaLaLexi2001 was her handle. She was in her mid-thirties, cool as hell, and we'd meet up on CU-SeeMe around the time I got home from work, which was mid-afternoon for her in L.A. She was a SoCal short-haired blonde with dark roots, who worked in Big Tech. I didn't really know what Big Tech was then, but she seemed to be doing okay for herself. When we were online, she'd grab her camera to walk it around her giant warehouse space in Studio City and show me around.

She and her crew rode dirt bikes *inside*. They had a wall of TVs just for video games, and every now and then she flashed stacks of cash to the camera. She was loaded. She said she was loaded, anyway. She called me, and everyone else, "bitch" before it was cool, and had the most incredible tan lines I'd ever seen over black-and-white dial-up video. I'd never met anyone like her. She was a little bit of Emily Valentine from *90210* mixed with Watts from *Some Kind of Wonderful* and a whole lot of Helen Slater from *The Legend of Billie Jean*.

Going into 1999, if you worked in TV, your life was consumed with Y2K and the millennium. There was mass-media mass hysteria, and everyone was losing their shit. Shows spent tons of cash to build over-the-top year-end shows. These meetings had been going on for months. In late fall, after weeks in a boardroom, and hundreds of ideas tossed around, someone suggested we do something around Hugh Hefner and *Playboy*'s millennium issue. Hef was hot at the time. He was freshly divorced, and he was back! *GQ* or *Esquire* had just done a huge feature on him, and how the mansion, after years of being a family home, was once again open for (sad and pervy) business.

I immediately shot up my hand and yelled over everyone, "I have a contact at the Playboy Mansion." I had *no* contact at the Playboy Mansion. I followed that up with, "I can get us an interview with Hef, and get a camera into their millennium party. No problem." Again, I knew nobody at the Playboy Mansion.

"Yes!" my boss yelled. "Sex 2000! Sin is *IN*!" She was already coming up with titles for the special.

I got to it. This was all I knew how to do. I worked the phones, lied, and promised the moon to anyone at Playboy who'd take my call. By the end of the next week, I delivered on everything I'd promised in that meeting. This was by far the biggest hustle I'd ever pulled, although that year I'd put some impressive shows together and booked more "impossible" guests than I could count. I really hated work, but I was goddamn good at it, and I built an incredible reputation as the guy who could book anyone. But the *Playboy* thing I was particularly proud of. It was a way to covertly get back at my boss for all the shit I'd put up with, *and* at the company that sat back and said nothing. We hired a kick-ass crew, got the budget approved, and off we went. A day with Hef, and full camera access to the millennium party at the Playboy Mansion.

The Playboy Mansion was in Los Angeles. La La Lexi was in Los Angeles.

"Roz! Get your ass in here, bitch!" These were the first words La La Lexi said to me in person. She was parked, taking up two spots, out front of my hotel in an old Jeep, standing up on the driver's seat hanging out the top, jumping and waving her arms around while screaming at me.

I didn't have a cell phone that worked in America, so this whole date was set up over email before I left Toronto. The crew and I had landed just a few hours earlier, and I was dealing with jet lag for the first time in my life. I was exhausted, and knew I had to be up early the next morning to head to the Playboy Mansion, so I promised myself I wasn't going to go too hard.

Lexi was fucking rad, and she was making a total scene. I'd never actually heard her voice clearly before and was blown away by just how L.A. she sounded. She didn't seem real. I didn't know her, and she sure as hell didn't know me, but when I jumped into that Jeep and kissed her for the first time, I was done. This was it. It was goddamn electric. She reached behind the passenger seat, grabbed a King Can of Bud, jammed it between my legs, and told me to keep it down as she peeled out of the parking lot.

"Do you want the bullshit PG tourist version of L.A., or the trashy version of L.A.—*my* version? Okay. Good!" She said all of this even before I had a chance to open my mouth.

For the next four or five hours we did it all, with the roof down. I was still a mystery to her. She knew nothing about me and didn't seem to care. I'd never felt so free. This was a total reinvention for me, a bloody awakening. After we drove through the hills, stopping every now and then to make out a little and crush another beer, she took me down to Sunset Boulevard. We passed the Whiskey, the Roxy, and the Rainbow Room. This was the exact strip of road that bred every band I ever loved growing up. It felt like home. Like I'd gone to the Mothership.

I was always drawn to Southern California. When my dad was eighteen, lost and broken, and in desperate need of a fresh start and reinvention, he wound up in L.A. He found his escape in the United States Marine Corps. I found mine in La La Lexi. A girl who within the first hour of meeting had me barefoot, standing with her on the front hood of her purple Jeep, with her face pressed against my back and her hands reached around my waist, jammed into my front pockets as we slow danced under the California stars. The whole thing was weird, wonderful, and totally embarrassing, but so was Los Angeles. La La Lexi kissed with her eyes open, tasted like vanilla and American cigarettes, and flicked the front of my pants and yelled "Whoopsie!" when she accused me of having a boner. I'd never even seen a palm tree before, and here I was, falling in love like a guy in a poorly reviewed Hollywood rom-com with a leading man nobody would ever pay money to see. All of this with a total stranger I'd met on the Internet.

California was everything my dad said it was. His stories of L.A. in the late '60s were fascinating, and like all his other stories, they evolved over the years. My story was evolving by the minute. As we drove down Sunset for the third time, I put my head against the back of the seat, closed my eyes, and rehearsed how I was going to tell my parents I'd met the love of my life on my first night in L.A. I was never coming home because there was no coming back from this. I was brand-new. I was writing my own love story, second by second, that would blow even my parents away.

"Here we go! Hang on," Lexi half-laughed/half-yelled, as she whipped the Jeep into a parking space right out front of a sex shop on Sunset. This place was nothing really special at all. Average, actually, but Lexi walked in there like it was her second home. She seemed to know where everything was and cruised the aisles loading up a basket like she was picking apples. Fuzzy things, hard things, leather things, things that took double-D batteries—all the things. I slapped my company Amex card on the counter, paid for everything, and she helped the guy who worked there load it all up into a black plastic bag. She was in a hurry, and I was nervous as hell.

As we were about to walk out, she grabbed a shirt off the last rack, whipped around, held it up to my chest, and said, "You *need* this. I love this for you. Try it on." As she let the hanger go, I caught it right before it hit the floor, then made my way to the change room. The shirt was hideous. It was a black mesh half-shirt with the number "69" spray-painted on the front in bright red bubble font. I was wearing super-casual pants because I'd come from dinner with the crew before we hooked up, so now I had to pull off pleats with a belly shirt. Not a strong look.

I walked out to do a quick spin in the mirror, dying of embarrassment, but still laughing. I could see pretty much the entire store in the reflection behind me. And Lexi was gone. I was alone. In mesh.

I awkwardly walked over to the guy behind the counter, covering my exposed stomach with both my hands.

"Did you see . . ." That's all I managed to get out before he looked up at me and shrugged. He didn't say anything. He just shrugged. Then he called me a cab.

On any regular day, the Playboy Mansion was just a sad old house full of sad old men. Everyone I met on staff was Hef's age and just shuffled around trying to look busy. My first day there was what they called an "off day," which meant no parties, no famous movie night, no naked shenanigans. No bunnies and no booze. But I did get to play with a monkey.

As we wrapped the first half of our interview, which took about ninety minutes, we were invited to have lunch with Hef out back on the patio beside the infamous Grotto. It was taco day! As we were slowly escorted out at a senior's pace, I took note of every single piece of furniture we passed. Everything was oversized, thick and heavy. Old wood, red velvet, and built for one thing and one thing only. Even the end tables looked strong enough to hold two people—comfortably. We toured the kitchen, which was huge and industrial, like something you'd see in the back of a restaurant.

One of the chefs yelled, "Who's ready for tacos?" as he and a few other people followed us out with trays and trays of food. I'd never had a real California taco before, let alone one handmade by a real Mexican chef, so I was pumped. My dad loved tacos and would always lecture us on what an authentic SoCal taco was supposed to taste like.

It took one bite, without even swallowing, for me to realize I was eating Old El Paso. Hef built his empire on the finer things in life. He had a half-dozen or so staff cook all his meals in a million-dollar kitchen, and there we were eating a store-bought taco kit with iceberg lettuce and pre-grated cheddar. To go along with everything else in that house, this was, hands down, the saddest lunch I'd ever seen. Don't get me wrong. I'm not above a taco kit—nobody should be, because they're delicious—but this was the Playboy Mansion, for god's sake. I wanted to appear appreciative and impressed, though, so I looked at Hef and said, "Man, these are just like the ones we have back home."

Hef smiled and grunted but said no actual words, while one of his guys chimed in with, "Yup. This is the chef's special. Hef knows what he likes." Which tells you just about everything you ever need to know about that place.

I've told this story a hundred times over the years, but I always add more boobs.

I never talked to Lexi again, but years later I looked her up. I couldn't find anything about her, or the company she said she ran, but I did read a story about a woman with her exact same name, who looked exactly like her, who got popped for fraud and identity theft in Florida.

Probably wasn't her.

LEARN
TO
DANCE

We often choose isolation rather than risk embarrassment. That's just what we do. Especially young men. That's why we rarely dance. Dancing is the single greatest example of just that. We'd rather sit alone at a table at a wedding, or stand against a wall at a junior high after-school dance. We'll watch our girlfriend out there by herself, or with some other guy, rather than run the risk of being laughed at. Being made a fool of. We're terrified of being embarrassed. We say things like *Not now, maybe the next one*, or *Can we wait for a slow song?* Isolation over embarrassment. Being alone always felt better than being singled out. Of course this is totally irrational. Really, it's a fear of something else: it's not a fear of dancing, but a fear of being vulnerable. We don't teach kids the value of vulnerability, especially young men. Nobody ever tells you that without vulnerability there's no intimacy. And without intimacy, what are we? What the hell are we even doing?

My old man danced. Long before Meredith and Cristina danced it out on *Grey's Anatomy*, my Pops danced it out on any floor that felt good enough under his slippers. Even when there was no music playing, he was still a fantastic, fun dancer. You'd never see him smile so hard as you would when he was whipping and spinning my mom around the kitchen on a Sunday morning. I don't know who taught him, or where he learned, but after everything he had been through, all the trauma, abuse, and war, my old man was two things: he was hard to kill, and he was a great dancer. There are levels to this—to life—and my dad reached levels of vulnerability and intimacy that I didn't fully see, or understand, until years after he was dead.

When I was working that job, I danced. Every night. In rock bars or gay bars, it didn't matter. I never danced to fit in, or to feel like I was a part of something. I danced to get lost. Alone, drenched, and drunk, eyes closed, head down, surrounded by a few hundred strangers. That was where I felt most comfortable.

You have to find something in your day that makes it all worthwhile. Otherwise, what the fuck did you just do? Complaining about your life to other miserable people does *not* count. Being angry all the time is exhausting, and I was always exhausted. I drowned the parts that hurt and burned the parts that didn't. I felt so goddamn heavy. Always. I looked for comfort and validation in anything and anyone that cared just enough to make sure I got home okay, but not much else. I was incapable of self-improvement, was tired from keeping secrets, and most days I was obsessively focused on finding the next exit sign. A temporary escape. A way out. That's what dancing was for me. It was the thing that made it all worth it.

So I danced. I danced my ass off.

Skin-tight black jeans, eyeliner, a wallet chain, three-buckle skull boots with a short heel, and a white undershirt. That was my uniform. Even in the winter. I never left the apartment in a coat, because I never wanted to deal with, or pay for, coat check, so I hustled or paid off the doorman when I arrived to avoid freezing in line. Once a week, I walked over to the mall up the street and spent sixteen dollars on a brand-new six-pack of Jockey ribbed white tank tops. I never wore the same one twice; I always thought of these as disposable. Most clubs had a dress code that at least required a shirt of some kind, but once through the doors, I grabbed a double vodka soda with a splash of cranberry from the bar, lit a cigarette, took off my shirt, tucked it into my back pocket, and made my way to the middle of the dance floor. I was like Jeff Spicoli walking into All American Burger in *Fast Times at Ridgemont High*. Every now and then, while standing at the bar, a bouncer walked up to say something like, "Hey, man. I know you had a shirt on when you came in here. . . ." But the shirts were always long gone by that point. Lost, thrown, or used to stop the bleeding from some new cut on my arm from getting bumped too hard, hitting the floor, and landing on broken glass. I never got home looking like I had a fun night out with friends. I always looked like I'd just come from Fight Club.

I have a lot of holes in my memory. Blank spaces, missing details, and lost time. Over the years, I've got used to it—I'm always the guy who, unknowingly and unapologetically, reintroduces himself to a person I've met four times before. But every time is like the first time for me. There are certain things I keep and certain things I don't.

I've spent hundreds of hours lost in the middle of a dance floor. I remember the feeling, but never the night. It was one of those nights when I met Summer, and the night I met Summer was the last night I went dancing.

I don't remember who said what first, or how we started talking, but we connected immediately. I think maybe we did a shot and arm-wrestled? Totally normal stuff. She wasn't wearing her regular clothes, though, I remember that much. These were club clothes, the type of late '90s gear we cringe at today, but she looked beautiful. She had blonde hair, dark freckles, and stunning eyes that darted back and forth as she tried to figure me out. I don't know what she thought I was, but I assumed she thought I was all dressed up too. That it was all for show. A costume.

Summer was an actor. I'd never met an actor before, and she had all the charm and confidence that only performers have. She was magnetic, and I couldn't take my eyes off her. She was also the first woman I ever met who ever called me smart, and from that first meeting, the two of us in the back of that dark club, we were instantly boyfriend and girlfriend. There was no first date or feeling each other out. She looked at me like nobody ever had before; I'm sure she saw some things in me that didn't actually exist, but that didn't matter. I made it work. I quickly became the thing she thought I was. I reinvented myself. I liked the way she made me feel, and nothing else mattered after that. Summer was my first actual grown-up girlfriend, after years of one-night stands and bar hookups.

I stopped smoking, quit dying my hair black, and didn't wear eyeliner anymore. I started dressing differently too. All her friends, her entire crew, were actors as well. They all had incredible style that I tried to copy. I didn't really have any good friends of my own. Summer's welcomed me with open arms, and I felt I was finally part of something. We were officially a couple, a great couple, and we spent every day together. Birthday parties, friends' weddings. We did *all* the coupley things that I hadn't done since high school. We spent the holidays with her parents for a few days, where I headed out to the garage with her dad to drink Scotch, smoke cigars, and bond. Her parents were wonderful people who really did seem to love me. My parents adored the shit out of Summer, too.

There's a difference between pretending to be someone else and trying to become a whole new person. That's where things started to fall apart for me. Summer and I had this incredible relationship, but the deeper we went, the harder it was for me to not fall apart. I liked the way things were in the beginning, but the longer it went on, the harder it was to avoid certain issues. I never really opened up properly or let Summer see any of the things I had stacked away. I wasn't ready to talk about the way I really felt about myself, not out loud. Even if I'd tried, I wouldn't have known where to start, or how to get the words out. So I started looking for a way out. I knew things had to end. I knew, one way or another, I was going to fuck this beautiful, fun, adult relationship up. I had a choice: be vulnerable and embrace intimacy, or run, burn it all down.

I could have been honest with her, but I wasn't. I could have told her how afraid I was, but I didn't.

So I married one of her friends instead.

THE WEDDING

Until my late twenties, the only person I ever really hurt was myself, and I was good at it. Up to that point, I didn't know what it felt like to hurt someone else, to truly let somebody down. I'd never lived with the regret and guilt that comes with being a shit person.

Summer and I had been together well over two years when she got an incredible offer to join the cast of a musical that was touring across the county. She was, and still is, one of the best singers I've ever heard with my own ears, and I encouraged her to go. I begged her. She was so excited.

"Do it!" I told her. "You have to do this! You'll crush it."

This was a once-in-a-lifetime-type opportunity for her, and she'd be gone for months. I was truly happy for her. She'd worked so hard for every single gain she made in that business. She fought for every inch. But I couldn't help but look at the trip as a way to pump the breaks, give me a bit of room to think, a way for me to catch my breath.

I did none of that.

I never do well on my own. I need accountability. I know that about myself. It's one of the reasons I've lived with my brother my whole life. Sure, I love him, and know I'd be crushed and miss him every single day if we moved away from each other, but also, having him around always makes me accountable. My brother being in our condo meant I had to get up and go to work every day, especially on the days when I had zero fight left in me. It forced me to eat and shower regularly, and to be social. I needed to show up sober and alive every now and then. I needed, and I still need, someone to come home to every day who's going to love me no matter what.

I needed that sense of accountability in my relationships, too. Although I didn't know that at the time. When Summer left, I lost all accountability *and* myself. The guy I was, the one who kissed her goodbye at the airport when she left, was gone as soon as I jumped in a cab to head back into the city. It was instantaneous.

Taylor was the younger sister of one of Summer's best friends, and we all hung out together. Those few months when Summer was away were a blur. If I wasn't at work, I was in a bar alone, and when I wasn't in a bar alone, I was in a bar with Taylor. That's when I fell in love again, over endless pitchers of beer, bar games, stories, reckless fun, pints of Long Island iced tea, and ashtrays overflowing with cigarette butts.

Taylor was different; she wasn't like any friend I'd ever had. She wasn't wired like anyone else I'd met. She was the first person I knew who actually grew up in the city, when everyone else seemed to come to Toronto from somewhere else. She lived by a different code and a whole set of rules I didn't know existed. She believed in things I'd never paid any attention to and saw the world in a completely different way. Her views on politics, social justice before that was even a thing, and what it meant to be a good person— your *own* person—all came from a place I hadn't been exposed to. Taylor was so fiercely independent that I don't think she'd ever had a real boyfriend before. She was so sure of herself that it changed my outlook on just about everything.

Nothing else mattered when I was with Taylor. I loved who I became when I was with her.

In all of it, though, in all this stuff about Taylor that took so much time to wrap my head around, there was one thing I knew for sure. Taylor was never going to get married. She didn't need anyone, and certainly not a husband. That wasn't her plan.

The day Summer flew home from her acting gig, I met her at the airport at nine in the morning, smelling like vodka and looking like shit. I had woken up at 5 a.m., still drunk from the night before. When she walked through those double doors, with all her luggage, what she saw was *not* the guy she'd left a few months earlier. She didn't get what she deserved. She didn't get the boy who said he loved her, the one who she went with on vacations, who she spent the holidays with. The one who told her to follow her dreams because he'd be right here when she got home. What she got instead was an even shittier version of the person she'd met in that club that first night.

At the airport I was stumbling around, wearing a long fake fur coat and jeans I hadn't washed in a month, and I hadn't showered in I don't know how long. I barely acknowledged her. I was so ashamed, and my head was pounding from guilt and from what-ever I did the night before, which I had zero memory of. There were no smiles, hugs, or welcome-home flowers. I was rude and distant. I ignored her castmates, and I couldn't get out of there fast enough. I was fucking cruel and embarrassing.

I dropped her off in a cab at her house so she could unpack, then I continued home. We planned to meet back up at my place later that afternoon.

When you dump somebody, when it's truly time to end things, you need to be blunt yet compassionate. You need to offer closure and leave no option for reconciliation if there isn't one. If it's truly over, you need to say that, as hard as it may be. People are owed that. You owe it to them to be honest and end things in a way that allows them to take the time to process and heal. It needs to be a clean break. That's what Summer deserved. But I did none of that. I offered every bad excuse and line a guy can chef up to avoid telling the truth.

"I need space. I don't know if I'm ready for this. It's all so hard. How can I love someone else when I don't even love myself? I'm unlovable." I ran the table on bullshit excuses that afternoon, all of which were to avoid saying the one thing I actually needed to say. What Summer needed to hear. The truth. "I don't love you anymore."

The only thing I remember Summer saying to me was, "I don't understand what's happening. Why? What happened?" She left my place confused and incredibly hurt, and I let her walk out thinking there was still a chance, that I just needed *to work on a few things*. Of course there was no chance of any of that happening.

A couple of months later I married Taylor, and Summer found out through gossip.

Taylor and I were engaged for less than a month. The whole thing happened so fast. Don't get me wrong—it was all so crazy romantic, punk rock, and came from a place of love that I'd never experienced before. We were alone, in my room, after another night out, lying side by side on my bed while I had one leg hanging off the edge. That somehow helped with the room spins and helped me make sure I didn't throw up. Taylor and I were messy, and we were in love.

"You have to make me a promise," I said. "If this, all of this, ever becomes too much and you want to bail, you have to give me time to clean myself up before you walk away. Give me time to get my shit together. Fix things. Promise me that."

"I don't have to," she answered. "I'll never get sick of this. I'm never leaving. Not you, not ever."

I rolled off the bed, landed on my knees, and started rifling through my nightstand looking for a pen and paper. "Write that down. Everything you just said. And sign it. We'll both sign it." And that's what we did. We made up a contract, and both signed it. "So what does this mean?" I asked.

"It means it's forever," she said.

"Yeah, but what do we *do* with that? If you're never going to leave me, and I'm never going to leave you, what do we *do*? Do we get married now?"

She smiled at me. I felt the world speed up around us. Everything made sense.

"Yes. That's exactly what we do," she said.

And that's exactly what we did. I went rooting through my jewellery box, which was a shoe box wrapped in yellow duct tape, and found a ring that fit her. It was nothing special, but she loved it, and didn't flinch when I told her that I'd found it, years earlier, in an ashtray out front of a dry cleaner.

There's still a huge part of me that believes this was a game of chicken that neither one of us was willing to call. We were holding hands about to drive off a cliff, both refusing to hit the brakes. It was like when you commit to doing something even though you can predict your inevitable failure, but you still follow through because you made a promise. There was no long-term plan. We had nothing. We hadn't had one single conversation about the future, or how any of this would work. But we were committed.

The plan was to do it all alone, but Taylor wound up telling her sister, which meant I had to tell my brother, and so there we were, six people at our wedding: the two of us, my brother and his girlfriend, Taylor's sister, and the British former fighter pilot who married us. Taylor wore a baby blue Betsey Johnson dress and knee-high black combat boots, and I wore a shiny black sharkskin suit and eyeliner. I catered the whole thing. In as long as it took to get a marriage licence and find someone to come to the house and marry us on my rooftop, we were married. I'd never felt more special. A woman who'd lived her whole life convinced she'd never get married, who didn't need any of that, had just married me.

The year before Taylor and I got married, Rich convinced me to empty whatever savings I had, sell what I could, and pool my money with his so we could afford the down payment on a new townhouse not far from where he worked. The neighbourhood was terrible, but developers were buying up all the land and if we got in early, we could be set. We could flip it in a couple of years and buy something even bigger. My brother's girlfriend, Leanna, started living with us not long after we got the place, so Taylor moved in with the three of us. We waited a week or two, then we told our parents.

None of this went over well with Taylor's mom and dad. They only knew me as Summer's boyfriend who'd showed up as her date a few times over the holidays when Taylor's mom hosted brunches for her and her sister's friends. Her father, who I really wanted to like me, was even less impressed than her mom. It's not that they didn't know me, or because Taylor was younger than I was—they were just worried. They were asking all the questions we should have asked ourselves but didn't. Everything was real now.

My parents, on the other hand, were ecstatic! The first time they met Taylor, they met her as my wife. We drove back to Acton, walked through the door, and just blurted it out. There were about thirty seconds of shock and confusion, then my dad got up out of his chair, danced over to us, dropped to the ground, and wrapped his arms around Taylor's ankles. He immediately started begging for grandchildren.

My dad wanted to be a grandfather more than just about anything, and he'd started buying presents for our kids when my brother and I were still kids. When I was about five and Rich was around eight, my Pop got us matching low-rider bikes called Green Machines. They were sort of like a Big Wheel, but infinitely cooler, and we lived on those things. We had only had them about a week before my dad went back to the same department store in Montreal and picked up a third, but *that* Green Machine wasn't for us. *That* Green Machine was for his future grandchild. He knew that handing that over to one of our kids would make him the coolest grandfather ever. "Every kid should have one of these," he told us. My dad kept that thing in the same box for over twenty years, and only got rid of it when he and my mom moved into a place without a garage and they needed the space. I know that broke his heart a little.

"Please, please! Grandchildren! Grandchildren now!" my Pop howled, lying face-down on the floor, half fake crying, while still hanging on to Taylor's legs with both arms and his whole heart.

Kids. That was yet another thing Taylor and I had never talked about before we got married. Not one conversation. But my old man was happy, so we let him have that moment.

My parents welcomed her into the family and told me that they expected this would happen one day. My mom had long come to terms with the fact that she would most likely not be at my wedding. She knew this was coming. She knew if it ever did happen, it would happen exactly like this. They were just happy to see me happy.

Taylor moved out of the townhouse, for the *first* time, three months later.

It was about a month and a half before Christmas and I was sitting at work doing what I normally did, pretending everything in my life was fine. Nobody had any idea Taylor had left—most of the people I worked with didn't even know I was married—and I had zero desire to sit and try to explain the whole thing to anyone. I was crushed and felt like a loser. I wasn't even sure at this point that I actually wanted to be married, but I sure as fuck didn't want to feel like a failure in front of my boss or anyone else.

It was just after lunch when my mom called my office phone, which was super unusual. She never called me at work. I hadn't told her Taylor had left, that she was overwhelmed and needed space, so as soon as I heard Mom's voice, I put on a giant smile, so I at least sounded happy.

"Hey, Ma, what's up?" I said like I didn't have a care in the world.

"Dad's in the hospital again. We met with the doctors today."

I knew my dad had been sick and dealing with pneumonia. But he'd had it before, tons of times, so during these last few weeks I hadn't thought too much about it. I hadn't talked to him in a while and just assumed, well, *nothing*. I was so consumed with what was happening with me and Taylor, I hadn't even bothered to check in.

"Your dad has cancer," Mom told me. At this point, she tried her best to keep it together and to be strong for me, sticking to the facts and remaining positive and optimistic. As she held in tears on her end, I did my best to hold it together on mine. I was in an office full of people. People who, up to this point, had never seen anything that even resembled an emotion from my corner of the room. I remember my hands going numb, and my back getting hot. I fought back tears so hard I thought my throat was going to close. I knew if I blinked, or even closed my eyes just once, there would be no stopping the flood, so I stared down at my notebook on my desk and wrote the word *NO* over and over again. My mom kept talking, but I'd stopped listening long ago. I didn't need to hear anything else. I had no questions.

"Yup, okay. Bye now!" I said in the happiest tone I could pull together, then I hung up the phone. I sat for a few more minutes as people buzzed in and out around me. Slowly, I put on my coat and walked out. I took those same two buses, subway, and streetcar home. I sat in the same seat I always did. I did what I always did. Nothing.

When I got home, Rich was already there, standing at the top of the stairs as I opened the front door. I kicked off my boots, dropped my bag, and walked up. The only thing Rich said to me was "Hey, brother." Then nothing, not a word. I kept my head down because I knew if we made eye contact, I'd start to cry. The baseboards needed to be repainted, the railing resanded, and the carpet hadn't been vacuumed in months. It was beige, but they called it Spiced Peach when we bought the place. I used everything around me as a distraction. I could tell Rich had had the exact same afternoon I did. I knew he hadn't told anyone either. Neither of us had said the words out loud. Then he hugged me.

As we stood there in the small hallway hugging, we both broke down. I didn't know much, but I was sure that from this point on nothing was ever going to be the same again. In that moment, hugging and crying seemed better than sitting and talking, so that's all we did. We just stood there together, quietly sharing the second-worst day of our lives. That is why I always need to come home to someone who's going to love me no matter what.

About a week later the TV network cancelled the show I was working on. I got fired.

Dad's official diagnosis was mesothelioma. He'd spent his entire career calibrating the instruments they used to build jet engines for airplanes. He was good at it, but his job was never his life. It was never his identity. He was always so much more than just what he did. He had worked for the same company for twenty-five years, in the same room with the same gear. The room he worked in was attached to what they called a test cell, where they ran these huge engines, alone, for hundreds of hours before ever putting them on a plane. Every precaution was taken to keep my dad, and everyone else, safe. These were jet engines, full of jet fuel, and this was the room that would determine whether they would explode or not. The walls, ceiling, and floor were lined with asbestos, and my dad worked in that room for most of his adult life. The place he woke up for at five in the morning every day, the place he worked so many night shifts and so much overtime to make sure we always had the best Christmases, was the place that killed him. His job killed him. My dad retired from that company early, a year before he found out his body was full of cancer. He was on *his* time now.

My dad had cancer, my marriage was ending, and I'd just lost my job. I didn't ask any questions that I didn't want to know the answers to, so I didn't look up anything about the kind of cancer he had. I did zero research. But every now and then, when I did start telling friends what he had, the reactions were always the same. If people didn't know what it was, I'd have to try my best to explain.

If they did, if they knew more than me, they'd just hug me and say nothing. If you knew, you knew, I guess.

I wanted to run, or rewind time. I just wanted out. But I had nowhere to turn. I couldn't talk to Taylor, my brother was going through all the same shit I was, and my mom had it worst of all. I'd never felt so alone. I had all these people in my life, and I had never felt so alone.

So, I called Summer.

Summer had heard about my dad though friends and agreed to meet for coffee. I was desperate and just wanted things to go back to normal. "I need you," I said. "I can't go through this alone. I don't know what to do. Just please help me."

"Roz, your dad is dying," she said. "He's going to die." Summer was the first person to ever say those words to me. She was the one who made it real, and as messed up as this sounds, I appreciated it, and thanked her. Summer did what, up to this point, nobody else had. She was blunt yet compassionate. She was all the things I wasn't. She gave me what I should have given her on the day that I broke her heart.

She gave me the truth.

ALL
DADS
DIE

THAT
ONE TIME
IN THERAPY

Those who feel the breath of sadness,
Sit down next to me.
Those who find they're touched by madness,
Sit down next to me.
Those who find themselves ridiculous,
Sit down next to me.
In love, in fear, in hate, in tears,
Sit down next to me.

—JAMES, "SIT DOWN"

It was three weeks before Christmas. I knew it was going to be my dad's last one: his favourite day of the year, and he only had one left. I was so lost, I didn't know if I was going to make it to the weekend, let alone the holidays.

I was never good at asking for help. Not because I never felt I needed it or could use it, but I always felt it ended with me in debt to someone. My goal was to always end my day without feeling

I owed anything to anyone. Every day needed a clean ending; that was the only way I could sleep. I was relentlessly independent, cripplingly private, and I didn't even know where to start when it came to finally asking for help.

I've always been susceptible to influence, so I avoided any situation, like therapy, where someone could put something weird or fucked up in my head that wasn't there before. I'm obsessive like that. When I was a kid, my mom casually told me that she could never go to Niagara Falls because *she always got the urge to jump*. That's exactly how she said it too, like it was no big deal. She couldn't really explain it, she wasn't suicidal, but she was drawn to the fall, to that quiet moment of nothing on the way down, to the freedom. Before my mom confessed that to me, I'd never thought about jumping off anything. But ever since, I've avoided the edge of *everything*. Even today, I always request low floors in hotels that have balconies. I'll never take that last step to look over anything no matter how beautiful the view is. Her thing became *my* thing.

That's why I was afraid of therapy. I didn't want someone putting something in my head that I'd never be able to remove. I didn't want anyone messing with the stuff that I'd meticulously filed away. I was afraid that if someone started pulling it all apart, I'd never be able to get it back together again. I was convinced that my feelings were far too complex and unique for anyone to understand, no matter how many diplomas they had on the wall. I knew that as soon as I started talking, saying shit out loud, then everything would become real, and there was no coming back from that. I once heard someone say that articulating your feelings is the first step to accepting them. I wasn't ready to accept anything.

Therapy wasn't my last option, but it sure as hell felt like it. I didn't need a hero. But I did need help, and I was finally ready to ask for it. I called up a psychiatrist I'd booked as a guest on the show over the years. We knew each other, and he was great at what he did. In my head, therapy was a luxury that people who grew up where I did didn't have. I'd never met anyone who had a therapist. This was some bougie and expensive shit that I didn't know how to do. How do you *do* therapy? How honest do you have to be to make it work?

My appointment was set up as a one-off. My therapist was unbelievably casual about the whole thing, too. I explained a bit over the phone when I first reached out, but I didn't get too deep as I didn't want to overload him. I didn't want him to know *how* fucked up I actually was. I didn't want to burden him with my problems, which I knew was sort of the point, but I didn't want to owe him. I blamed myself for everything, and in a messed-up way I needed him to tell me it was all my fault and that I needed to take responsibility. That was my plan.

Shrink sessions are usually forty-five minutes. I figure this is to give them enough time to run patients in and out in one-hour blocks. I was his 11 a.m. that day. Getting to his midtown office took about an hour. One streetcar, a few subway stops, and a long bus ride. I made a CD the night before with "Sit Down" by James, off their 1991 reissue of *Gold Mother*, burned over and over again. I listened to that track, on repeat, for the entire trip, while I rehearsed what I would and wouldn't say. I prioritized what I felt I needed help with the most, and looked for ways to dumb down or totally avoid all the rest. This was a one-time deal. I had one shot.

What I didn't know then is that therapy is hard as fuck. But it's supposed to be. If you find it easy, find a new doctor.

I sat on that couch, in the psychiatrist's eclectic but messy office, and told him what I thought he wanted to hear. I never wanted to burden anyone, and I hated being fussed over, so I skimmed over my feelings of failure and my own self-worth. I was the furthest thing from an open book, and even sitting there distracted by all his important junk piled everywhere, I still wasn't ready to say most things out loud. I opened myself up a bit and let him take a look.

This is where, for me, it all went to hell. This is where I started looking for a way out. I wanted to stay in the moment, to fix the things that hurt *now*. I didn't want to look back and map out every single event that got me to his couch that morning. I didn't want to be judged because I was afraid that I'd disappoint him. It felt like an audition, like I needed to say all the right things to keep him interested. To prove I wasn't wasting his time. I needed to come off as therapy-worthy, but not too big of a project.

I quickly explained what was killing my dad as best I could, and I touched on the guilt I had over Taylor leaving. I told him I believed the world was full of monsters, and I was incapable of seeing the good in anyone. I explained I was convinced that everyone I'd ever met was an opportunistic phony who would fuck me over in a heartbeat to gain even one inch in life.

"Yeah, you might not be wrong," he said with a cool casualness that confused the hell out of me. I sounded paranoid and all over the place. I'd never talked about any of this before and I didn't really know how to. I was performing for him, treating him like an audience. Even the stuff that hurt the most, I tried to say in a way that would make him laugh.

"Tell me about your mom," he said.

"Good cook. Believes in ghosts. Taught me how to sew." I wasn't dragging my mother into this. She was about to lose the love her of life and was hanging on by her teeth.

"What about your brother?"

"He's smart. Funny. A nerd, but like a *cool* nerd."

I was doing a routine. I'd really only ever bonded with people over two things—sex and humour. I knew enough about myself to know these were a defence mechanism. That was my escape.

The doctor didn't even flinch. While I told him most of what I was willing to say, he barely moved his pen across the pad propped up on his knee. At first I thought I was failing, wasting his time. What I quickly realized was there was nothing I was saying that he hadn't heard a hundred times before. None of this was unusual, and this guy had me figured out top to bottom in the first thirty minutes, which infuriated me. The only thing worse than someone thinking you're fucked up is someone telling you you're *normal*. This was actually all good news, and I should have been relieved, but screw that guy.

I sat there in pieces as he mapped out a way to put me back together.

By the end of our session, the one-off, the favour for a friend, he told me he wanted to see me again on the following Tuesday *and* Thursday. Then the next Tuesday and Thursday for the foreseeable future. He knew I was holding back. In forty-five minutes I'd gone from having never done this kind of thing before to being a twice-a-week shrink patient.

I was pissed.

Realizing there's a path to success isn't the same as following that path. I wasn't ready to do the work to get where I wanted to be. I had told him maybe one-tenth of what I should have, and I was already a career patient.

That was my last appointment.

I'm pretty good at giving advice, but absolute shit at taking it, although I do try to learn from my mistakes, my biggest being that I judged my individuality, the thing that separated me from everyone else, by how much hell I could go through and still carry on. I judged myself on how much pain I could mask from my friends, family, and co-workers and never ask for help. I chose to hide my scars, self-destruction, self-sabotage, tics, loss, abuse, and failure and manage to never let it show. By opening up just a little in therapy, I let the light in, and it burned like bloody murder.

I didn't know then that individuality, the thing that actually makes us special, doesn't come from how much we can handle. It comes from what we can *offer*. I had so much work to do, but instead of getting on with it, I walked away and torched the path behind me. I wasn't ready to put every thought I had on trial or attach meaning to things I'd spent years trying to forget. I got back on the bus and managed to get the same seat I always did. I reached into my bag, pulled out my notebook, and flipped to the page with my dad's Christmas list on it.

He had one Christmas left and I hadn't even started shopping yet.

A
CHRISTMAS
STORY

My dad had this beautiful way of always fucking up Christmas morning.

We were Christmas people. There was no Secret Santa single-gift exchange, and we never got too old or bored of seeing a tree exploding with presents on Christmas morning. Even when Rich and I were grown up and had long since moved out, my family didn't set budgets or come up with restrictive rules, we just bloody went for it. All of us. Every single year. My old man was the undisputed king of Christmas and he'd always spend way more than he had to make sure we got everything we asked for, and a ton of stuff we didn't. My mom did the vast majority of the Christmas planning, prepping, cooking, and shopping. She still tells us stories from when we were kids of her coming home with bags and bags of gifts for us. And my dad would look at her and always say the same thing: "That's not enough. We'll go back out tomorrow. Together. We can carry more." When it came to my Pops and Christmas, *everything* was never enough.

When Rich and I started making our own money, big money, was when things really went bonkers. The weeks leading up to the holidays became a frantic but well-oiled glorious pain in the ass. Each of us would write up and pass out a list of everything we wanted, then everyone else would sneak off and talk privately to divvy it up. Rich would always figure out who was getting what for who. He was by far the most organized. My mom's list was, without question, the most important, though. She did all the work, so she got the most attention. She got everything she wanted.

My mom's list was the one thing we couldn't fuck up, but every year my dad would. Even as adults, long after we had moved out, my brother was still the master of the lists, and he took that job seriously. He'd write down everything Mom asked for, divide it up, and assign things to me and my dad to get. He'd break it down by price, priority, and store location to make sure she was fully taken care of. We all knew what we were in charge of getting. We'd spend that last week checking in with each other to make sure nobody forgot anything. Of course, my mom couldn't have cared less about what she got as long as we were all home and together, but making her feel like a kid on Christmas morning was always our way to thank her for being such a great mom. And then my dad made a mess of the entire thing.

Aside from the giftsplosion we'd wake up to every year, we didn't really have too many big family traditions—but we did have a million little ones. Anne Murray or Boney M. would always be playing as Mom walked out of the kitchen with a fresh pot of coffee and a bottle of Baileys. She'd set out a tray of sausage rolls straight from the oven and a huge bowl of those little round potatoes from a can that she'd fried up in a pan with hot oil and herbs. There was always leftover tourtière from Christmas Eve and enough chips and chocolate to keep us awake and full until dinner. We've eaten the same thing every Christmas morning for our entire lives.

For years, my mom had suggested, "Maybe one time we could all wake up, shower and get dressed, and have a nice breakfast in the dining room before opening gifts." That was never going to happen. We were not *those* people. Between me, Rich, and Dad, if even one of us managed to get dressed for dinner it was seen as a Christmas Miracle.

A few weeks before the holidays my dad went in for laparoscopic surgery. They explained that they wanted to go in with tiny cameras to get a better look at the tumours. Just a few small holes, no big deal. The day he went in, he was ready. My dad had a process that he went through before any of the appointments with doctors or surgeons. He did this alone. We'd do one last group hug, then he'd tell us he had to *get ready*. I'm not sure what he thought about or said to himself in those moments, but whatever it was, it always got him out the other side. No matter what the doctors did, Dad always woke up ready for whatever was coming next.

I went to see him in the hospital the day after the surgery, and he was sitting up at the end of the bed when I walked in. Even up to this point I had never actually seen my dad *lying* in a hospital bed. He was always propped right up. Or sitting off the side. It was clear he did this for me.

"Wanna see what they did to me?" he asked as he slid his gown off one arm. "They cut me in half." He pulled down the other shoulder, and I didn't even know what I was looking at. There was a slice so big I couldn't tell where it started or where it ended. He had bandages covered in dried blood with exposed staples sticking out the sides from the centre of his chest, down in a half-circle to his hip, then up his back to between his shoulders. A giant U-shape.

Yeah, they cut him in half. That wasn't supposed to happen. These were supposed to be tiny holes for tiny cameras. But the doctors said they'd needed a better look. They did all of this without telling us or even asking, and there was no coming back from it.

There was no way dad would be strong enough to enjoy Christmas.

I don't know how he managed to get himself to the end of the bed, or why he felt he had to, but he wasn't the same man he'd been two days before. He was about to go through as much chemo and radiation as any one human being is supposed to be able to handle, and the fight was fixed.

He had nothing left.

Dad's first gift from me was the same thing that year as it was every year: new slippers. They were totally expected but always appreciated. Every year, he pulled them out of the box, kicked off the pair he'd got the year before, and tried the new ones on while knocking his heels together and wiggling his toes around inside them. My old man did everything in slippers. Sure, he had shit style and never cared if anything he wore even matched, but he knew how to be comfortable.

"Okay, sweetheart, your turn," Dad always said as he dug through the mass of colourful paper, bows, and ribbons to find one for my mom. "This one's from me."

Most years, my mom carefully tore through the wrapping and opened one of the things she'd asked for. Something straight from her list. It could be anything, but let's just say a curling iron, and not just any curling iron—the exact, very specific curling iron that she'd wanted for months. The exact curling iron my *brother* was supposed to get and *did* get for her. Rich mumbled, "What the hell, Pops?" as he passed my dad on his way to root around under the tree for the exact same box in a slightly different wrapper to hand to my mom.

"Okay, and *this* one's from me, I guess," Rich said while shooting my dad the same look he always did. Mom peeled back the paper, doing her best to look surprised, to reveal the *exact* same curling iron. She thanked Rich and Dad, then casually stacked them on top of each other beside her La-Z-Boy.

My dad laughed. "Well, now you have *two*! Nothin' wrong with that! You can keep one in the basement." As if my mom had big dreams of doing her hair in the same bathroom where we kept the cat's litter box.

This would go on and on, all morning long, gift after gift, every year. After all the organizing, all the work, the sub-lists from the main lists, and reassurances that we all knew what we were responsible for getting, my dad had taken Mom's entire list and bought it all, top to bottom.

We always joked and goofed on Dad for his flakiness and inability to follow simple instructions. It took me forever to realize it wasn't that at all. This wasn't my dad not paying attention. This was him being unable to leave anything off my mom's list. He didn't have it in him. If my mom asked for it, my dad was going to get it for her, regardless of the rules. So, she got everything. Twice.

It was a predictable and hysterical mess. It was beautiful.

But that Christmas, my dad's last, was the first year I can remember that not happening. No double gifts for my mom. My dad was too weak to shop, so my brother and I took care of it for him. Rich and I joked that we should buy Mom two of something just to keep the tradition going, but I think that would have crushed him.

When someone's dying slowly, piece by piece every day, you do everything you can to never point out or remind them of the things they've already lost. There was no way we were going to make my dad feel like he was no longer the guy who gave his wife everything she asked for.

Dad still got his slippers that Christmas, but I had to put them on for him. I got a size smaller than I normally did, but he was still swimming in them. He'd lost so much weight that nothing fit properly. He looked like a little kid who got into his father's closet and tried everything on. I rested his foot on my knee, and helped him get the slippers on, but there was no heel-kicking and toe-wiggling this time.

"They okay, Pops? Not too tight?" I asked.

"Nah. They're perfect, son."

It wasn't supposed to be like this. It wasn't supposed to happen this fast. As happy as I tried to look that morning, I was livid. We all were.

My dad couldn't keep food down, and I'm not sure he ate one entire meal in the week leading up to Christmas Day, but he wasn't going to miss my mom's turkey dinner, and she wasn't about to let him down. Mom slayed dinner that night. It was a work of art. Absolute perfection. That dinner, on Christmas Day, was always my dad's favourite ninety minutes of the entire year, and this one was going to last a lifetime.

Before we started, Pops asked if he could say grace. My parents weren't particularly religious people, but there's no shame in turning to God when you need a little extra help or have a prayer you hope has a chance of getting to someone who gives a shit. Dad talked for a few minutes, stopping and starting, wiping his tears with the sleeve of his sweater that was now two sizes too big for him. He reached out and held my brother's and my hands on either side of the table. All we could do was let him take his time.

I don't remember how he started, or what he asked for, but I remember how it ended.

"Thank you. Thank you for my life. I had a really good life." His head was down, and his eyes were closed, but my Pops wasn't praying. He wasn't thanking God. He was thanking us. "Amen," he whispered to himself. "That's it."

ONE
GOOD
DAY

When someone's dying, they have good days and bad days. Doctors ask that question all the time to people who are dying: "Was today a good day or a bad day?" Of course, what they mean is, How's your pain? But dying people actually do have good days. A good day can be nothing more than a few quick moments of normalcy, so it doesn't take much. Walking a few extra steps, laughing at an old joke that never gets old, or having the strength to hug you back with both arms. My dad's good days were built around exactly that. Anything that let him forget, even for a second, that he wasn't going to be our dad for very much longer. He wasn't in denial, he knew what was up, but on days when he needed a win, he usually found one.

Early on in his treatment, after maybe his third surgery, I went to visit when they had him at a downtown hospital not far from where Rich and I were living. I walked in with a double banquet burger, fries, and gravy stuffed deep in the bottom of my bag so nobody would smell it as I made my way through the long halls, avoiding every nurse I saw.

Dad was propped up in bed, wearing the VR goggles I'd got him for Christmas, playing his Sony PlayStation. I wheeled his tray over. I tapped him on the leg and squeezed his foot to let him know I was there.

"Hey, son!" he said with that big smile I hadn't seen in forever. It had been months since we laughed together, and even longer since I'd seen him excited about something. "Guess what happened?" he whispered, really dragging out that last word, while slowly raising his hand as far as he could for an incoming high-five. "I got a boner this morning." This was a *good* day.

When someone you love is dying, you have good days and bad days too. For me, a good day was one I was able to get through without being reminded that my father was dying. At the beginning of all this, I really did try my best to do all the things and really be there for him. I made him kale soup, because I read in the *New York Times* that dark greens were good for cancer patients. He hated it. I tried to get him up and walking around. He did his best. I sat with him during chemo a few times. On those days, when this all started, I was the good son. I didn't know what to do, so I did everything I thought I was supposed to do. In a lot of ways, I was acting the part of someone who was about to be half-orphaned, because that seemed easier than the alternative. This wasn't denial—it was just the truth.

My dad had shit hair his whole life. A great moustache, but shitty hair. I don't think he ever had a full head of it. He wasn't a vain guy, so it never bothered him, until the day his hair didn't do what it was *supposed* to do. I actually think, in a weird way, he was looking forward to losing it during chemo. But that didn't happen.

They pumped his body so full of poison that he should have had nothing left, but his thin, wiry, three-toned shitty hair refused to fall out.

While he was in the middle of his second round of chemo and radiation, we drove out to see him and my mom and spend the night at their house. I brought my clippers. I sat my Pops in a chair in their kitchen, wrapped one of my mom's good towels around his thin, bare shoulders, and took care of it for him. Row after row, I slowly shaved it all off, gently wiping away whatever was left with my hand and kissing the top of his head as I went. I remember standing behind him because if I saw his face, I wouldn't have been able to get through it. I took my shirt off too, so it didn't get covered in clippings, and every time I reminded him to sit up as straight as he could, his back would touch my chest. He leaned into me, and I held him up with everything I had. When I was finished, I wrapped my arms around him from behind, and tried not to hug him too tight. He was too tired to lift his arms to hug me back, but he managed to turn just enough that our foreheads touched. That was the best he could do and all I could hope for. That was the last time I remember hugging my dad while he was still alive enough for it to mean something.

That was the night I said goodbye. He still had time left, but that was it for me, and I knew it. That's the last memory I have of me and my dad together while he was still *him*. Thanking me and telling me *I was a good kid*, and me saying "Thanks, Pops" as I kissed the top of his head. Those are the last words I remember sharing with him.

Not too long after, he went in for what would be his last surgery. This is the one that should have killed him—it was so incredibly invasive that he shouldn't have made it out alive. But he did.

The plan was to go in heavy and rip out anything that didn't belong. His body was so riddled with tumours the surgeons didn't know where start, or when to call it. Taylor was with me in the waiting room that night. We weren't officially back together, but she was right there with me through it all. Somehow, I managed to fall asleep slumped over on a chair with my head on her lap, while my brother, his girlfriend Leanna, and our mom slept on the floor. I don't know what time the doctor walked in, but it was late, maybe almost morning. He flicked the light on before saying anything, and we all jumped awake the same way you do during a lightning storm or a bad dream.

"We did what we could," he explained. "We managed to get a lot of it out, but we couldn't stop the bleeding. He's still in there. We packed him with all the cloth, gauze, and sponges we had in the room to try to get it under control. That's all we can do right now."

I put my head back down on Taylor's lap and waited it out. I was more numb than sad. The sadness I did have wasn't because my dad was in there dying. It was because he was in there dying alone.

I'm not sure how much time that last surgery bought him, but he made it home for one last stretch. The good days, from that point, were hard to come by no matter how much fight he had left in him. There was no optimism, and there wasn't going to be a miracle. It was only a matter of time, and the best he could hope for would be a few minutes on the phone with his boys. That would have been a good day. He didn't want much, he just wanted a couple of minutes a day to forget all this and just be a dad. He needed to feel that he still mattered.

I took that away from him.

In a lot of ways, I killed him off long before he died. In my mom's kitchen that night, when he was wrapped in a towel, while

I shaved his head, that's when I let him go. I did my best to start living my life without him, trying to get over his death while he was still alive. It was almost like some morbid obsession. I knew losing him would never get better, but I hoped it would get easier, and I wanted a head start—to just fucking get on with it, already. My dad went through his last months alive without me. He was dying, but I was the ghost.

My mom called, after Dad had fallen asleep one night, to beg me to talk to him. "You know he sits by the phone all day hoping you'll call, right? Please call him. Just talk to him. Can I tell him you'll call?"

"Of course," I replied. I promised I'd call after dinner the next night. I didn't. I never called.

"When's the last time you talked to Pops?" my brother asked. He wasn't so much asking as confronting me.

"I don't know. Not that long. The other day?"

"It's been three weeks. You haven't talked to Dad in *three weeks*."

I knew exactly how long it had been. The only times I did talk to Dad is when I walked into our living room while he and Rich were already on the phone. Rich would hand me the receiver. Even then, I couldn't get off quick enough. It was cruel. This was a man who'd given me his absolute best his entire life, and I couldn't give him five minutes on a Tuesday.

I never learned how to grieve because I refused to acknowledge loss or the sadness of being hurt. My entire identity was built around coping mechanisms and distractions. It was easier to take responsibility and ownership over things that happened *to* me than it was to deal with, or even admit to, being hurt by someone else. I owned it all.

Hiding scars from burning myself was easier than admitting what they were actually covering up. I was never sad, rarely angry, and I would never dream of taking anything out on another person. I was just stuck. I was stuck in that closet with that family friend when I was nine. I was stuck in every moment where I wished I could have said *no*. Every burn, every drink, every hotel room or back seat of a stranger's car. Every fight I knew I couldn't win. All the times I cancelled plans at the last minute because I was too paralyzed with fear to leave the house. I was stuck in every situation I'd made myself a target because it was easier than trying to fit in. I hid my tics the same way I hid my wife leaving me. I let the things that hurt me continue to hurt me every day.

Nobody teaches you how to grieve. It's not something they go over in school, and it's always the one topic you try your best to avoid with anyone who's already gone through it. We all grieve differently, and no matter how many people you surround yourself with, we all do it alone. Grief is natural. That's why most of us don't need medication or counselling and usually find or fight our way out of it. We're built for this. We don't know it, but we are. We're built to deal with incredible loss, pain, and sadness.

I didn't understand that then.

If you Google "grief," or how long it's supposed to last, what you'll find, right there at the top, are the famous five stages: denial, anger, bargaining, depression, and acceptance. What they don't tell you is these don't always happen in that order. It's not a map. I skipped the first four and forced my way to acceptance, and I was never going to look back. There was no anger and no room to bargain, but I deliberately and selfishly denied both myself and my dad the experience of losing each other.

It wasn't meant to be cruel. I tried to convince myself that this was all coming from a good place, a place of love. I wanted to get on to grieving with love, and not because of heartbreak and immeasurable sadness. I wanted this year to be over. I knew that if I did this, that eventually, when the time came, when that phone rang in the middle of the night to tell me it was time, I'd be better prepared.

It was only much later I realized that none of what I did was done out of love.

Guilt isn't one of the five stages of grief, but it should be. I was dealing with such incredible guilt. I blamed myself for all the things my dad wouldn't experience. When someone dies young, your heart breaks for the things they'll miss out on. I took all the blame for this. I blamed myself for not being good enough or fast enough for my Pops to see me shine. His whole life, I was always on my way to *becoming* something, and he was never going to see his hard work fully pay off. I jumped into a marriage that was never going to work out and I robbed him of the chance to be the best grandfather any kid could ask for. He didn't get to stand beside me at my wedding, and as my marriage fell apart, I realized that any woman I met after Taylor would have no idea how incredible he was.

And to my own kids, if I eventually had them, my dad would be nothing more than a story I told. For those last few months, when I didn't call, it wasn't because of denial. It was guilt. I'd let him down, and I didn't know how to say sorry.

GOODNIGHT, ROADRUNNER

If I asked you to tell me the moment you grew up, could you answer? Like, the moment your life changed forever, when you moved forward from whatever kid innocence you may have had left? The moment where you separated from that *other* person forever. The old you would now be a memory, and nothing could ever be recaptured or repeated with any sort of honesty. A total reset. That's what happened to me the night I sat with my brother in a small beige office under fluorescent light, as a doctor slid a DNR form across the desk and asked if we wanted to sign it.

A DNR is a fuck of a document. This is a do-not-resuscitate order, which instructs health care workers not to perform CPR if a patient's heart stops beating or they lose the ability to breathe on their own. This is also a way for them to inform you there's nothing more they can do—it's about compassion, not survival. It's a way of telling you the fight is over. Coming from a family of fighters, this was bloody hard to sign off on. It felt like a betrayal. My brother and I put our names on it, slid it back across that desk, and walked out carrying all the guilt and shame that comes with giving up on someone you love. In writing.

My dad survived more than anyone should have to, but this was us committing to not fight for *him*.

When we got to the hospital that night, that last night, he was already too far gone for anything to really matter. He wasn't conscious and couldn't talk or respond to anything we said. This was the end. These were the walls he was going to die behind, under shitty fluorescent lights in a room with a window that didn't open.

When it came to his family, my Pops would have chewed through brick to make sure we were safe, but there we were about to stand there and do nothing. We knew he had to do this alone. All dads, eventually, have to do this part alone. Doing nothing was the hardest thing I've ever had to do. When you sign a DNR, your family story changes, and everyone has to be on board. The story becomes less about motivation, less about the fight, and more about abandonment of all hope. I was still my dad's cheerleader and his champion, but instead of telling him to get up and walk, to eat something, to think positive and fight, I was leaning in whispering that it was *okay to go*. Instead of telling him how much I needed him, I was letting him know it was alright to say goodbye.

I sat by his bed and held his hand.

I repeated, "Don't worry, Pops. You did a good job," and "We're all going to be okay," over and over, hoping these words would make their way in. And I thanked him.

This is when I first truly understood what I was actually losing. It was everything. I was losing everything.

I never thought for a second about what the last words I'd say to my dad would be. This isn't something you rehearse. Nor should you. All dads die. There's no other way to say it. That's not a reminder, or a reality that I get any sort of joy from writing, but it's the truth. There's no lesson here and you shouldn't, for one minute, waste your time wondering how you'd handle it. It's not something you can or should ever try to prepare for. Don't put it in your head, and don't run the scenarios. It won't help.

When someone you love is dying, people try to relate to you, while still offering whatever support they can. It's awkward, but sometimes beautiful too. They'll ask how your loved one is doing, without pressing too hard. They'll give you space, but still want the updates. They'll praise your strength, while wondering, out loud, how they themselves would handle it. This happened a lot in those last few days—I heard it all. *I don't know how you do it. I couldn't imagine. I don't know if I'd be able to go through that.*

I know people weren't being shitty, I know they weren't making my very-soon-to-be-dead father all about them, but people can't help it. It's just what we do. My answer to all of them was the same. Very simple. "Don't. Don't spend one second playing that out. Don't imagine anything. Don't put yourself in my position. Just call your dad. If you're pissed off? Call him. If you're busy? Call him. If you hung out yesterday but miss him today? Call your dad, and if he doesn't pick up, leave a message and let him know you're thinking about him."

I couldn't remember the last time my dad and I talked, or what we actually said to each other. But I do know that I didn't say goodbye. At least, not in any way that would have meant anything. And this kills me. Even today. Those last few months, when he was alive, were a gift I left unopened. I didn't have what it took to walk that road with him. I knew that the next part of me to break was going to be broken forever, so I walked away. I couldn't tell him how hurt I was. I couldn't put that on him. I was young and I wasn't ready for any of it.

I play those last few months out in my head all the time, and how today I would do it all so differently. I would empty my bank account to find him the best care at home. I would find a place in the country with no neighbours and with windows that opened. He deserved to go out with morning sun on his face and wet feet from sitting on a porch in one last rainstorm. I would take one of those hands of his, the ones that could fix anything, and hold it against my chest every night until he fell asleep. I wouldn't force him to get up and walk, but I would ask him to dance. I would beg him to finish telling all the stories that still had holes and felt incomplete. The ones without endings. The ones I was now going to have to tell for him.

My dad had this Roadrunner belt buckle that he always used to show off when I was a kid. I was fascinated with it. It wasn't anything fancy, didn't look like it cost more than a couple bucks, but I knew it meant something to him. I don't remember a lot of stuff actually meaning much to my dad, but this did. I hadn't thought about that belt buckle in over twenty years, but for some reason, as he was lying there dying, I couldn't get it out of my head. I wondered what happened to it. Where it went. I used to think it was the coolest thing, and I remember asking to borrow it one time for a costume I was putting together for school. He told me no for the first time in my life. The story behind it meant more than the buckle itself, but that little piece of tin with a cartoon Roadrunner hammered into it was all that was left of whatever he did to earn it.

In the Marines everybody got a nickname. Dad's was Road-runner because, he said, "Nobody could ever catch me." Like most of his stories, that one evolved over the years too, but I'm not sure he ever finished it. I'm not sure I ever got the whole truth behind the Roadrunner. My dad was never proud and never bragged about anything he did in the Marines, but this was different, and I'm still not sure why. That's all I could think about that day. That belt buckle and the unfinished story behind it.

The lung floor of any hospital is a different place from all the other floors. Most people on a lung floor are dying prematurely from totally preventable deaths. Every hallway, bathroom, and waiting area reeks of cigarette smoke. It's filled with dying sixty-year-olds who look eighty, with most of their friends and family looking the exact same. I was a great smoker: even after both my lungs collapsed a few years earlier, I was still a great smoker. I was ticcing like crazy and fighting off panic attacks. I couldn't smoke in Dad's room, so I'd sip on a premixed bottle of vodka and orange juice I kept in the bottom of my bag. Drinking always helped with my tics and anxiety. Or maybe I just cared less when I was half-drunk.

I'd go from wanting to be there, right by his side, to needing an escape; from wanting to make every second last to wanting it all to be over. One minute I promised myself I was never going to let go of his hand, and the next I was making every possible excuse to go and do anything else. I'd go on coffee runs, or pretend I had to pee so I could hide in a bathroom to stand beside a urinal and cry. Then I'd smoke. I'd take the elevator down three flights and walk out to the sidewalk to sit and smoke with dying addicts. I'd smoke with people wearing robes and slippers, in wheelchairs with oxygen tanks attached to the back. I'd put on my headphones and listen to "Pink Moon" by Nick Drake two or three times, and we'd smoke. In the rain. This somehow made me feel better about myself. And I'm sure, in some fucked-up way, it made them feel better about themselves too.

You'd think walking back up to the lung floor smelling like wet cigarettes would be frowned upon, but it was the furthest thing from that. You could hear people take in deep breaths as you walked by. I wasn't gross or some reminder of bad decisions. The exact opposite, actually. To them, I was delicious. I smelled like home.

After one of my long smoke breaks, I walked back into Dad's room and found myself alone with him. Rich and Leanna were off getting food, Taylor was probably with them, and I'm sure my mom was out on the phone updating friends or somewhere catching her breath. It wasn't for long, but me and my Pops were alone. After the DNR was signed, I'd stopped asking questions about recovery and procedures. I had no interest in what happened next, or how long Dad had. The only question I remember asking was, "Can he still hear me?"

The doctor replied, "Yeah, I'm sure he can. Talk to him."

But what do you say? How do you even come up with the last thing you'll ever say to someone? All I wanted to do was hear his laugh. I didn't want to say anything to him, but I wanted to *hear* everything. I wanted him to snap up and tell me where he'd been these last few days, and whether it was beautiful. I wanted him to open his eyes and say something funny. I wanted that awkward high-five followed by a kiss on the forehead he'd always give me, sometimes for doing something great, but most times for no reason at all.

I knew this was going to be my last time alone with him. I knew this was it. I'm sure he did too. I couldn't fix him, or make any of this better, but I owed him something. I had to just be the fucking kid he raised. The words I said would be a direct reflection of him. All his hard work, advice, and sacrifice.

I pulled my chair in close, rested my head on his chest, and said, "Happy Birthday, Merry Christmas, I love you, and goodnight," which were all the things I knew he'd miss hearing the most. Those four things, said with a kiss on the forehead, were always guaranteed to light him up. That was my dad, and that was the last thing I ever said to him.

When it was time to say goodbye, when his body fought like hell for that last breath, my mom gave that moment to me and my brother. We climbed into bed with him, me on Dad's left and Rich on his right. Mom stood at the bottom of the bed rubbing his feet. She didn't move, break down, or say a single word. She was built for this, and she knew this was the way my Pops would want to go. Exactly like that. That was the day that hollowed me out, and it was perfect.

Goodnight, Roadrunner.

FUNERAL CLOTHES

Truth is, I have no idea when my dad died or how long it's been. I don't want to know either.

The day I said goodnight to him was the day I stopped counting time. I never wanted to be reminded. I refuse to acknowledge the anniversary and still avoid all reminders and conversations that would timestamp it. I simply don't ever want to know when I hit the point where I've lived more life without him than I did with him.

How long does it take to get over someone you love dying? Years ago, my answer was always the same: "I don't know. I don't know if anyone knows, but I'll tell you when it happens." Today, my answer to that question is: "Forever. For as long as my dad is dead and I'm still alive it's going to hurt. It never gets better, but it does get easier."

We know how to handle death when it happens to someone else. We bake a lasagna, break out our funeral clothes, and offer "whatever you need." We know how to be there for people, even when it's the first time. Instinct takes over, and we put a few words together from the heart, even though they're not even close to being enough. But they don't have to be. We don't have to do it all, because that's what all the *other* people are for—to build a net and make sure the person suffering doesn't fall too hard. There's no timeline for grieving, and it's something we all have to do at our own pace. Generally, people give you whatever time and space you need, even if they've never gone through it themselves. They get it, and there's an understanding that people *just need time*. What everyone has difficulty with, however, is when someone climbs out of that net too soon.

We know how to handle someone who's hurting. We *don't* know how to handle someone who should be hurting but isn't.

I was that person for a very long time.

I took an extra week off work after my dad's funeral because I thought people would think me and my Pops had a shit relationship if I went back too soon. Like somehow five extra days off would make some huge difference, but it did. To them, not to me. And when I did make it back to work, I made sure I looked sad enough that people knew I had a heart, but not so sad that I made anyone uncomfortable.

When you finally make your way back into the life you left, most people you know will ask you the exact same, well-meaning question: "How are you doing?" It's simple, doesn't ruin your day, and usually comes from a good place. You can answer that question a thousand different ways, but what you *can't* say is, "I don't know. It hasn't hit me yet," and just carry on.

I cared too much about protecting other people from *my* pain, and *way* too much about what I'd eventually have to do to pay back whatever support came my way. Everything was about balance: I told myself never to take more than I'd be able to give back. I had nothing to give and couldn't see myself ever being able to return any of the goodwill or kindness that people seemed so eager to lend, so I left all offers on the table. I didn't trust people when they said it was no problem or they were happy to help and do whatever. I looked at support like a loan, or favour-banking. I was skeptical, paranoid, and hollow.

Every night after work, I'd head to the Black Bull Tavern on Queen West. The Bull was one of those loud, "established in 1800-something" rock 'n' roll pubs, filled with thick smoke, thick blue-collar bikers, and a stacked staff of hard women who could more than hold their own. The Bull wasn't the toughest place, but just like the women who ran it, it could be when it needed to be.

This was my church. I'd go to fit in *and* disappear, always sitting on the last stool around the back corner of the dark, sticky, carved-up hardwood bar. I'd always have a notebook and a few pens with me, so it seemed like I had some creative or artsy reason to be there alone every night, but the truth is, nobody cared.

Half the other people were in there alone. I'd see the same guys every night, usually older, ghostly looking men who'd flirt with the bartenders while nursing the same beer for an hour before they'd drift home to whatever *they'd* been avoiding, or to the next bar hoping another drink would be the one that fixed everything. We were exactly the same.

I'd leave work to sit in the dark and in my own head, surrounded by strangers. Sometimes I'd manage to write a few notes, or a song lyric or a bit of what resembled poetry, then I'd rip the pages out of my book and throw them in the garbage by the front door on my way out. I took nothing with me. Mostly I'd dive. I've always had the ability to check out or zone out, whatever you want to call it. I can find a spot on a wall or out a window, anything that catches my eye really, lock onto it, staring a hole through whatever it is, and dive. I don't black out, but I can easily lose fifteen, twenty, or sometimes twenty-five minutes doing this. Doing nothing while silently building a case against every decision I'd ever made. I was listing my mistakes and losing count.

"Hey! Where'd you go?" said a voice that finally broke my concentration one night. Nina, who looked like Britney Spears and talked like Courtney Love, was my favourite bartender. She was waving her hand in front of my face to interrupt, or disrupt, whatever the hell it was she thought I was doing. I clearly made her uncomfortable, curious, or both.

"Huh? What?" I replied, snapping out of it.

"Where do you go when you go? You do it a lot." She whipped her body around, putting her back against her side of the bar and faced away so she could see what I saw, trying to make sense of it. What could have possibly held my attention for that long? A cash register, a few bottles of Wild Turkey, a Budweiser poster with bikini models?

"Nowhere. Just in my own head," I told her.

"Anything good up in there?" she asked, while pointing a straw between my eyes that she'd just pulled from her own mouth. Now, this wasn't so much a question as a cheeky comment. She wasn't really asking and didn't *really* want to know. This wasn't an opportunity for a "moment." She wasn't trying to connect or help me through whatever it was I was going through. She wasn't flirting.

It was the perfect opportunity for me to deflect or throw some fun comment back. Which is what I usually did instead of actually saying anything from the heart. Just be fun. *You can fake fun*, I thought while taking *way* too long to answer.

"No. There's nothing good in there," I said in a rare moment of honesty.

Her eyebrows shot up to her hairline.

You fucking idiot, I thought to myself.

"You want another one?" she asked with a half smile while grabbing my empty pint glass.

I nodded and opened my notebook and started writing to at least give the impression I knew what I was doing. To not look so bad for business. "HOPE DIES LAST," I wrote.

When is all this going to finally knock me on my ass? I'd ask myself. *When's it going to hit? When am I going to be normal?* I wanted so bad to cry myself awake and drink myself to sleep.

So I waited. I waited for the sadness to creep or even jack-hammer its way in. I didn't know much, but I knew the way I was grieving couldn't be right. It sure as shit didn't *feel* right. I wondered if I was just really bad at it, or maybe, *just maybe*, really bloody good at it. Maybe this was my thing. Maybe letting people go was my superpower. After all, I'd long been more than fine to let friends go. Great friends, friends that I told secrets to that I'd never say to anyone else. I was in my late twenties by now, and my closest friend was someone I'd met three years earlier—if that. My child-hood relationships had all expired or run their course, and I never thought about any of those people. Ever.

"What do you call a fish with no eye?" Nina asked, holding my drink off to the side until I answered.

"I don't know. What?" I gave her enough of a beat to deliver whatever was coming next. I've always had respect for a good joke and would never think of stomping on someone's punchline.

"Fsssssshhhhhhhhh," she answered with wide eyes and a huge smile. She gave me the same look parents give to their kids when they try to cheer them up after they bonk their head on the edge of the counter. "Don't spend too much time up there," Nina added as she slid my fresh pint glass across the bar. "You gotta get out of your head sometimes. Give yourself a break."

I hadn't cried since the funeral, and here I was months, maybe even a year later and still nothing. I wasn't in shock, I was vacant. My body was built for resilience, not grief. Maybe I got this from my old man, or maybe it was the same defence mechanism I'd unknowingly used over the years, I wasn't sure. I wasn't proud of how I was dealing with it, and I certainly didn't think I was tough. I was embarrassed. I read every room I walked into and over-analyzed every conversation around me so I could look and sound like someone who was still struggling, because that's what you're supposed to do when you're in the net.

My mom was just as lost as I was, but she had it ten times worse. I still don't know how she did it. Six months after my dad died, *her* dad died, which meant she had to move my grandmother from Montreal to live with her in Acton. My nan was your classic petty, passive-aggressive, sweet-but-bitter English-speaking Montrealer, and now the two of them were mourning their husbands under the same roof. I'm still surprised they didn't kill each other. Nan was a retired nurse who raised four kids on her own before meeting and marrying the man who was the only father my mom ever knew. My mom's birth father died in a work accident when she was three, leaving my grandmother alone to raise my mom and her three older brothers during their teenage years.

Nan loved a good joke, a "lovely ham," canned peas, and a boiled potato, but if you ever asked what was for lunch, you'd only ever get one of two guaranteed answers: "shit on a stick" or "cows' cocks and dandelions." Nan was funny, but she also held grudges and was a master manipulator. She made sure Mom knew how much she hated being there with her after their husbands died.

ROZ WESTON

My mom did it alone, all of it, and never asked anything from anybody. At home she was dealing with more than any one person should ever be expected to—fighting back tears and fighting for air every second of her day—but she never complained or once felt sorry for herself. She never let it show. We were the same.

Not long after Dad died, the phone calls stopped. People, other couples, and friends from church, people my parents had been tight with over the years, cut her off. There was no support system. Nobody wanted the widow at the barbecue. "Screw them," she told me on the phone one night. "I'm sick of this." She packed up my grandmother and everything she owned and moved out east to Newfoundland, leaving the small town where she'd spent her entire adult life. The same small town where she had just buried her husband. If she was going to be alone, she was going to do it in a town where she didn't know anyone.

Taylor and I were back together, but not living together. I fought like hell to keep our marriage going, not because I thought we were great, but because I was afraid of being judged if it ended. That I'd be accused of only keeping her around long enough to get me through my dad's death. That I used her just for the support. And I felt I'd somehow be betraying my dad if I ended it. He really loved Taylor and was one of the only people who truly believed we'd last.

We instinctively do our best to avoid judgment. This is especially true of how we act after someone we love dies. I hear these stories all the time when people call in to the radio show or write to me on social media looking for advice. Someone loses the love of their life and they're wondering when it's okay to move on and maybe even fall in love again. How much time is enough time? When is it okay to be normal?

Because I've spent years seeing only the worst in people, when I go looking for it, I always find it. When someone overlaps grief with new love or happiness a little too soon, even friends of friends you hardly know become pearl-clutching, judgmental assholes. Okay, how long is long enough, then? When is it okay to dance again? How long do you think somebody needs to be alone before you stop questioning if the love they lost was real or not?

I felt that pressure. The same pressure felt by all those people who've reached out to me over the years. Like we have to perform, like we have to *do* grief, but not go too fast. I hadn't accepted or processed anything. I dressed for a funeral I refused to let myself remember, and I chose isolation, in my own head and at the end of a bar. Nothing mattered. This wasn't the heathiest way to deal with it, but nothing I ever did was the healthiest way of doing anything.

I wrote Nina's fish joke in my notebook, ripped out the page, and stuffed it in my pocket. That was the only thing I ever took home with me from that bar.

LAST CALL

Have just enough to drink to be able to do it, but not enough that anyone could tell. That's how I hosted my first TV show. Every night.

Last Call was a live late-night experiment that lasted less than a year, and was so bonkers that people still bring it up with me today. Seriously, it was on the air for maybe seven months, and twenty years later people still ask me about it. It was a wild, drunken disaster created by wild, drunken disasters. We shot the show in an actual working bar every weeknight at eleven. I'd sit with a fake bartender and a few other hosts and talk shit about the day's headlines, interact with the actual customers, and interview whichever celebrity had a publicist insane enough to book their star client on our show. The *Globe and Mail* described it as "a bunch of C-list celebs chatting in a bar about their C-list lives" and "an hour of tedium with a trio of hosts most would walk a block to avoid drinking with." An instant classic.

I had no business being on that show. I didn't have any confidence and I'd never hosted anything in my entire life. The only things I had going for me were that I was a great producer, a better writer than most, and I didn't give a fuck. Most nights, that last one really showed. I was ticcing like crazy, and my stage fright was so bad that earlier that year, when I was asked to say a few words at a friend's wedding, I had such incredible panic attacks that I lay down in the back seat of the cab the entire way there. I strapped one seatbelt around my upper half and the other one I wrapped twice around my legs, convinced I was going to pass out and hit the floor if the driver stopped too quickly. I couldn't catch my breath and reconsidered that entire friendship the whole way to the church. But there I was, not long after, on live TV, on a show that bothered people so much one viewer turned up and sat at the bar for the entire taping, with the sole intention of attempting to smash a thick-bottomed cocktail glass over my head when I walked off set. I was pulling in $55,000 a year, making me, without question, the lowest-paid host in the history of late-night television. And I was almost disfigured by a weak-armed fan with bad aim in my second month on the job.

"Hey, fucker! Fuck you!" he yelled, right before the glass went flying by my face and one of the bartenders—a real one, not our TV one—tackled him to the ground.

I don't know whether I just have a punchable face or what I was doing to rub people the wrong way even on TV, but I felt like that glam kid again, the skid whose hair was too long, legs too skinny, wearing homemade costumes and yesterday's eyeliner. The shit magnet always running away from a fight in jeans with no give and shoes with no grip.

I didn't want to be hated, and most nights I did really try to do a good job. But no one needed me to do a good job; they just needed me to do all the crazy shit nobody else was willing to do, and if I could do it wearing only bikini bottoms, then even better. Anything for a laugh—and *that's* what people had a problem with.

ROZ WESTON

There's a pretty sizable part of the population that hates seeing other people having really dumb fun, especially when they're getting paid for it. It bothers them because it's not them. That's why Instagram influencers and TikTok stars are as hated as they are loved. I looked like somebody else's waste of money. But with me, on *that* show, people skipped right past jealousy and went straight to rage.

I'd roll into the station at ten every morning, sit through a few story-pitch meetings, and say yes to doing whatever crazy ideas they had. I never refused anything.

"Can you review *The Passion of the Christ*, but as a comedy? Like with a laugh track?"

"Sure, of course. No problem."

"Then can you sneak your way into the Liberal Party convention and ask party members embarrassing questions? Like about sex and stuff? But don't be too blatant. Don't let them know it's about sex—we'll take care of that in editing. Does that make sense?"

"Of course it does. Like butt stuff, but not really butt stuff. Do you want me to wear bikini bottoms or regular clothes?"

"Maybe wear a suit there but have the nut huggers underneath."

"Done."

My mom didn't care what I did. She just cared about the hours I worked, and the amount of sleep I didn't get. While working this show, I'd fall asleep around 2 a.m. and be up again at seven. Mom was terrified that I was going to work myself into the hospital, like I did when my lungs collapsed. Whenever I checked in with her, she always ended our conversations the same: "Okay, hon. Just don't work too hard. You can tell these people no sometimes." I could hear her using every ounce of Mom Restraint she had.

"I know, Mom. But the only reason they keep me around is because I'm the guy who doesn't say no. I'll try. I promise."

I broke that promise every time.

After the morning meetings, and a full day of writing, producing, and shooting stories, we'd all have from 7 p.m. to 10 p.m. free before we had to be across town to shoot the live show at the bar. That's when the most talented crew of people I've ever worked with would head to a pub and get more drunk than I've ever seen people get, yet still be able to do their jobs. All of us. Every night. The show's main advertiser was a beer company, which meant during the show the hosts were expected to drink, or at least pretend to drink, their beer on-air. I hated beer, so, just outside of the camera view, I always had a double vodka soda in a pint glass to pound during commercial breaks. Everybody who worked on that show had a drink within reach. I had two.

I went in every night, sat at that bar, and did the best I could. I wanted so desperately to make somebody proud. That's what I lost when my dad died, and what I missed the most: the person who was always most proud of me was no longer with me. He would have loved all the crazy shit I did on that show.

I'm pretty sure Taylor hated the show. She didn't say as much, but she also never brought it up. I actually don't remember much about our marriage. But I remember how much it bothered me that she never asked about the show, and I don't have one single memory of her asking how my day went. We never fully agreed on art, or entertainment, or what it meant to have a voice and a platform or what you put out to the world, but I had a pretty good handle on what she thought was shit. Everybody likes doing foolish things, but nobody wants to look like a fool doing them, and

I started to get a sense that Taylor thought she'd married a fool. I remember feeling like I'd let her down.

It kills me that all these years later this is what I remember of our marriage. I have no memory of us doing normal married-couple things. I don't remember us ever cooking dinner together or having a favourite show that we'd never miss. I don't remember what I'd get her for her birthdays, or when we stopped having sex.

I can't say for sure that my doing this show had anything to do with why Taylor and I broke up for good, but I can't say for sure that it didn't, either. We went through too much too soon. Our marriage started with most people we knew wishing us luck but telling us to our faces that they didn't think it would last. I probably spent more time trying to prove them wrong than I did trying to be a good husband. Proving people wrong was always what drove me. I think maybe I held on too long because I knew that if my marriage ended then I'd never be able to put my dad's death fully behind me. If I met someone new, even years later, then they'd want to know his story just to be a part of my life. But I couldn't see myself ever wanting to retell or relive any of it.

I spent the days leading up to the night we ended our marriage coming to terms with the fact that maybe this was it. Maybe this would be my last actual relationship. This was my rock bottom. You always hear stories of people's "rock bottom"—that last bender, huge loss, or catastrophic mistake. My rock bottom was different. My rock bottom, my lowest point, was when I came to terms with the fact, and convinced myself, that I was okay with never becoming a father. I couldn't see myself ever getting married again. The risk was too high, and I didn't have anything left.

I remember the night we broke up, like officially, but I have no idea why it was that night as opposed to any of the others.

The conversation happened in our bed, fully clothed, lying on top of the blankets with both of us staring up at the ceiling. We never made eye contact, and neither of us fought for a single thing. We didn't so much end our marriage as we let it go. Even today, if anyone asks what happened or why we split, the only answer I give is, "Sometimes you need a whole lot more than love to make a marriage work." We loved each other with everything we had, but it wasn't enough. It was never going to be enough.

Nothing was ever going to be enough again.

LOOK FOR THE HELPERS

Have you ever met someone who is so much like you, it's frightening? I'm not talking about someone who looks like you or does the same job or grew up where you did. I'm talking about someone who is *exactly* like you. These people never seem to walk into your life when you're at your best; they always find you at your worst—in those moments when you're stuck and feel like everyone else is running at a different speed or moving in another direction, or when you can't tell if you're on the outside looking in or right in the middle without anyone noticing you. I've spent a lot of time in that very spot. That's where I met Reagan.

Now, the best thing you can do when you're there, when you're lost, is to follow Mr. Rogers's advice and "look for the helpers." This quote, as well as his song "What Do You Do with the Mad That You Feel?," go viral every couple of years, usually after a school shooting or something else equally heartbreaking and inexplicable. His "helpers" quote goes like this: "When I was a boy and I would see scary things in the news, my mother would say to me, 'Look for the helpers. You will always find people who are helping.' To this day, especially in times of 'disaster,' I remember my mother's words, and I am always comforted by realizing that there are still so many helpers—so many caring people in this world."

But what if the disasters are happening *inside* you? We can't claw our way out when everything is spinning so fast, so we stand still and convince ourselves that this is now our life. Maybe it's what we built, or what we deserve. Maybe we're just broken and we need to get on with accepting that. This is when you need the helpers. Helpers will make a difference. What *won't* make it better is if you find someone exactly like you. Someone in the same fucked-up spot. These people are bad for you. They feel glorious and for the first time in a long time you'll feel whatever normal used to feel like. But they're so very bad for you.

I didn't want help, and I didn't need a friend. I needed a partner, someone to race to the bottom with. Someone who also believed the world was a cult of cruelty and full of monsters—because they'd fought them too. Someone with scars and secrets. That's who Reagan was. She and I would meet at a filthy diner up the street from me at 9 a.m. on weekends and start drinking. The diner didn't sell alcohol that early, but Reagan had a way of convincing anyone to do anything, especially when it came to breaking the rules, so they'd serve us secret beer in coffee mugs with our breakfast, and we rarely had to pay for any of it. She was magnetic and wild, and I just wanted to be around her. Everybody did.

Reagan was an expert at getting people to do all the things they never would, good or bad, humiliating or exhilarating. But when you were doing them, you never felt manipulated or taken advantage of. You felt free. I felt free. She was another vice, another distraction, but I loved who I was when I was around her. Nothing mattered, and we used each other.

There's a power in irresponsibility. A freedom. It gives off the sense that you have nothing to lose, and that's an intoxicating quality to certain people. Living without consequences can be goddamn sexy.

Reagan and I would drink from early morning until after midnight, getting lost in heady conversations and co-commiseration, then we'd jump in her borrowed minivan, drunk, and she'd sideswipe a half-dozen parked cars all the way down the narrow one-way street around the corner from my house.

This went on most weekends. Just the two of us, hammered, cheating death, and pouring our guts out to each other. It was all so incredibly self-indulgent, yet validating.

"Do you think you feel things differently than other people?" she asked one morning, in that diner, drinking beer out of mugs.

"I don't know what I feel. Sometimes I don't even know if I *do* feel." If I didn't play the part, I knew she wouldn't want to hang with me anymore, so I told her what I thought she wanted to hear. She looked at me like I was special, broken and fucked, but she somehow made me feel good about it, like I was doing everything right.

"Do you *want* to feel?" Reagan grabbed my hand, laid it out flat on the table, took a long drag off her cigarette, then hovered the tip of it over the back of my wrist until my hairs curled and burned. "Do you feel that?"

I couldn't tell if this was like a sex thing or if she thought this was helping, but I went with it. "No," I said. And that was the truth. I'd spent hundreds of hours locked in a bathroom burning myself, so the hot end of a Camel Light an inch above my skin didn't even register.

"What about this?" She touched the end of the cigarette to my hand and quickly pulled it away.

"No," I said again. I started to feel less like I was part of something and more like her plaything. Like a toy. I'd been in this situation before, and I knew what to do. I became the thing she needed me to be.

"How about now?" she asked, and she snuffed what was left of the cigarette out on the meaty part, right between my thumb and index finger. The end of it sunk right in and the skin turned black around the edges. I knew enough about burns to know this one was going to take forever to heal.

"No," I said again, shaking my head without breaking eye contact. Maybe this *was* a sex thing. I couldn't tell if she had just fallen in love with me or lost all respect. She reached across the table, took *my* cigarette from between my lips, took a long drag, put my *other* hand flat on the table, and did the same thing, only harder, and I helped her. I put my hand on top of hers to make sure she didn't flinch. To make sure she knew I felt nothing.

She held my cigarette there until it was out.

That was the last time anything hot ever touched my body in any sort of deliberate way. Half of me was pissed because I knew Reagan just ruined my favourite thing, my ritual, but the other half was relieved. I was done. A better story would have been that I got the help I so desperately needed or found a healthy way to deal with it through honesty and growth. But I didn't.

These were my first burn scars that other people could actually see, and that's when everything changed for me. I don't exactly know why I stopped hurting myself, but I just did. I knew I needed to start actually feeling life, and this was step one of a million, but it was a damn good start.

You can still see those scars almost twenty years later. I'm not embarrassed by them anymore, but I've never told anyone the truth

ROZ WESTON

about where they came from. I told my mother I got them from the broiler when I reached into the oven and the door came back up and slammed my hand inside.

"You got the clumsiness from me," she said.

I told my co-workers the burns were from a hot motorcycle engine, or my barbecue, and I even used fishing as an explanation when I was bored one day in a car with a cameraman.

"How the hell did you burn yourself fishing?" he asked.

"You've never been fishing with *me*," I answered.

These were all lies: addicts lie, and I was a liar. I used humour to get me out of most awkward situations, because I was in a constant state of pain and anxiety. Hurting myself was an addiction. I was addicted to using physical pain for emotional release. It was my way to deal with and ease all the awful stuff inside—the psychological pain. There's a romantic, almost punk aspect to seeing yourself as a weirdo or outsider. Living on the margins, by force or by choice, can be wonderful. But you can't stay there. You have to have the courage to grow, and that first step is always the hardest.

"Life is about choices," my dad always used to say. "Sometimes you're going to make the good ones, sometimes the bad ones. Just don't beat yourself up too hard over the bad ones. We all make bad ones. But the worst thing you can do, after you really screw up, is not ask for help."

My old man was certainly no Mr. Rogers, but I always knew what he meant. I'm not saying that all of this was a choice, because for most of us, the ones who hurt to not hurt, it's not. But not asking for help was.

For anyone who self-harms, as I did for half my life, you owe it to yourself to exhaust all your options when it comes to help. There's an end to it, and your world is filled with helpers. They want to help. Let them.

ALL THE MONEY IN THE WORLD

My Pops never saw me on TV or heard me on the radio. Which kills me. I was never the last thing he watched before bed, or the first thing he listened to in the morning, but, even back then, he knew I worked hard. Too hard, most days. Years before he died, Dad could already tell I was letting life get away from me. "Don't forget to pump the brakes," he'd tell me. "Work is work. It's the thing we all gotta do, but it can't be your everything. It doesn't mean you can't do a good job, but it can't be the thing you love or hate the most in life. That's what your friends and family are for."

I don't remember my dad ever once coming home and complaining about work. I'm not saying the job or the people didn't ever drive him nuts, but he never wore it home. He was never emotional about work, he was efficient, dependable, and always on-time. He didn't love it, but he *was* damn good at it. "You can work your entire life for a company, every goddamn day," he'd say, "then on a routine checkup your doctor will tell you, 'Sorry, Mr. Weston, you've got an ass full of cancer.' Then what? That job you just killed yourself for is going to seem pretty insignificant. And what have you been doing this whole time? For what? For who? Don't forget to pump the brakes. Your job shouldn't be the thing you look most forward to in your day. Save your best for the people who matter the most. They could pay you all the money in the world, but none of it'll mean squat."

I'd like to say that I took my dad's advice, but I so obviously didn't. I mean, the part about not getting emotional or letting my identity get too tied up in the job came easy. I've spent most of my adult life doing what a lot of people would consider dream jobs—playing on TV, hanging with celebrities, travelling the world. But I've never used those two words, "dream job," to describe what I do. I've never said I loved any job I've had or told anyone this was something I've wanted to do ever since I was a kid, like it was some sort of boyhood dream come true. For the most part, I've kept work and the people I work with on the outside. I wanted to see how far I could get in the industry without having to buy in to the community. I refused to kiss anyone's ass, schmooze, or network. I wanted to do this all on my own, with no help, and I became obsessed with success, and not just my own. If I overheard a co-worker talking about how their husband who worked at a bank got a promotion, I'd be infuriated. It would bother me all day. I'd obsess about it. I never felt like a victim, or that anyone was holding me back or was out to get me. I just couldn't stand the feeling of not doing enough. Like there was someone else out there, at a bank, working harder than me. My jealousy was fuelled by incredible feelings of inadequacy, and it was impossible for me to acknowledge, let alone celebrate, whatever success I had. It was never enough.

For my whole life, I'd felt like I was running on an alternate timeline to everyone else. Although I was the same age as the other kids, I seemed to go through all the big "growing up" bits way before anyone else. But all that was starting to shift by this point, and I began to feel I was being left behind. I was turning thirty and I was working my first on-air job, which is super late in that world. I was no longer the young kid with the big future. Suddenly I was the late bloomer.

This was the early 2000s and the industry was exploding. People who did what I did, playing on TV, were getting incredible opportunities in America. There was a pipeline of talent flowing from Toronto down to the U.S. to work for MTV, VH1, E!, and just about every other cable network that needed a snarky talking head with cool hair. I was all those things too, but I didn't know the first thing about finding a job in the States, and I refused to ask anyone for advice. I didn't want anyone to ever know what I wanted in case it never happened. I couldn't stand the idea of anyone knowing I'd failed.

Seven months after it debuted, the network cancelled *Last Call*, the bar closed, and I didn't have to get drunk at work anymore. Most of the production crew and I were moved over to the station's new entertainment show, called *The A-List*, which was very much like *Access Hollywood* only without the access. This was before *TMZ*, social media, and gossip blogs, and we were doing Perez Hilton–level shit talk before Perez Hilton was even a thing. The show was stacked with talent, and I was doing a ton of celeb interviews. This was another one of those "dream jobs" that made me miserable: my skin would crawl every time I walked into that building. It wasn't enough. I needed more, I always needed more.

I was pretty sure my new boss hated me, and I was more than sure I didn't like him either, but we got along in a weird way. Like two people forced to collaborate on a common goal that's mutually beneficial. Like two divorced parents who've vowed to not screw up their kid, so they suck it up and make it work. My boss and I had this thing—this show—in common, and we were both determined to use it as leverage for the next opportunity. I needed him, he needed me, but fuck did we ever *not* get along. He didn't know it yet, but he was also my ticket to America.

I spent months researching New York talent agents. Then I paid a video editor who worked on our show a hundred bucks cash to cut together a demo reel for me out of the best of what I had. I remembered someone saying that agents never watched anything past four minutes, and usually decided within the first thirty seconds whether they wanted to work with you or not. My demo reel was three minutes and fifty-eight seconds, and the first thing you saw was me, wearing only a pair of super-small, super-shiny black bikini bottoms, strapped to a bench, getting whipped by North America's third-best dominatrix. I'm not sure how one becomes a third-best dominatrix, but it was great television. That, by the way, was one of four clips of me doing crazy shit in bikini bottoms that I included on my demo. There was also a clip of me interviewing Paris Hilton, another one with Pauly Shore, and a few seconds in the studio from one of the rare times I'd been allowed to host the show. And not much else. But it was a killer edit, and it moved fast as hell. Was I proud of it? No, not really. But people loved it, and that's all that mattered.

I sent that package to twelve New York agents. Six got back to me and four of those wanted to set up meetings. I couldn't afford the flight, so I had to wait for my boss to send me to New York to do interviews for *our* show. That way I'd be able to piggyback on the work trip and get him to pay for the whole damn thing.

One meeting lasted less than three minutes, one agent didn't show, another turned me away while I was still sitting in the lobby.

I'd been sitting in the waiting area for about ten minutes when he walked out of his office to introduce himself. I stood up and did all the right things.

"Hang here for another five minutes," he said, while looking me up and down but pretending to check his watch. "I'll be right with you." He disappeared back into his office.

Twenty-five minutes later someone else walked out and told me I could leave.

"Do you want me to come back later?" I asked. "I can change my flight no problem."

"Noooooo, that's okay," she told me. Really stretching out that "no" part.

However, the fourth agent loved me and wanted to sign me on the spot. That's how the agent game works: three will think you're shit and maybe even tell you to your face all the things wrong with you, then one guy likes you so much they prep the paperwork even before you arrive. This agent, the one who liked me, ran a mid-level shop out of a tiny office on Lexington Avenue and had helped a few Canadians deal with the immigration and visa stuff in the past. He knew what he was doing. He was around my age, had thin hair, and was much shorter than me, but his suit was incredible. Two-button, single-breasted, and custom as hell. I'd never seen that colour blue in my entire life. This dude looked like he loved money. His clothes were beautiful, but his desk was a disaster. He had all the paperwork already out, propped right on top of a huge stack of files and headshots, ready for me when I walked through the door. I signed on the spot.

He talked like a New York agent from the movies. "Loved the stuff with the whipping. The dominatrix stuff." He beamed. "Really edgy. Really real." I could tell that he'd only watched the first thirty seconds of my demo, but I didn't care. "We can make money together," he said. "We're going to make some good money together."

We shook hands and I skipped across town to do the interviews for the show I was *currently* working for, then hopped on a quick flight back to Toronto. I didn't say anything to anyone. Not even my family.

Two months later I had my first big-time American TV job offer. In Orlando friggin' Florida!

"It's a morning show they're building—a brand-new show," my agent told me. "They're looking for four hosts, and they really like you. No crazy sex stuff, but they liked your interviews."

You have to believe me when I say that even though it *was* Orlando, this was just about the most flattering thing anyone had ever said to me. It charged me up. I racked up more confidence on this one phone call than I'd felt in years. This was the validation I was looking for. It was pure, and I did it all on my own.

But Orlando?

"It's a syndicated show, which means it *will* be national," my agent continued.

Okay, go on, I thought. *Now we're talking.*

"Syndicated to small and medium markets throughout the States. So, no New York, no L.A., no Chicago or Dallas...." He went on and on, in detail, about all the cities the show *wouldn't* be in. But still, this was America—my way in. I just needed to get there. This is what people do: go down with a job offer, have someone else take care of all the visa and immigration nonsense, crush it, and hunt for the next opportunity. That had been the plan for years. I needed this.

"I've dealt with this team before," my agent said. "They've produced a ton of syndication, and they're really great with moving expenses. People tend to not want to move to Orlando, so they'll take care of everything, put you up for a few months. And they pay well too." Before I could even ask, he added, "We can negotiate, but you're probably looking at something in the two-fifty, two seventy-five range."

He was so casual about it, like a $275,000 a year offer was normal to him—and it probably was. To me, this was more money than anyone had ever made in the history of my family. I felt I somehow owed it to every single one of them to jump at this. To me, this *was* all the money in the world. Even if I went down for two, maybe three years, I could live like a king in friggin' Orlando and still send enough money back home to Rich so he wouldn't have to carry our mortgage without me. I could even double up on payments and pay that sucker off years before we thought we ever could. This job, and all that money, would kickstart our future in a way I could never have dreamed.

"Think about it," my agent told me. "We have a little bit of time. Let me know when you can jump on a quick call with them, then we can get you on a flight down to meet them. But they're really into you, so I think we have some power here."

This was a shit ton to take in. It took me three days to even get over the shock of it all, and when that happened, when the shock wore off, it took me about one hot minute to decide I wasn't taking the job. There was no way. I didn't want to call them, or fly down, or even see how high we could negotiate that number. I didn't want to know because the number didn't matter. I wasn't going.

My agent was pissed. He begged and did that agent manipulation thing they all do, trying to get me to at least talk to the Orlando people, to hear them out, to wait for a formal offer in writing before deciding anything. After all, there was a ton of money on the line here.

"No," I told him. "No, thank you."

That was the last time I ever talked to that agent. I never told anyone about the Orlando offer, or how much I turned down. It was like it never happened.

I didn't want to be alone. I've never wanted to be alone. That's the simple and the from-the-heart truth. That's why I turned down that kind of payday. How long would it be before I made even one friend down there? I couldn't come home to an empty house. I've *never* come home to an empty house. I couldn't work those hours, up at 3 a.m., crazy long days, and work *that* hard to not have anyone to share it with. I couldn't do that, any of it.

Rich was my anchor. I still hadn't processed Pops dying, and I was scared I might crack. What if all the stuff I had stacked came crashing down? What if I needed my brother and he wasn't there? There was an emptiness in me that for years I filled with self-destruction, self-loathing, and self-harm. But loneliness was what I really feared. I couldn't be alone.

Not for all the money in the world.

HEART-SHAPED TATTOO

1984

The first concert I ever went to was in the summer of '84. It was June 26, the third night of Bruce Springsteen's *Born in the U.S.A.* tour down at the CNE Grandstand in Toronto. It was hot as hell that evening, but it was an outdoor show so every now and then you'd catch a quick, cool lake breeze that would blow through your hair and give you a couple short seconds of relief.

We lived about an hour outside the city, so going in for a concert downtown was more like an adventure than it is now: you left early and made a day of it. It was magical.

This show was just three days before Bruce released the video for "Dancing in the Dark," the one where Courteney Cox was planted at the front of the stage and got pulled up near the end to dance, *not* in the dark, with Bruce. The video where we all fell in love with her and had no idea that she was actually hired to be there until years later. "Dancing" hit at the midway point of the show that night—it was the fifteenth song Bruce played. Two songs after "Born in the U.S.A." and ten before "Born to Run."

I was nine, about to turn ten in the fall, and the summer of '84 is what defined so much of who I am today. I don't think you forget those magical summers when you're nine, ten, and eleven. Those are your peak kid years, when you maybe kiss a girl for the first time, get into your first fight, fall in love, or get that ticket stub from your very first concert. That was the first night I ever got lost dancing in a crowd full of strangers, and the first time I saw another human being stand on a stage and have absolute control over the bodies and emotions of thirty thousand people. Not only was 1984 the most significant year of my youth, but it was *the* most significant and incredible year in pop culture history. And that's a hill I will die on.

In 1984, I went to the third night of Bruce Springsteen's Born in the U.S.A. Tour and became a legend among my classmates.

My dad's co-worker Penny had become more like a family friend. She'd been to our house a few times, and I remember her being a little younger than my parents. She was cool and pretty, and she always talked to me about the music I was into. My parents really had zero interest in what I liked, so I was always happy when we'd see Penny. She lived in a fancy high-floor apartment close to the city, and every now and then Dad and I would drive out there so they could hang out together.

I was totally blown away by her balcony when we arrived.

"Can I go out there?" I remember asking. I'd never been in a condo before, *or* on a balcony.

"Sure! Of course you can." Penny set me up on the balcony with her portable tape player and a stack of her cassettes, and I burned through *Born in the U.S.A.* as many as times as I could before my Pops dragged me in because it was time to leave. Penny's apartment was exactly how you'd picture a modern '80s condo—

glass block divider wall between the kitchen and living room, white metal spiral staircase up to the bedroom, and a built-in and fully stocked bar with four high-back, dusty-rose stools. I loved it there.

Another time we went, another Saturday afternoon, I was allowed to swim in the pool off the back of Penny's building while she and my dad hung out upstairs. On about our third or fourth visit, I remember Penny and my dad in the kitchen pouring bottles of alcohol down the kitchen sink. I looked over at the bar and it was empty. All the bottles that were there the last time were now on the kitchen counter. I didn't know what the hell was going on. Why would you do that? Maybe the booze had gone bad?

I do remember Penny crying that day. She was sad, an absolute mess, and my dad was trying to console her and calm her down by rubbing her back and whispering in her ear. I felt bad for her but stayed in the living room with my back to the kitchen, still wet from my swim, trying not to make too much noise. I could see everything going on behind me through the reflection in her TV. She was having a rough day, and I wished she wasn't.

"Hey, Roz," Penny yelled to me as she walked out of the kitchen, wiping tears from her eyes. "You ready to have the best day of your life?"

"Yeah, okay," I said.

My dad was still in the kitchen, leaning against the counter putting tops back on empty bottles. Penny grabbed her purse off the coffee table, dug her hand down to the bottom of it, and pulled out a small white envelope. "Here," she told me. "These are for you. For us, actually," and handed it over.

I opened it up and pulled out three concert tickets. I'd never seen a concert ticket before, so I didn't really know what I was looking at. "What is it?" I asked her.

"Bruce Springsteen," she explained. "Tickets to his concert. It's in three weeks and your dad said I could take you and your brother. The three of us will go together." To be honest, I didn't fully understand how concerts worked—like, was Springsteen coming *here*?

"Yes. Springsteen is coming *here*. And we're going to see him. Live."

"Will they have T-shirts?" I asked. I don't remember why that was such a concern, but it was the only question I could think to ask. Concert shirts were the only thing I knew about concerts.

"Yeah," she said and laughed. "They will definitely have T-shirts and we can definitely get you one."

I spent the next few weeks bragging to all my friends that I was going to a concert, and that it was Bruce friggin' Springsteen. None of my friends had ever done anything like that before. This was another one of those things that I did way before any other kid I knew.

In the days and weeks after the show, I was a hero, an absolute legend. I would be at a friend's house and even their parents were jealous of me because they'd tried and failed to get tickets to one of Springsteen's three nights in Toronto. I knew all the songs in order. I told them how he started with "Badlands" and ended the night with a cover of "Twist and Shout" by the Beatles. I told them how I danced on my chair and screamed until I had no voice left. I told them about how incredible our seats were, third row floors just off to the left, and that I was *pretty* sure Bruce pointed at me but was *definitely* sure Clarence Clemons did. I remember telling anyone who asked that yes, I did get a T-shirt, but forgot it in the bathroom after the show, and I was pissed about it because it was twenty-five bucks. I told everyone everything.

I've told this story for almost forty years. I've told it to friends, I've told it on the radio, I've gone into detail about that night on TV and mentioned it in interviews when anyone ever asks me what my first concert was. Hell, I even told Bruce himself that he was my first concert when I met him, briefly, on a red carpet years later. I had maybe four seconds with the man as he was ushered past me, and I told him *he* was my first. "That's really great, man," he told me. We shook hands and he was gone. How many people get to do *that*?

But it never happened. It's all bullshit. A lie. All of it.

I never went to see Bruce Springsteen that night. I never danced on a chair, sang along, or lost my T-shirt. The tickets were real, that's for damn sure. But I didn't make it to the show because a week before it happened my mom kicked my dad's ass out of the house because he was having an affair with Penny. He was cheating. They were fucking. And it broke my mom's heart, and almost destroyed our family.

I don't know exactly how he told her or how my mom found out, but I remember being up in my room and hearing my mom yell, "Well, you're a hell of an actor, Ralph!" as she slammed the door behind him. It had obviously been going on for a while.

"Your dad's gone and he's not coming back!" she shouted up the stairs when I poked my head out of my room to see what was going on.

I didn't know how to react, I didn't know what to do with sadness and rage, so I picked up a small metal shelf in my room and threw it into the beige wall over my bed, just to the left of my Loni Anderson poster. "No!" I yelled as I grabbed it again and put four more holes in the drywall from the sharp feet on the bottom of it. Then four more holes. I pounded that thing as hard as I could, as many times as I could, until I fell back onto my bed, next to my Chewbacca stuffy, and cried in my hands.

Out of all the things that happened in 1984, this is my most vivid memory. I have no recollection of seeing *Ghostbusters* in the theatre, but I remember my mom calling my dad a liar and kicking him out. I didn't want to remember it because I didn't want it to be real. I wanted everything to be normal again. I didn't want my mom to cry, I wanted my dad back, and I didn't want to have to tell the other kids why I didn't get to see Bruce Springsteen.

So I lied.

The day after the show I was riding my bike around Prospect Park, which was right across the creek from the old flour mill where Rich and I got our first jobs. Two older kids, maybe late teens or early twenties, were standing around and talking about the concert the night before. I rode circles around them, without getting too close, as they went on and on about how great the show was, and I memorized everything I overheard. Then I rode up to Ed's In-N-Out Variety and grabbed a copy of the day's paper that reviewed the show and printed the entire set list. I memorized that too. Twenty-eight songs. "Dancing in the Dark" was the fifteenth, two songs after "Born in the U.S.A." and ten before "Born to Run." That's all I needed to know.

I hated my dad for doing this to me. For putting me in a position to lie for him, because the truth hurt too much to tell. So I lied, and I've lied about this for my entire life. Maybe because I've never told anyone about my dad's affair, and those two things are somehow tied together in that little part of my kid mind that still exists somewhere. Maybe I kept this story in the same place I kept that afternoon in the closet with that family friend, and the same place

I put the possibility that I may have fathered a child when I was thirteen going on fourteen.

My dad broke the rules. He broke the rules of his marriage, of his workplace, and of Alcoholics Anonymous. There's a long-standing rule in AA when it comes to sponsorship: the boys with the boys and the girls with the girls. That's the rule when someone sober is helping someone else through the early stages of their recovery. It's not an official rule, but it is code among recovering drunks. Most try to stick to it.

The relationship between the sponsor and the sponsee is an emotional one based on trust between two equals. But we're all only human. My dad and Penny were human, and they broke the rules. They weren't in love, and he was never trying to destroy our family because he'd found someone else. He simply went too deep and became just as vulnerable as the person he was trying to help. That's why the boys stick with the boys and the girls with the girls. My dad was the in-house counsellor at his work and had been for years. He'd helped countless friends, strangers, and co-workers get into recovery, and he was great at it. But for the first and only time, with Penny, he broke the rules. He lied to my mom, and I've lied about him my whole life.

Mom took Dad back before the school year started, and by Christmas you couldn't even tell. We never talked about it.

But out of all the things that went down in 1984, in that year that shaped so much of who I am today, both good and bad, the most significant event happened on May 24 in Guernsey, which is a small island in the English Channel off the coast of Normandy. That's when Katherine Holland was born. My Katherine. And in 2005, exactly twenty-one years, one month, and five days after I *should* have been at that Springsteen show, we met.

SHE WAS
A PAIR
OF SHOES

I was about a week out from starting my first day at *Entertainment Tonight Canada*. A job I fought like hell to get but didn't even know if I wanted. I was at a going-away party for a new co-worker of mine who was leaving his old job at MuchMusic to come and work for us at *ET Canada*. The party was at the Guvernment, a huge club down on the Toronto waterfront. I felt I had to be there. Attendance wasn't mandatory, but a ton of people from the new show were going, and I figured I should put on a suit, style up my brand-new but boring "*ET Canada* haircut," and try to bond. Or at least show up.

I was standing at the bar, alone, doing what I did best: judging people for having fake-fun and wishing I was any place else. I arrived by myself and had every intention of leaving the same way. I wasn't looking for anything, let alone a good time. I'd spent hundreds of nights in places just like this, lost and alone in the mayhem of a dance floor, or making out with a stranger in a filthy bathroom stall. But those nights and that life was over and I had zero connection to the person I was a decade before.

I hated clubs now and I hated going out. Club nights were now "events" and always had some sort of promotional purpose attached to them, and *nobody* danced. They weren't fun anymore. The only reason anyone showed up to these parties was to hustle their way into the VIP area to look special, or to kiss the ass of someone with bottle service to look even more special drinking $500 vodka Red Bulls all night that someone else paid for.

This was one of those parties. Paris Hilton was in the corner, in her own roped-off section, on display like she was for sale. A good 80 percent of the people there were *only* there to try to get in close enough to get a good look at her, catch her eye, or maybe grab a pic on their BlackBerry. I'd met Paris a year earlier, and we got along great and already had our moment, so I was hanging by myself in the back, in the dark, watching this shit show unfold in front of me. Watching Paris build her empire one low-res BlackBerry fan-cam pic at a time.

"Hey, you're Roz, right?"

"Yeah," I said, barely looking to see where the voice was coming from, but it's a good thing I made the effort, because if I hadn't looked *down*, I would have missed her. I'm six foot four, Katherine's five foot one, and this first conversation played out with a combo of me bending down a full foot and her popping up on her tippy-toes to try to meet me halfway.

Katherine looked like trouble, but the good kind of trouble. She was goddamn beautiful. The kind of beautiful that you quit your job for so you can stay home to stare at her all day. She had that chaotic energy that only twenty-one-year-old dreamers have, and I immediately adapted to it and followed her lead because with Katherine there is no other choice.

I realized suddenly that I'd missed that energy and optimism that you don't know you no longer have until someone holds up a mirror. Katherine had on a pair of beat-up bohemian moccasins, tight-ass jeans, and a vintage rock 'n' roll T-shirt with the sleeves cut off, and every time she put her hand on my shoulder to talk to me, I could see her bra as I bent my head down to listen. It was a *great* bra. The more we talked, the closer we got, and the closer we got the more I realized she was something special. She wasn't looking for anything or trying to network, and she was just about the only person in that place who was actually having fun.

Katherine was all the things I wasn't, and I knew that from the moment I met her. I didn't know how she knew me, whether it was a mutual friend or if she saw me doing dumb shit on TV wearing only bikini bottoms, but it didn't matter. I never asked.

She was so kind, and not yet jaded. She smiled at strangers and shimmied her hips to the music every time she took a sip from her straw. She was fun, which is something I hadn't been in a very long time. I'd stopped looking for fun, and had zero desire to jump into another relationship, so I avoided places like this. And women like Katherine. But I was all in that night.

"What are you drinking?" I asked her. "Can I get you another?" Casual question. *If she says yes that means she wants to stay*, I thought. *Please say yes*.

"Water," she said. "And yes, please."

Water, I thought. You're locked in a room with two hundred Paris Hilton superfans, on a *Wednesday*, and you're drinking water? "*Just* water?" I asked for clarification.

"Yup! *Juuuuust* water," she replied. And smiled. "It's too loud. Come with me," she yelled over the music, as she grabbed my hand, and her water, and dragged me through the Paris Hilton mob, through a black curtain, and into a deserted purple neon-lit

VIP room. This was obviously the room they'd set up for Paris and her crew. It was tacky as hell and clearly Paris hadn't used it. Katherine and I sat side by side in that empty room on a horrid silver fake leather couch, still holding hands.

I finished the rest of my drink with my left hand because there was no way I was letting go. I was about to start a new job that I was nervous about, I still hadn't processed my dad dying, I was technically still married, and I wasn't over *any* of it. I told her everything—in tiny bits, like some depressing highlight reel or the world's worst Lavalife profile. Within the first half-hour of us meeting, Katherine already knew more about me than the people I'd worked with for years. I held nothing back, but she didn't flinch. She didn't ask any follow-up questions either. Nothing other than what was happening in *this* very moment was relevant to her. Where I'd been, what I'd done, or what I'd been through changed nothing. There was no judgment or hesitation. She just held my hand.

"How old are you?" I finally got around to asking, while still hanging on tight.

"Twenty-one," she replied with all the confidence of a twenty-one-year-old.

"So you were born in, what . . . ?" I asked, trying to do the math.

"1984."

"Of course you were." I said just loud enough for her to hear me.

"What does that mean? 'Of course'?"

"Nothing," I answered. "It's a good thing. It's perfect. Love '84. It was a big year for me, I saw Springsteen for the first time." *Lies.* Nobody born in 1984 actually remembers 1984, and any love they have for it was something they had to learn on their own years later or from stories they were told. If Van Halen's *1984* was the best thing to come out of that year, Katherine Holland was a very close second. I knew that right away.

"Do you wanna get out of here?" she asked, suddenly squeezing my one big hand with both her small hands.

"Yeah, we can do whatever you want, Panama."

"Panama? What's *that* mean?"

"Nothin'. You'll figure it out," I told her.

"Or I won't." Katherine didn't fuck around. "Where do you want to go? What do you feel like?"

"I don't live too far from here," I said with all the hesitation of a thirty-one-year-old who was in way over his head but trying like hell to not look too old or too confident.

"Okay. Do you want to go 'not too far from here' with me?"

"Yeah, I'd like that. That sounds real great, Panama. Let me get my shit."

"Still don't know what that means," she said.

Track three, side one of Van Halen's *1984*. She had no idea, and I had zero game. That was my best. I was starting to sound old and douchey, but I was committed. I doubled down. "You'll figure it out," I repeated.

"Probably not," she told me.

Katherine wore my coat out of the club because she had a brand-new nipple piercing and told me she'd be "screwed hard" if it was even slightly cold outside. I remember when I first got my nipple pierced, in 1991, by someone who used a thick sewing needle and had no business sticking anything into anyone, so I knew exactly what she meant. "A rock-hard nipple and a fresh piercing is *no bueno*!" she yelled over the music, loud enough that the bouncer at the door tried to sneak a peek as we passed by.

We held hands as we walked out, and she didn't even let go when she flagged a cab. I woke up the next morning *still* holding her hand, with her curled up on top of me. I don't remember much of what happened when we left that club, but I do remember having the best sleep of my life. I hadn't had a good night's sleep in years, and she fixed that on night one. I don't know how, but she did. I wanted to thank her, but what woman wants to hear that? *Thank you for putting me to sleep.* Even though it was the truth.

Katherine was even more beautiful that morning after. She was uninhibited, but not a show-off. She had a history, but no sense of regret. And that morning, she sat naked with a coffee, curled up in the chair in the corner of my room, and didn't even ask for a robe or one of my oversized T-shirts to wear.

"I don't normally do this," I told her.

"I've *never* done this," she said with the type of honesty I wasn't used to. There was no awkwardness, walk of shame, or that empty feeling after a one-night stand. Katherine was the best start to any day I'd had in my whole life.

Katherine was the first woman I'd been with in any serious way since my dad died. I wasn't looking for commitment and, up to this point, my perfect woman would have been an orphan dog owner. Someone who had no hometown or family, so I wouldn't ever be asked to meet them or spend any amount of time with someone else's parents. I wouldn't have to bond with a father who wasn't mine. And a dog owner, well, because when you date a woman with a dog, no matter how much they want to stay, they'll always have to leave at sunrise, without you ever having to ask.

Katherine's parents lived four hours away in Ottawa, and she *did* have a dog, but this annoyed me more than anything else. I never wanted her to leave. This was also my first relationship since

Taylor, who I was still married to. As I hadn't yet told the majority of people I knew that we'd broken up ten months before, this very much felt like cheating. I didn't know how to do this out in the open, and I was so terrified of being judged. I didn't want this, whatever we were on our way to becoming, to look like an affair that broke up my marriage. Or people to think I went from first to second a little too fast. I didn't want to put Katherine in a position to be judged either. She was magic, and if anyone ever saw her as something other than that it would have broken my heart. So I kept her, and us, a secret for as long as I could.

My brother will tell you that for the first year Katherine and I were together, to him, *she was a pair of shoes.* Even though he and I lived together in a small townhouse, Katherine and Rich never met. He only knew she was there with me when he'd see her tiny boots by the front door as he left for work in the morning. Then I'd sneak her out while the house was empty like we'd just pulled off a heist. Sometimes secrets are sexy.

I'd spent too long confusing guilt and love. I still had this loyalty to Taylor, even though I knew whatever it was we'd had was long gone. There was no more *us*, but because it wasn't a clean break and we were still friends, I feared my moving on in any way would somehow hurt her. I felt terrible for wasting those years of Taylor's life. Our marriage was never going to work, and I knew that when we got married. I should have walked away, but I didn't, and now I was feeling like a shit person for moving on even though I knew Taylor had already done the same. I felt like I still had to pay that price.

Love and guilt are two very different things. Love is supposed to feel good; guilt feels awful. But they both hit you in the same place. I had been consumed with so much guilt for so long that

I couldn't tell the difference between what felt good and what didn't. I was just happy to feel *anything*, while also trying to make up for *everything*. I could never look objectively at any of my decisions. I could never separate the person who I knew I was from the choices I'd made. I took full responsibility for everyone else's feelings, but the idea of falling in love seemed way too much of an indulgence. It seemed selfish.

Katherine and I were together maybe three months when she told me she loved me. I had started spending more time at her place, and in her bed. Always in her bed. She lived in a small bachelor apartment so the bed was the only option, and I used it as an escape. Katherine didn't have some fancy job or a ton of money, but she spent everything she had on expensive bedding and things that made her place smell nice. Her bed wasn't big, and my feet always hung off the end, but it didn't matter. In her bed, with my head on her stomach, is where I felt most comfortable. Wrapped up in 800-thread-count sheets, and wrapped around her, was the only place in the world I felt good about myself.

But when I'd leave, that feeling would stay behind. I never took it with me—because I wasn't strong enough to hold it.

"I love you, Roz," she told me that night. She just said it. There was no lead-up, no "We need to talk," no nothing. She just said it, and when I picked my exhausted head up off her lap and turned to look at her, I could see that she meant it too. But this was more of a statement, a matter of fact, than it was an invitation to say it back.

My initial reaction was simple. "Don't," I told her. "Don't say that. Please. I'm not going to say that back to you. Not that I don't have incredible feelings for you, but I can't. I'm just not there. So please, just don't say that." I was almost begging, like this was going to be the beginning of the end. I couldn't move this fast—I couldn't move *at all*—and I knew that this was going to fuck the whole thing up. I was comfortable in her arms and in her bed, but the idea of taking up space in her heart terrified me.

"No," she told me.

"What do you mean, 'no'?" I asked. "No what?"

"No, you don't get to tell me that. You can feel however you want. You can take your time, or not feel anything at all. That's fine. But you don't get to tell me who I can love, and you certainly can't tell me what I can and can't say. You don't have to love me back, but I need you to hear it. For me. This is how *I* feel, and I want you to know that *I* love you. Because it's the truth. And that matters."

When you're the type of person who doesn't believe you deserve nice things, you do whatever you can to avoid them, and you push them away when they show up. When you feel like you'll never be able to return the good, or give as good as you get, you consistently avoid doing all the things that would bring you closer to whatever idea of happiness you think only exists for everyone else.

That was me. That's the person I was for the first two years Katherine and I were together. I was broken. And she was patient.

WILDFLOWERS

When *Entertainment Tonight Canada* started, we were a small crew that put together a big show from two rented wood-panelled mobile trailers that smelled like old cigarettes and fresh raccoon shit in the parking lot of the network building. This was the same building where I'd produced that talk show years before and blown twenty-five grand of their money on that trip to L.A. to meet a girl only to be left stranded at a dildo store at two in the morning. I kept that story to myself even though the entire company had been bought and sold *twice* since I last worked there. They weren't paying me enough to pay them back, but the show wasn't making enough that I didn't think they wouldn't try, so I kept my mouth shut.

This wasn't a flashy downtown media headquarters like the other places I'd worked. This building was in the suburbs north of the city, and smack in the middle of a residential street. It was a pain in the ass to get there, but a trip that I was more than used to. The network had big plans for *ET Canada* and were dumping a ton of money into it. They were building us our own offices and a state-of-the-art control room, but until all that was done, we produced the show from that parking lot, in the blazing heat with no personal space.

I was sweating buckets through my borrowed suit as my thick caked-on and layered TV makeup liquefied and dripped off the tip of my nose onto my desk when I was writing scripts. This was a glossy production, but I was far from a glossy guy, so the brilliant contradiction between how the show looked on TV and what it all looked like behind the scenes suited me just fine. I was a skid with a little bit of shine on him now, but I was still far more comfortable in that parking lot than I was on set of the show.

The first meeting I had with my boss was when he made it clear why I was hired. "Interviews and voice-overs," he told me. "That's what—sorry, that's *all* I need from you." I'd worked with this same exec producer when I was doing *Last Call*, so we had enough history that we could be (somewhat) honest with each other. But clearly he didn't like me enough to give me anything more than a series of one-year contracts, when *everyone* else was getting two- and even three-year deals. I had to constantly prove myself, continuously auditioning for my own job.

"I need you to ask the questions nobody else will," he said. "I don't care what the rules are, or what they're promoting: we ask what *we* want to ask, and we make news. That's what you do for this show. That's your job. These people aren't your friends, and we owe them nothing. They need us more than we need them."

So that's exactly what I did. I spent the first two years of that show pissing people off while building a great reputation for getting people to talk about all the shit they said they wouldn't. This was the kind of structure and discipline I was looking for. I was a tool. I had purpose. But I wasn't proud of any of it. If Robert Downey Jr. was promoting a new movie, I'd ask about his past drug use and jail time. I'd go hard on people's relationships, their break-ups, and their breakdowns. I said horrible things about Britney Spears during her 2007 head-shaving episode, and have apologized for it, publicly, every opportunity I've had since. I'd unfairly ask about pregnancy rumours, how much money people made, affairs, weight gain, eating disorders, and anything else that might make some news and get us some press. My philosophy was, it was *way* better to have Lindsay Lohan pissed off at me for five minutes than have my boss be pissed off at me for five days.

One of my first trips to L.A. was to interview Colin Farrell. He had a new movie, *Miami Vice*, that he was promoting, but the *big* story was that he had recently, and secretly, married. This was huge for us. He chain-smoked for our entire interview, and in the final minute I said, "Can I ask you a personal question?" to which he replied, "Can I snuff this fucking cigarette out in your eye?" But because of his accent, his mumbling and the ten feet between us, I didn't hear any of it, and asked the question anyway. He didn't answer, but I had to ask. That's all that mattered.

These first few years at *ET Canada*, I was crushing it. I didn't love the job, but I was good at it. They hired me on as a senior reporter, but it wasn't long before I started doing all the work of a co-host, which in that world, are two *very* different jobs. I was great on the teleprompter, showed up on time and prepared, and could always get the show back on track if we were ever running late. I was fast and didn't fuck around. I was consistent, dependable, and had amazing chemistry with Cheryl Hickey, the host of the show, who I'd known for years. I didn't mind my life as a reporter and really had no desire to be the face of anything, let alone *ET Canada*, but it drove me crazy that they *used* me as a co-host but never let me forget that I *wasn't*.

This had nothing to do with money, either—it always felt personal to me. I obsessed over why I was never asked to co-host the show officially. I didn't particularly want the job, but I did want to be *offered* the job. My boss had absolute control over my life and future on that show, and when I asked him if he'd ever promote me to a co-host, he told me flat out: "No. Never. You're just not dashing enough." He actually laughed while answering, like me thinking I could co-host this show was hilarious.

He was right, though—I wasn't dashing. I was never going to be dashing. I didn't even like the word "dashing." But for some reason, this all messed with my head and crushed my confidence.

"I didn't hire you for your looks. You should be happy about that," he told me. I felt like that skid I had tried so hard to erase. And fat. I felt fat. I spent the next four months pounding Hydroxycut, an over-the-counter miracle weight loss supplement that years later was recalled and banned. According to the FDA, "Hydroxycut presents a severe potentially life-threatening hazard to some users. Although Hydroxycut-induced hepatotoxicity has been reversible in most patients . . . in certain instances acute liver failure has resulted that has required liver transplantation to ensure survival."

At the time I didn't know any of this, but I knew it was wrong. It felt wrong, and I didn't care. I didn't have a weight problem, not even close—I had a self-image and confidence problem. I'd always hated my body, but now I was pissed off. I was going for the kind of drastic change that a new haircut and a few hours in a tanning bed wouldn't even come close to achieving.

I was ashamed. I didn't keep the pills in the bathroom vanity or in the medicine cabinet like any normal medication. I kept the bottles in my sock drawer, hidden and buried so deep it was a pain in the ass for even *me* to find them every morning. But they were working, and doing exactly what they were designed to do. Fix the outside and destroy the inside. Our wardrobe stylist was taking the waist of my suit pants in an inch every couple of weeks. I shaved all the hair off my body, ankles to neck, so I could better see the progress, and would stand naked in front of my full-length mirror in my dressing room for twenty minutes every morning before getting dressed for the show.

After routine blood work, my doctor called me at nine one night. He had never called me personally before; I'd only ever talked to his assistant or one of the nurses at the clinic. He told me he was testing me for hepatitis, and asked big questions about my family history and if I had travelled anywhere sketchy recently and needed to know if I was taking PCP or ketamine in "large amounts." I was six four, 146 pounds, and my liver enzymes were off the charts. I was killing myself with diet pills in some stupid quest to prove I was "dashing" to a person I wouldn't have taken the morning off work for had he dropped dead. I knew what was hurting me, so I stopped taking the pills and played dumb. I lied. My second round of blood tests, about five weeks later, came back totally normal. It was a miracle.

I found a new doctor and stopped watching myself on television. I haven't seen an episode of *ET Canada* since.

For about a year, early on in the show, Suri Cruise was the most famous baby in the world, and the show paid an obscene amount of attention to her. A baby. For months, it didn't matter who we sat down in front of, or what they were promoting, we had to ask *every* interview what they thought of the baby. If you were a TV chef promoting your cookbook, with zero connection to Tom Cruise and Katie Holmes, or if you were the bassist from Metallica, if you were on our show you're goddamn right you were going to talk about *the baby*. Our boss was obsessed.

I was assigned to interview Penélope Cruz, which was a huge deal, as she dated Tom right before he and Katie were married. Penélope was an actual connection—she was Tom's ex, and a comment from her would *blow the fuck up*, I was told. My boss sent me in to do what I was hired to do, and nothing more. The script for the show was already written. I had no choice. They created big flashy graphics with the word "EXCLUSIVE" in huge shiny font and everything was ready to go. Did I really want to ask a woman about her ex-boyfriend's new baby? No, but that's what I was hired to do, so that's what I did.

"No personal questions," her publicist told me before I sat down. "No relationship questions. No games. Stick to the movie."

"Yeah. Of course, man. *Nooooo* problem," I reassured him.

I was an expert at lying to publicists. I *was* a huge fan of Penélope Cruz, though, and under different circumstances I think we probably would have had a lovely chat. Her movie was really great. But none of that mattered, because *the baby*.

I don't remember if Penélope Cruz stopped the cameras or if we were still rolling when this happened, but I do remember our interview ending early with her hunched forward in her seat, her finger pointing at my face, darting closer and closer after every word, as she cussed me out in a lightning-fast combo of English and Spanish. To be honest, it could have been one or the other, I don't remember, because I wasn't listening to a word of it. The only thing I remember wondering, as she rightfully read me the riot act for that gross overstep, was did she say the word "happy" before going off on me. If she said the word "happy" like she was "happy for Tom," we could run that. We could isolate that one word and build an entire show around it. *That's* the exclusive. I didn't apologize or try to justify the questions I asked, and I didn't even stand up or say *thank you* when she stormed past me out of the room.

I'm pretty sure she said happy, I thought. *I fucking hope she did*.

I felt horrible after that interview. But I got high-fives when I got back to the studio with the tapes.

I left the office that night around six, feeling gross about myself. I took the same two buses, a subway, and a streetcar back downtown to Katherine's tiny apartment. "How was your day? How was the show?" she always asked when I walked in.

"Fine," I'd say. That was the only way I ever described my day. *Fine*. Then we'd flop on her bed, on those incredibly soft sheets that she couldn't afford, as she quietly sang along to whatever was playing. Usually something by Bob Dylan. I'd put my head on her stomach, close my eyes, and fade into her while she ran her fingers through my hair until I was me again.

I didn't want to break up with Katherine, but I had to.

Most of the truly horrible decisions I've made in life, like this one, have been based around the same made-up mathematical equation that has no specific formula or defined rules. It goes like this: I take all the people I've hurt, add that to all the people who've hurt me, then I know *exactly* how much I need to hurt myself.

Do you know how much you have to dislike yourself to dump a woman like Katherine, who is pure fucking joy, optimism, and kindness, for someone who tells you: "You're so worthless that when you're not around me and my friends call you Peso?" Like some cute nickname? That's where I was at. That's what I did.

I'd started feeling guilty, like I was taking advantage of Katherine and her kindness. We were in love, and it was crushing me. I knew where this was going, and I couldn't handle the weight.

In the years we were together, Katherine never asked me to define myself or our relationship. But I could feel that we were getting to a point where that wasn't going to be enough for too much longer—not for her, but for me. Her patience was my anxiety, and she deserved more. She was worth *all* the work it would take for me to start putting the pieces back together again. But people started to look at me like I was a big deal now: I was on national TV, I had an audience and free clothes and people seemed to love my flirty, awkward, and brutal interviews. And as much as *most* of what I did made me sick to my stomach, I did love the attention. I didn't mind being *that* guy. *That* guy felt nothing. But I wasn't that person around Katherine. Katherine was genuinely proud and encouraging.

But if I stayed, I was going to burn it down.

I couldn't be both people, and I wasn't ready, even after all this time, to process the loss of my dad or anything else. If I started to fall apart now, I'd lose it all. I didn't know how to be happy, but I was an expert at being a fraud. So, I ran. I started to put space between Katherine and me, and began to undo all her hard work. Travel became my new distraction. I was more comfortable alone in a hotel room in a city I'd never been to than I was at home or in Katherine's bed. I told our assignment editor to just send me anywhere. It didn't matter where. "Just keep me on the road," I told her. The U.K., L.A., New York, Aruba, all over Mexico, northern Alberta, South Florida, Egypt, Rome, Vancouver, Chicago, Moscow, Paris. I'd be gone for weeks at a time.

I felt if I ran far enough, I'd find what I was looking for.

On one of those trips, I met a writer from back in Toronto who was covering the same story for the paper she was working for. Nothing happened between us on that trip, but I could tell we had a connection. I probably paid a little too much attention to her and she definitely didn't mind. She looked at me like I was someone else, someone I clearly wasn't but was already interested in becoming. Being *that* guy felt good. It felt easy. She didn't care about my story and never asked me to open up. She was into fashion and fancy shit that I didn't know anything about. I *still* don't know what "couture" means. I never once saw her wear the same thing twice. She had rich friends, she was popular, had beefcake male models blowing up her inbox *way* before Instagram, and clearly had never waited in line for anything her whole life. The polar opposite of anyone I'd ever been with. She was the exact kind of woman who would *never* date a skid like me. But she never met that guy. She didn't know my life, or where I came from, and didn't ask. And she was never going to ask. This woman was going to hurt me, and I went all in.

At first, we really did have a few good days. Her friends seemed to like me, we had a couple of fun nights out, and I'd always do my best to take note of what I did on those days, to make sure I didn't do anything to piss her off the next day. She was super easy to piss off, and could easily freeze me out for two or three days at a time, making me work my way back in.

The good days started to fade, then became non-existent. What I was chasing were the days that weren't just total shit. I convinced myself that a "not total shit day" was actually a *good* day, because the bad days had quickly become volcanic and cruel. But there were no more good days. Two months into our relationship, I was so beaten down that I was taking Viagra just to be able to sleep with her because nothing worked. Nobody has ever made me feel worse about myself so fast. Then we'd have one *not total shit day* where I'd feel like I was her entire world, and the whole wicked cycle would start all over again. I'd call her friends to ask what I was doing wrong.

"Everything," one of them told me. "You're doing everything wrong. Last week at brunch you made a joke about blowing your nose into your hand in the shower and pushing the booger down the drain with your big toe."

That sounds like something I'd say, I thought.

"She dumped a guy for that."

Excuse me?

"For blowing his nose in the shower. How do you not know that?"

How would *I know that?*

"She needs a *man*," another friend told me. "So you need to get your driver's licence. We think it's weird that you don't have one."

She said this like they were all part of some collective hive. That was the truth, though. I was thirty-four and I'd never driven a car. I never got my licence because I was afraid I was going to kill somebody, but how could I admit that to the most judgmental person I'd ever met?

My Tourette's had progressed over the years and was cranked up by the amount of stress I was under. It was made especially bad by having to be awful in interviews but flawless on TV. I'd gone through a few years now where all my tics were in my eyes. I would blink rapidly, squint, or roll my eyes back into my head. I didn't trust myself to drive a car, because *one* tic could take me out of the world long enough to miss something. I worried if I lost even a single second when I should have been paying attention, I'd cause an accident. I was afraid I would kill somebody.

I'd never mentioned my Tourette's to her, and I wasn't planning to either.

"If you want her, you have to fight for her," the friend instructed me. "I want you to win. I'm on Team Roz over here."

I didn't know it was a competition.

We were in bed one night at my place when I saw her texting someone because she thought I was asleep.

"Be home soon" were the words I read from the corner of my eye.

I asked to see her BlackBerry. She refused, even though she went through mine every night before we went to bed.

"I need to know I'm your boyfriend," I told her. I was ready to fight for us. "I need to be more than just another guy in your phone." I'd never tried this hard with a woman before. But it wasn't about love. It was about validation. I felt like shit, but I was in too deep and had walked away from whatever life I'd lived before her. This was it. I wanted to become the exact thing she needed. A whole new person. I needed to win, and tried to prove my worth by being able take whatever toxic abuse she threw at me. More than anyone else. That was a fight I *knew* I could win.

"Do you know how hard this is for me? Being with you?" she asked while I was still lying naked on top of her. "Do you realize that every time I kiss you, I have to close my eyes and pretend you don't have tattoos, *that* haircut, or all those bracelets? You're not my type, Roz. I *told* you that, but I'm *really* trying here. What more do you want from me?"

She finally saw me for the skid that I was.

Asshole is what I thought. "I love you" is what I said. And I didn't mean a word of it.

What I should have done was gather up whatever self-esteem and pride I had left and walk the fuck out of her life, giving her the finger from the end of my bracelet-filled wrist. What I *did* do was start to wear long-sleeve shirts to cover up my tattoos and put every bit of rock 'n' roll jewellery I had in a box under my bed. I tried to do better.

—

On one of those bad days, when she hadn't returned my calls for a full twenty-four hours, I had a few drinks while out and then wandered next door into a tattoo shop to get a small heart done on the inside of my middle finger on my left hand. It didn't really mean anything, but heart tattoos are always pretty. Also, I wasn't burning myself anymore, and the process of getting a tattoo reminded me of that feeling. If I walked past a shop that had an open chair, I'd ask if I could get in for a quick touch-up on one of my older tattoos just to feel the needle darting in and out of my skin. I knew the tattoo would piss off my girlfriend, but I did it anyway. The heart tattoo took all of ten minutes, then I walked back next door, ordered one more drink, and settled up the bar tab I'd opened before I left.

Our entire relationship lasted maybe five months. I knew it was going to end, and it wasn't going to end well. It was only a matter of time. The last time we talked was when I found out she was *also* dating a friend of mine the entire time we were together. She had a whole second boyfriend. They went home for the holidays that Christmas, back to her parents' house, and *he* got to meet her family while I was at her place, back in Toronto, putting together her new bed frame and reorganizing her closets.

I've listened a lot in my life. Listening is the one skill that has helped me more as an interviewer, entertainer, and person than anything else. But I've never listened to the universe, not in any sort of Oprah/Higher Power kind of way. I'm not religious, I don't remember my dreams, and I've never looked for signs. I've never been *that* guy. I wouldn't even know what to listen for anyway. I don't believe in fate, or that everything happens for a reason, and I still have no clue what it means when Mercury is in retrograde. I've never once taken my guard down long enough to surrender to anything, and the only whispers I've heard were my own, bouncing off the inside of the walls I built around me.

But if it *was* the universe (and Paris Hilton) that brought Katherine and me together the first time, maybe the universe could do it again.

I called Katherine right after I ended that relationship, like the same night. Maybe an hour later. I'd spent so long hurting myself that I didn't once think about how it affected anyone else. I'd never gone back, or even looked over my shoulder to see what I was leaving behind. I was self-destructive and self-centred, which always does as much damage to the people who love you as it does to yourself. But I was done. I was done hurting myself.

Katherine picked up the phone and asked me if I was okay, if I needed help. She knew. There was no lecture, no yelling, no guilt, no price to pay.

"Can I come over?" I asked.

"Of course, always," she told me.

Katherine didn't look at me like I was someone who broke her heart, or an ex-boyfriend who showed up to beg for a second chance. She welcomed me in like I was a teenage runaway who'd finally made his way home defeated and lost, or an addict fresh out of rehab after a relapse promising *this* was the last time. Again. She was kind, but rightfully cautious. There was no big hug, but she did take me by the hand, like she had that night we met, and led me to the couch. She was in a new apartment now, and I didn't know my way around.

"What happened?" she asked me, while still holding my hand on her lap.

As I sat there trying to put the words together, I looked down at our fingers intertwined, both of her hands on top of one of mine.

"What is that?" I asked.

"What is what?" she answered. I had to wiggle my hand free to make sure my eyes weren't fucking with me.

"That!" I asked again. "When did you get *that*?"

"Oh, the tattoo? Maybe a couple of months ago." It was a small heart on the inside of her middle finger on her left hand. I slowly opened *my* left hand to show her mine. They were identical.

"What!" Her eyes opened wider than I've ever seen them, and Katherine has *big* eyes. "When did you get *that*?" she asked.

"A couple of months ago," I told her.

Now tell me, if that wasn't the universe, then what was it? How do two people, who hadn't talked in months but who were still so obviously in love, go off and get the exact same tattoo, in the exact same spot, at the exact same time? Like, are you fucking kidding me?

After talking for hours, and me telling her everything, we spent the night together. I was too exhausted to head home, and I didn't want to leave anyway. I don't think she wanted me to, either. I had the second-best sleep of my life that night. We woke up naked and started the day slow. There was no awkwardness, or remorse. I loved this woman and was never going to push her away again. I just didn't know if she wanted me. I'd hurt her more than I'd ever hurt myself, and I was never going to hurt either of us ever again. I wanted to heal. I took the week and tried to put everything together in my head. Everything that I wanted to tell her. Katherine came over the following Friday, maybe eight or nine days after that night at her place, and I took her by the hand and led her to the living room.

"I'm going to stand, if that's okay," I told her. "I've got tons to say. I'm probably going to ramble and pace around, but please hear me out. I'm going to try to make all this shit makes sense—please let me try." The ceilings in my place were tall, and my couch was huge, and Katherine looked so small sitting there alone, but she sat up straight with her shoulders back, confident as hell. She never broke eye contact.

"All right," she told me. "I'm not going anywhere."

"I never stopped loving you," I said right out of the gate. "I was never *not* in love with you." I needed her to hear that first and I needed her to know that I meant it. I talked for three or four minutes, waving my hands around like a maniac while walking rings, perfect circles, into the rug. Katherine never said a word. She just listened. I tried, as best I could, to explain that yes, I was a little bit broken, but I was not ruined. I just hurt all the time. I let the things that hurt me continue to hurt me every day. But I was done. No more.

"I think about dying. All the time," I told her. I still felt so much guilt over the way I handled those last few months when I still had my dad. That his death put me on the clock, and I'd lost sight of the purpose of all this—of being alive. Awful things happen to really good people, to all of us. But none of it, none of the hurt, abuse, or cruelty from the past, should define who we are today.

"I just want to fill a house full of love and see what happens," I told her. "And when it's the end, when it's my time to go, there's only one person I want by my side holding my hand and telling me goodnight. It's you. It's always been you."

"Do you mean that?" Katherine asked me. Finally breaking her silence *and* eye contact.

"Every word. I've never meant anything more in my entire life," I told her.

"Good. Because I'm pregnant."

—

I dropped to my knees and cried. I crawled over to her on the couch, sat on the floor in front of her with my head on her lap, and cried. I cried harder than I had in my entire life. Every tear, from every time I should have cried but didn't, came pouring out and they haven't stopped since. I can't say that I cry every day, but I do *almost* cry every day, and on the days when it does happen, it's beautiful. It's a recharge. It's always the exact thing I need at the exact time I need it. Like a rainstorm finally hitting a field of wildflowers after a long, dry summer. That's what we were going to be—wildflowers. Beautiful, full of joy, and free. Strong enough to grow through concrete, and resilient enough to thrive under whatever punishing conditions came our way. I learned to love the rain that night.

"I guess I should man up and get my driver's licence, huh?" I said when I finally stopped crying enough to put a few words together.

"Why?" Katherine asked while wiping her own tears from her chin.

"So I can take the kid to karate."

"Nah. I can drive us. We can go as a family."

A family of wildflowers.

THE BEST
DECISION
I NEVER
MADE

How do you replace everything? That, right there, is the question I've asked myself almost every day since my dad died. It's an overwhelming and impossible thought. Of course, you can't actually *replace* the people you've loved and lost. Not my dad, anyway. He was irreplaceable. When someone dies, they leave *things* behind, and at the start those little reminders are the ones that hurt the most. You miss their voice, their laugh, their smell, and their hugs. You miss their advice and the way they said your name. You miss the fun. You take months to finally clean up the puzzle in the basement on the folding card table that they never got to finish, and you leave their slippers by the front door right where they left them.

But after a while I realized that Dad's stuff was just *stuff*, and that it wasn't even his laugh, hugs, or unfinished stories that I missed the most. It was the space he occupied in the world. When someone dies the world keeps spinning, with all of us on it, and that empty space is what you feel the most. That's what always hurts. It's almost cruel. That was *his* spot. So was *that*. And my dad's space in this world, the one he occupied with strength, pride, compassion, and fart jokes, was empty and *that's* what killed me for years. The void. When he died, the world lost a great dad, but that night Katherine told me she was pregnant, *everything* finally made sense. I finally got my answer.

How do you replace everything? Well, you can't. I knew I couldn't replace my dad, but I *could* fill his space. This kid was the best decision I never made, and I was going to even everything out. The world lost a great father when my old man died. I was going to give it another one.

Mom was still living on the East Coast with my grandmother, both of them trying not to kill each other, and Katherine's whole family, who I'd met *once*, were in Ottawa, about a four-hour drive away. Neither of us had a large group of friends, and none of the friends we did have had babies of their own. So there was very little outside influence, which suited us perfectly. Katherine was building our kid, and we were building a home, and we did it all *our* way.

We bought a few baby books, like everyone does, but I didn't read a single page. The only people I wanted telling me about this pregnancy were our doctors and Katherine. Katherine became the teacher, and I became the student.

"Hey, did you know that I'll be pregnant for forty weeks? That's *ten* months. What kind of fuckery is that? Who started the nine months hoax?" she yelled to me when I was making her hundredth ham and cheese on a ciabatta one night early on. "Also, in three weeks I'm going to be growing hands and fingers down there, so I'll be busy that day. Don't book anything. That sounds like a shit ton of work. I'll probably need like *two* naps that day."

I'm not sure Katherine had ever even held a baby before she was pregnant with her own, but she became an expert, and I listened. I didn't want to ever come at her with my own info from something I had read or try to explain what *I* thought was going on with *her* body. I wasn't absent, or uninterested—the exact opposite actually—but we knew very early on that there were parts of this that we were going to go through together and others that she was going to handle on her own. Like the puking part.

If I can offer one piece of advice for first-time fathers-to-be it's that you *have* to have the puke conversation with your girl. Have it early and establish the rules. Katherine is one of the greatest pukers I've ever met. The complete opposite of me. Whether it's the flu, mild food poisoning, the rare times she's been drunk, *or* pregnancy, Katherine pukes with such ferocious efficiency and speed that it's actually impressive. Usually it takes her no longer than it would to walk into the bathroom to blow her nose. Then she'll be back on the couch sipping a tea like nothing happened.

But the *sound*. My fucking god, that sound. I've never heard anything like it. It's violent and aggressive, like she's being run over *while* drowning, or having her hips broken with a cricket bat *and* throwing away old soup. It's demonic. Katherine didn't have morning sickness, she had all-day-maybe-we-shouldn't-leave-the-house-today sickness. And it was So. Very. Loud.

"I need to know what you need from me when you're in there," I said after the first time it happened and I heard what I heard. I was paralyzed, in shock, and ready to call 911. "Do you need me to come in? Hold your hair and rub your back? What do you need me to do?"

"Nothing," she replied. "I need you to pretend it's not happening. You don't hear anything."

"Can I turn the volume up on the TV, or it that too rude? Do you want me to pause our show? Or keep watching? I can leave—do you want me to leave?" These rules were important.

"*Do not pause* anything. When you hear the toilet flush, just rewind to wherever it was before I went in."

"I can do that," I told her. And that's what I did. I'd listen for the flush, then the sound of her electric toothbrush, and then I'd hit rewind and wait for her to walk out of the bathroom, always amazed she still had both her arms because it really sounded like someone just sawed them off in there. She'd flop on the couch and I'd hand her tea to her, kiss her shoulder, and tell her I loved her. Then I'd press Play and we'd pretend *none* of that just happened. We never talked about it.

Katherine and I were building our House of Love—one that we also shared with my brother, Rich, and his now fiancé, Leanna—but we loved them too. Katherine and I hadn't ever lived together, and when she did move in, she was already pregnant, so it was game fucking on! We weren't dating: we were a family. Rich and I were about two years into living in a big, hundred-year-old Victorian house that we'd bought with the money we made off the townhouse. The previous owner of the place had used the entire main floor as an art gallery and moved all the "home" stuff, like the kitchen, bedroom, and full bathroom, up to the top two floors.

It was perfect for us. Rich and Leanna took the upper floors, and I spent the first year after we moved in renovating the main floor for myself. It was a blank slate I turned into the perfect bachelor pad. One bedroom, huge living room, and a bar. This house was *not* built for a baby—hell, this house wasn't built for Katherine. Glass-topped coffee tables, hard-as-hell limestone floors, poured concrete countertops with sharp edges, and everything was built *up*! I didn't want the kitchen to take up too much space, so I stacked everything high, and because I'm so tall it was perfect. For me. The upper cabinets were doubled, two full rows on top of each other, all up the ten-foot ceilings. Katherine had to use a step stool just to get a coffee mug.

"I'm going to rip all this out," I told her. "We need a second bedroom. Babies don't shower so we'll definitely need a tub. And how are you going to feed this kid when you can't reach any of the food?"

I was still paying off the first reno, from two years ago, but was ready to do it all again.

"No. You're not ripping anything out," Katherine replied. "We're fine. We need a changing table, a bassinette beside the bed, and the sink is more than big enough for a bath. We're not buying things until we need them. I don't want to have to sell a mini dresser or a mini anything else in six months just because we thought they were cute at the time. But the glass coffee table has got to go. That thing will kill a kid." Katherine has always had a way of slowing me down. The only thing our house needed was love. . . . And a baby gate. She *did* let me buy a baby gate.

Katherine found two old pictures of my dad in a box in the basement and framed them and put them on a shelf in the living room one day when I was at work. Until then, there were no reminders or memories of my father in my house, except for his cardigan on the far left side of my closet. But these weren't pictures of my father when he was my dad: they were of him when he was younger. Looking at those pictures every day was like looking into a mirror. In those little frames I saw someone who, despite having gone through hell, only wanted to do his best. He was flawed but determined, a man with secrets that would eventually become great stories, and one who was built for fatherhood but didn't yet know it.

Those two pictures sit on that same shelf in those same frames even today. And they're still the only two I have of him.

EVERYTHING

In the summer of 2009, my family life was better than I could have ever imagined, but I still felt *off* about my career. Like I had more in me that I wanted to do. I just didn't have a place to do it. Katherine and I were in sync, crazy in love and about six months away from becoming parents. We were having the time of our lives and would spend most of our evenings laughing until I cried and she peed. We were a wild and free army of two, soon to be three.

Also, I was about to sign my first multi-year deal with *ET Canada*. The show had gone through some major changes, but so had I. I wasn't being asked to be shitty in interviews anymore, so *that* was good. There were no more invasive and gross questions and no more lying just to get me in the room. And we, as a show, moved on from obsessing over, or running pictures of, celebrities dropping their kids off at daycare. But I *was* asked to flirt. They *loved* a flirty interview. I'd be assigned to interview every young female star in hopes there'd be some kind of connection that played out in the four minutes we had together. That kind of shit didn't often happen naturally, so I'd have to force it most of the time. When it worked, it worked.

"That was gold!" they'd tell me, or, "She really loved you!"

When it didn't work, it *really* fucking didn't, but they'd always cut around it in editing and the worst bits would never see the light of day. I didn't know it then, but years later, *those* would be the interviews that would come back to haunt me, not the ones where I was digging too deep, or getting shut down or walked out on.

Other than those interviews, I was having fun. Patrick Swayze showed me how to air hump while teaching me the dance from *Dirty Dancing*. I rode a camel through the Egyptian desert, then crawled down to the tombs beneath the Great Pyramid of Giza. I've done high leg kicks with Liza Minnelli, hugged Carrie Fisher, *and* witnessed Alec Baldwin verbally destroy an assistant over the phone, spitting venom and profanities at a volume I didn't think was possible, while I sat quietly waiting for him in the next room. I watched the Super Bowl in Rome, made Al Pacino laugh, and discovered Steve Carell is one of the nicest people you'll ever talk to and Adam Levine is *not*. I got to interview every single action hero and rock star I idolized as a kid. For most people in the business, this was a dream job, but I needed more. As wonderful as *ET Canada* was for me, I felt constricted. I still spent most of my day wearing clothes that weren't mine while standing in front of a teleprompter speaking words I didn't write.

On June 25, I'd taken the day off and was with Katherine at a doctor's appointment when I got a call telling me to be on standby to come in because Farrah Fawcett had just died. This one hit hard. She was an icon, and I cherished my Farrah poster when I was a kid, the one where she's in the red bathing suit, which hung *right* next to my Loni Anderson poster, also in a red bathing suit. I told work that I needed a couple of hours but would be free if they needed me after that. Then, four hours later, my phone exploded; I'd stepped away for thirty minutes and I had twenty-six missed calls. The first email

I checked was an open-ended ticket to Los Angeles and the flight was leaving in less than three hours. Michael Jackson was dead.

I always kept a carry-on bag half-packed and ready to go. It had a toothbrush, hairdryer, makeup bag, pair of shoes, three pair of socks, and four pair of underpants stuffed in there. There was never any scrambling on flight day. I'd grab my passport, a couple shirts, and a suit, then kiss my girl and I was out the door. I was at the airport less than thirty minutes after getting that email, and it's a twenty-minute drive.

When you travel as much as I did, people just assume you love it. I lived every weekend like I had just scored the grand prize on *The Price Is Right*—"You've just won an all-expenses paid trip to Hollywood, California, staying at the *luxurious* Four Seasons hotel in *beautiful* Beverly Hills, where you'll attend a red-hot red-carpet movie premiere, rub shoulders with the rich and famous, *and* dine at world-renowned five-star restaurants. We'll also throw in seventy-five dollars a day to go on that shopping spree you've always dreamed of!"

This was my life almost every week, and I can *not* stress enough how much I had grown to hate it. Not to mention the fact that seventy-five bucks wouldn't even cover breakfast at the Four Seasons. I just hated everything about travelling. I hated being away, I hated being alone, and I hated flying. I'm not *afraid* of flying; I just don't fit on airplanes. Over the years I had spent as much time building contacts and making friends with key people at all the major airports as I did on my actual job.

The goal was to always get upgraded to first class. As soon as work sent me my ticket, I'd start working my contacts. For anyone who's never flown first class, let me break it down for you. The difference between first and coach goes way beyond the bigger seat, free wine, and warm cookies. If you manage to get yourself on the other side of that curtain, you'll discover that *first class* isn't about the in-flight service, it's about how you're treated as a person.

If the seatbelt light is on and you get up to go pee during mild turbulence in the back of the plane, a flight attendant will literally put their thumb in the middle of your forehead to push you back down in your seat. If that same thing happens in the *front* of the plane, one of them will take you by the hand while the first-class cabin crew lock arms and form a human chain to make sure you get to the bathroom safely. *That's* the difference. You're a first-class person.

Gabby was my contact in Toronto, and as soon as I got to the airport that day, I started texting her. She'd worked for the airline for twenty-five years and knew all the tricks. If she couldn't find me a seat, she would always hack the system and try to bump someone else out. The airport was madness that day, and the customs line snaked all the way back through security. Gabby texted back asking where I was and telling me to hurry. She couldn't get me upgraded on *my* flight, but there was another flight leaving for L.A. in twenty minutes that she could get me on.

"I'll do my best, but I can't make this line go any faster," I texted back. There were at least two hundred people ahead of me. I wasn't going to make this flight.

All anyone could talk about in line was Michael Jackson dying, and the people who recognized me from the show knew exactly where I was headed. "Michael Jackson?" one woman asked. "Yup. Michael Jackson," I replied without looking up from my phone, still furiously texting Gabby.

"Thanks, Gabby. But I'm not going to make it. I appreciate you trying," I wrote.

"Stay where you are! Don't move!" she texted back. "I'm coming to get you!"

Skipping the line at customs and immigration is impossible. We all know that. If you're late, you miss your fight. That's the rule. That's on you. Being my height made flying brutal, but it did allow me to look clear over the heads of most people. I could see all the way to the back of the terminal, and as I scanned the crowd for any sign of Gabby, I finally saw it. A flag. And not just any flag— a bright orange flag on the end of an eight-foot pole. An eight-foot pole that was attached to the back of a fucking wheelchair that Gabby was pushing through the mob towards me.

"Get in," she mouthed to me. Gabby had big hair but she couldn't have been any taller than five two, so I leaned way down and whispered, "There is no fucking way I can get in that thing."

"If you want to get on this flight," she whispered back, "get in. It's the only way I can get you to the front of the line."

"I've been standing with these same people, in this same line, for forty minutes. I can't just suddenly *need* a wheelchair. I just took a picture with a fan!"

Gabby reached up and pulled me in close by the back of my neck, the same way a mom does when she wants to give you shit for acting out in public. "If you're not going to sit, then you're going to have to limp," she told me. "Can you limp?"

Yeah, I thought. *I can limp.*

Gabby put my luggage on the seat of that wheelchair and my hand on her shoulder, and I limped my ass to the front of that line and all the way to first class.

When I landed in L.A., it was a boots-on-the-ground and all-hands-on-deck type situation. I met my producer and cameraman at the airport, and we worked through the night building stories. At sunrise, we made our way to the L.A. County coroner's office to grab a good spot for the press conference that was going to start in a few hours. That's when my phone started blowing up *again*.

But nobody had died this time. These were all messages from people I'd worked with over the years but didn't really talk to anymore, and all of their emails and texts had the same message: *KiSS FM needs a morning show!*

Years earlier, when my dad was in his last few months, when I was out of work and my marriage was ending, I took a job at KiSS 92.5 FM—a Top 40 radio station in Toronto that blew up riding the wave of boy bands, Britney and Christina, and those early seasons of *American Idol*. The program director and my boss was Julie Adam, a maverick, hell-raising, and rule-breaking executive who hired me to produce her morning show. On my first day, and right after I told her my dad was dying so I'd need a couple weeks off soon, she handed me a printed-out five-point list of rules. Her rules for radio. I don't remember what the other three were, but I can tell you that points one *and* five were both *Have fun!* In a lot of ways, Julie and her *Have fun or fuck off* attitude saved me, and I never forgot that. She was exactly what I needed at the exact right time.

And here she was again.

It was ninety degrees in L.A. that day and I was standing, for hours, on Mission Road at the end of the drive-thru at the Jack in the Box across from the coroner's office interviewing people, who were eating in their cars, about Michael Jackson. That's when I got to work on my pitch letter to Julie. In between every interview, around every on-camera intro and throw, and while I sat for hours in Los Angeles traffic. Through all that, I was on my phone writing, trying to come up with a shred of an argument to convince Julie that I was the right choice for that new show. I needed that show.

I started with facts and the hard truth. No, I'd *never* done this before. I'd never hosted a radio show before. But fuck it. I'd never been a DJ, or ever introduced a song, or run a contest live on the air. I'd never done the weather, and I had zero clue how all the commercials and music worked. But fuck that also. I told her I knew she had hundreds of tapes and resumés from qualified and professional hosts because an opportunity like this was the Holy Grail of radio, but she needed to take a chance on me: I was different. I was going to sound different. And I wasn't going to play by the rules because I didn't *know* the rules. I was an out-of-tune voice in an autotuned world, but I understood an audience.

I wrote the first draft of that email over two days surrounded by grieving Michael Jackson fans, while getting an up-close look at the connection an entertainer can have with an audience. Not that I thought there was ever a chance I'd achieve *that* level of fame, but it was clear how incredible that relationship can be. An audience isn't something to take for granted, and unlike so many other people I'd worked for in radio over the years, I knew I'd never do that. I'd always put the audience first, I explained. Then I hammered home the most important point—I already had a full-time job with *ET Canada*, so if it all went to hell, she wouldn't have to feel bad about firing my ass.

I knew I could do this. I promised her I'd be the most open, most relatable, and best storyteller she'd ever hired. I had no clue if I could pull any of this off, but I knew in my head and my heart that I had to try. I finally had something to say, and for the first time in my life I wasn't afraid to fail.

By the time I flew back home to Katherine, Julie had offered me the job.

—

I wrote my new boss at *ET Canada*, Tamara Simoneau, and told her we needed to talk, but assured her I was *not* quitting. Nobody likes getting the *we need to talk* email without context or explanation. She wrote back saying, "Good. I need to talk to you too. And no, you're *not* getting fired." Love that woman.

Tamara is as tough as she is smart, and she always brought out the best in me. She's Australian and only ever called me Rozzicle, which I didn't mind, because we'd built a great relationship over the years and her accent always made it sound sort of sweet.

So we met on a patio on a sunny Toronto day and both agreed that we needed at least one drink in us before we started talking about anything serious. As soon as round two arrived I went first.

"I've been offered a job to host and build my own morning radio show." I explained all this hiding my tics behind a pint glass and dark sunglasses. "But I want to do both shows, the radio show and *ET Canada*," I continued, even though these were two full-time jobs for two massive and competing networks. "I think we can make it work. I can do both if you let me," I said.

This was a shit ton for her to take in. A bonkers and *way*-out-of-left-field proposition.

"Okay, now you go," I told her and pounded back what was left of my second drink.

We ordered round three.

"I want you to move to Los Angeles."

Fuck.

"You'd be our L.A. correspondent but still working for *ET Canada*. You can do all the freelance work you want down there, we'll pay for your move, give you your current salary in U.S. dollars plus 20 percent, *and* help Katherine to get a visa after she has the baby so she can work too."

Fuck Fuck Fuck. The idea of me and Katherine, who hates winter more than any human I've ever met, in L.A. with an American baby raised on the beach with sun-kissed asscheeks and waves nipping at her heels was more than appealing. *How the hell do I say no to that?*

I didn't have to. Katherine did. And it wasn't even close.

"L.A. isn't what you want," she told me. "You're going to be doing the same job you already do just in a different city, and for what? Do you even like L.A.? You need to do the radio show, Roz. That's where you're going to make a difference. That's where your heart is."

She knew.

Now it was a matter of finding a co-host for the radio show, and convincing two massive companies, which didn't have a great history of playing nice, to share me. But that's what lawyers are for, and mine was great!

If I can offer some advice here. If anyone *ever* hands you something that has been touched by a lawyer, grab it with your thumb and pinky like you would a bag of hot shit and hand it directly to *your* lawyer. Don't try to understand it, make sense of it, or negotiate it yourself. You hand it off and let lawyers do what lawyers do. My lawyer, Domenic Romano, has spent years getting me maximum money, freedom, and protection in all my contracts. I explained, "I want to do what nobody else has ever done in this country. I want to work two full-time jobs, on two massive shows, for two different networks. I want to wake up at 4 a.m. and work until 6 p.m., and do it all. I don't know if anyone has ever successfully pulled this off."

"Maybe not," Dom replied. "But you'll be the first, Roz. Leave it with me."

He's the best.

While hardcore negotiations were happening and lawyers were doing lawyer things, I spent weeks going through cassette tapes, MP3s, and CDs of people who had applied to be my co-host.

I'd never done a radio show before, and all my insecurities and fears were raging from the moment I woke up to when my head hit the pillow at the end of the day. Every tape I listened to, I felt worse about myself. I was shitting my pants because I was looking for someone who was all the things I wasn't: I needed a quarterback who could run the show, but also someone who was an improv master and would never let me fall, no matter how much I rambled. I needed a comedy partner and someone to do the heavy lifting at live events because I knew my anxiety in front of crowds would be too much for me to handle.

I listened to dozens and dozens of audition tapes. They were *all* the same, and I would have failed with every single one of those people.

Then I heard Mocha.

He was crazy but he was no-bullshit. He was a master at what he did and was already hired by the station to do another shift. He was perfect. He was all the things I wasn't—he was *everything*. We put champagne on ice (but not really) and offered him the job.

Aaaaaaand—

He said no.

I was beyond crushed, but I wouldn't give up. It took me three weeks to convince him to build this with me, to take a chance on ourselves and create something great. He finally came around, but I understood his hesitation. I wouldn't have wanted to wake up at 3 a.m. to do a show with me either.

I had been listening to a ton of punk during all this. Punk wasn't perfect and neither was I. Most of those bands could hardly play their instruments, and the ones that could never bothered to tune them. These guys never wanted to be the most popular or best *anything*, but they made noise and they made a point. They built something great long before anyone would have considered them ready, or even competent. They shook up the industry because they had something to say. Three chords and the truth type shit. That was me. I was a little too rough, a little too loud, and I *hated* rules. I had to make this work.

After a few months, and more than a few thousand dollars in legal fees, the deals were finally done. My lawyer managed to pull off two new contracts for two shows *and* a bridge deal between the two companies to share me.

"There's a few things that worked out in your favour," Domenic told me. "The first is that I got the sense from both lawyers that neither company thinks you'll be able to sustain this schedule."

Yes, I can, I thought.

"That it'll be too hard on your body."

They have no clue what my body can handle.

"That after a few months you'll have to pick one or the other, and they both think it'll be them."

No, I won't.

And I didn't.[†]

[†] Anyone who's ever written a book has that *one* friend who's going to skim through the entire thing looking for their own name. Maurie Sherman, this is for you.

THE
GOOD
FRIEND

It was New Year's Eve, the last day of 2009. I was standing in the middle of a hundred thousand people at the edge of Niagara Falls freezing my ass off and hoping Katherine, who was at home watching me on TV, didn't go into labour.

ET Canada was hosting a monstrous live New Year's Eve special from the Falls. It was a free concert with big bands, fireworks, drunken tourists all trying to stay warm, and a few million viewers. I don't know why I agreed to do the special and nobody else did either. I have no memory of that show, who the bands were, or what I said on TV when we were live. I just remember sitting on a lighting box in between segments with my BlackBerry on my lap trying to make my frozen fingers work, texting Katherine to make sure she was all right.

"Hey, Rozzy! You okay?"

That's what I heard in my earpiece during a commercial break. When you're doing live TV, you have more wires attached to you than someone on life support. Our director, Frank Samson, was back in the broadcast truck and could see every camera on the monitors in front of him at all times—even when we weren't live. He had a direct and private line to my ear, and he knew I was freaking out. He knew me well enough to see it. "Listen, I think you're doing great, but what are you doing here, man? Isn't Katherine about to give birth like *now*?" he asked.

"No, I'm good. She's fine. No baby action yet," I whispered back into my mic. I was having the worst time, and my head wasn't at *all* in the show.

"What's your plan?" Frank asked.

"Plan for what?" Now keep in mind, I was on a podium surrounded by a sea of people and my legs were too cold for me to walk, let alone run.

"What's your plan if Katherine says it's *go-time*?" he asked.

"I don't have one," I whispered again, while looking out at the chaos. I was a two-hour drive from home in *no* traffic, and the crowd was so big it had taken me forty-five minutes to walk five hundred metres from the hotel to the broadcast site at the beginning of the night. There was no easy way out. "I really don't know. I don't have a plan."

"Well, don't worry about it," he said. "I have a helicopter. I'll get you home. I got you."

That wasn't bullshit: Frank *did* have a helicopter. He'd hired one to shoot all the aerials of the crowds, the fireworks, and the Falls, and he was just crazy enough to use it for a badass first-time-father extraction mission if he had to. "Now let's finish this show so we can all get out of here." Then he told me to *suck my gut in*, get *into position*, and counted back from five. We were live again.

I didn't need the helicopter that night, but I did need a friend.

—

One thing you should know about me: I'm not a very good friend. But I am a *great* friend. There's a difference. I'm never going to be the guy who organizes wing night, I'll always have to be reminded it's your birthday, I'll forget to RSVP to your wedding, and if I *do* show up, I'll probably leave early. I'm rarely there for the little things, but I *am* the friend you call when everything goes to hell. I'm the "in case of emergency break glass" kind of friend. When your marriage is ending, or someone you love is dying, you just got fired or cheated on, or feel like your world is being pulled apart— I'm *that* friend. I'm the *great* friend.

Frank is too, *and* he's a vault. He's the only person I ever told about my Tourette's, how I hide my tics on TV. He's directed me on three shows, including *ET Canada*, and has spent more time staring at my face than anyone else I know.

"When I'm standing there, on set, and my head is down," I explained one day in his office with the door fully closed, "or I turn my back to the camera or walk off set, I'm not being an asshole or trying to hold things up. I'm in hell. I have tics, and before we go on I try to get as many out as I can, then fight like hell to keep all the rest inside until *you* say we're done. It sucks, but I manage. I just might need an extra minute every now and then."

Frank never asked a single question. He didn't want to know how long I'd had them, what caused them, or if I could show him. "No problem," he told me. "I got you." And that was that.

Midnight came and went, and it was officially 2010, and I held what I'm sure was one of the longest fake smiles ever attempted on live TV. I drank more champagne than I sprayed and hugged a hundred strangers as I pushed my way through the crowd trying to get the hell out of there. As I sat in traffic for more than three hours in a car hired to take me home, I realized this wasn't going to be a one-time thing. This wasn't the last time I'd feel like this. With the hours I work, the decisions I'd made, and the life I'd built, the feeling of missing out was going to be constant. Something I was going to live with daily.

I wanted to quit everything right then and there. I was going to miss the little things. I'd never be able to do school drop-off or pick our kid up when she was done. I'd miss birthday parties and whatever shows or recitals she'd have on weekends because I'd be god knows where interviewing who the hell knows about whatever movie they were trying to sell. I was panicking and convinced that every decision I had made to make sure we were good, taken care of, and free would result in my kid growing up feeling ripped off.

As soon as I walked into the house, still smelling like tourists and winter rain, I told Katherine all of this, in tears. "I don't know if I'm going to be a good dad," I told her.

"You don't have to be a good dad," she said. "Because you're going to be a great dad."

THE
PAPER BAG
PARENTS

I don't think you truly become a man until your father dies. You can be seventeen or sixty, but if there's still that someone in your world who calls you *son* and means it, there's always that part of you that still exists. That boy. When you lose a father, or the man that raised you and kept you safe, you can feel it. You can be forty-five with kids of your own in college, but when you say goodbye to your father it happens—instantly.

When we're kids, growing up like I did, and our dads take us camping, it's never about dinners around the fire or adventures down a river. I didn't know that then, but I do now. It's about taking us into the dark. It's about their presence and protection. It's about being there for us no matter how dark it gets. When we wake up in the middle of the night and it's so dark we can't tell if our eyes are open or closed, terrified and convinced that *every noise* on the other side of that thin panel of nylon is there to kill us, it's *their* presence that gets us through until morning.

After my dad died, I stopped looking for him in the dark.

When Roxy Alabama Weston was born, I became the light.

Becoming *that* person isn't something someone can teach you. Not even your own father can show you how to do it. You won't find out how in any book or course, and that light won't be there for you to use until you're ready to hold it. The same thing happens to women—I saw it happen to Katherine—when they become mothers. It's instantaneous and life-changing. It's primal. When Katherine met Roxy for the first time, she decided right then and there what kind of mom she was going to be, and she hasn't once second-guessed herself. She's the perfect combination of strength, courage, and *just* the right amount of crazy. These are the best moms.

Katherine wanted to make sure Roxy loved the rain, and I wanted to make sure she'd be able to handle spicy food. These are what you call Priorities. Katherine taught Roxy how to listen with her heart, and I made sure she knew the difference between hurt and injured. I made sure she knew how to ask for help, and Katherine made sure she helped others, and was kind and brave. I would teach her how to make the perfect soffritto for a Bolognese sauce and made damn sure she knew the difference between a nap and a sleep.

Which, by the way, are two *totally* different things. Katherine doesn't nap—she full-on sleeps during the day if she's tired. In bed. When Roxy was born, Katherine and I had been living together for less than a year, and even though we'd been together for years, there were still a few surprises and new things we learned about each other. Like napping. We will *never* agree on napping.

The first time Katherine caught me napping, I was snapped out of it with her standing over me asking "What . . . the hell . . . are you . . . doing?"

"What the hell am I what?" I asked, rubbing my eyes, straightening myself on the couch. "I'm taking a nap."

"Why don't you just go to bed? Go to bed if you're tired," she told me. It was about 2 p.m. and the spring sun was pouring in through the back window, lighting me up. Katherine refused to believe that this was in any way comfortable for me.

"I don't want to go to bed because I don't want to go to sleep."

"But you *are* sleeping."

"No. I'm napping," I said.

She was *not* prepared for how seriously I take this shit.

"You don't nap in a bed, you *sleep* in a bed," I tried to explain. "Maybe, like *maybe*, you can nap in a bed, but you have to be on *top* of the covers. If you get *under* them, then that's a sleep. I'm napping. That's why I'm on the couch."

"Okay. But why do you have to nap so weird?" She pointed her finger up and down my body as she stood over me, blocking the sun, in perfect and beautiful silhouette.

She wasn't wrong. I *do* nap weird. I like to nap on the couch flat on my back. Always on my back. I take four throw pillows and line them down my body—one on my chest, another on my stomach and two more for my thighs and shins. I tuck my arms under the top pillow and cross my arms across my chest the same way a vampire sleeps. The same way they tell you to hold your arms when you're going down a water slide. *That's* a nap.

Katherine and I were still figuring each other out while we also wrapped our heads around parenthood. Neither was all that tough, although there's just so much shit they *don't* tell you.

Like pin worms. Pin worms are *high* on the list of shit they don't tell you before you become a parent.

There's this skill, or maybe even superpower, that most mothers have—it's called Mom Restraint. Dads do *not* have this. Dads have the exact opposite. When dads want you to calm down and not panic, they usually yell something like, "Calm *down*! Don't panic!" This, of course, has the exact opposite effect on everyone involved. Moms, on the other hand, can be confronted with just about anything—a broken bone, road rash from wiping out on your bike, an infected piercing, or a split forehead from a botched cartwheel on the sidewalk—and they always react the same: "Mm-hmm. Yup. Okay. Come with me," with the inflection going up at the end of each word. Absolute Mom Restraint. This is when they gently put their hands on their child's shoulders, slowly spin them around, and march them into the bathroom to assess the damage. The bathroom is where moms do their best work when everything goes to hell. Dads are more like a World War II field doctor, whipping off their own T-shirt on the driveway to stop the bleeding from a cut that should have been taken care of with one, *maybe* two Band-Aids.

Which brings us to pin worms.

There's no situation, not a single one, that personifies Mom Restraint more than the first time your kid walks out of the bathroom with their little arm stretched out holding a tiny worm dancing on the tip of their finger to tell you, "Mom, this was in my butt." Pin worms live in your butt, and at night, in the dark, they crawl out and go on missions to lay eggs on everything you own and crawl up the butts of everyone you love. When one person in the family has pin worms up their butt, you *all* have pin worms up your butt.

I've never done what anyone would ever call *well* with medication. I get every single side effect on the side of every single bottle, and for the most part avoid anything that will take me out of my own head. Even pin worm medication messes me up, but when I come home and see my portion of pin worm meds laid out on the counter, I take the damn pills. Because that's what families do. That's parenting.

THE KING OF STUPID SHIT

What makes a great dad? To be honest, I'm still trying to put it all together. I've been going at this alone for a little bit now, just like anyone who lost their father young. I don't have a map and my Pop isn't around to offer advice.

My old man was lot of things. He was a dreamer, a fixer, a bit of a schemer, and a total skeptic. He loved any kind of discount and never minded bending the truth a little to make a good deal happen. My dad played the lotto twice a week, and at least *once* a week we'd all sit around the dinner table talking about what we'd do with all that money. Dreaming. One spring afternoon, when I was still in grade school, my family got rocked to its core. This was the day a dreamer's dream came true. *This* was the day we got one of those *You just won $10,000,000* sweepstakes letters in the mail.

I was the one who brought the massive envelope in after school, and wanted so bad to open it, but knew what would happen if I did. When Mom and Dad got home, he snatched it up off the counter and immediately called a family meeting. Rich and I made our way to the dining room, which was weird because it wasn't Christmas, so whatever was about to happen was going to be big and formal.

"Sit," Pops said to us. So we sat. "You see this? There's a ton of pages here. I want you and your brother to look through it and see if you can find anything fishy."

"Fishy like what, Pops?" I asked.

"Like the scam part. I'm not sure how they got my information, or what they want, but if this is legit, we need to figure out what we're going to do. And if it's not, we need to find the scam."

We'd all seen those commercials on TV where the old guy with grey hair shows up with a giant cheque and helium balloons. The idea that my dad was taking this even a bit seriously was mind-blowing. He must have seen something. They had all his info, middle name and everything, and the longer we read, the more we thought this might actually be legit.

"See anything? Anything weird?" he kept asking.

"Weird like what? Like what's weird?" I asked again.

"Look for the part where they ask me for money. It's always about money. That's the scam."

As Rich and I flipped through the pages, back and front, Mom sat there saying nothing, humouring us, as we planned how we'd spend the million.

"We need a lawyer," my dad told us. "Your first move is to get a lawyer to protect it. To invest it." I'm not sure my dad had ever met a lawyer, but his head and his heart were in the right place. "We get a big place out in the country, we build it and live off the interest."

I don't ever remember my dad having a ton of wild dreams, but that's the one I do remember. Pops always wanted a place in the country, with no neighbours. Something he could build from the ground up, with his own hands and his boys by his side. He'd often show up at home after work with these glossy brochures full of artist renderings of log cottages and cabins and floorplans you could buy and build yourself. I'd usually grab a few from the stack and head right to my room and construct a scaled-down version of my favourites with Lego. I'd pick out where to put my bedroom and the perfect spot for the TV in the family room, then run the whole thing downstairs and set it on the floor to see what he thought. "Looks perfect," he always said.

I could see all that, *the dream*, playing out in his eyes as he flipped through that ten-million-dollar package. It was the same look he had every Saturday morning when he checked his lotto numbers. It lasted a few seconds, then it was gone, but he was never too broken up about never winning.

"There it is!" he shouted, slamming the stack of papers on the good table. "They want me to buy magazines. Right there! Look! If we want to *qualify* for the next round, to *maybe* win the millions, we have to subscribe to their shitty magazines." That look faded from his eyes again and we all walked out of the dining room, shutting the lights off behind us.

Dad hated the idea of being taken advantage of—I *know* I got that from him—and he was always on the lookout. "If someone's asking for your money, your vote, or your faith, they're probably lying to you," he told me. He also used to say the same thing about military service, and his credit card number. My dad protected his Visa number like it was it was the launch code for nukes. Cash was his thing, and anytime anyone ever asked for his credit card number, he'd lose his shit and they'd walk the gauntlet.

In the mid-1980s, when I was in junior high, we were a Beta family living in a VHS world. At first, things were pretty even, but after a few years they just stopped releasing the good movies on Beta. Rich and I would beg Dad to take us to the video store to rent a VHS player so we could load up on all the movies we weren't able to rent on Beta. You know, to really make a weekend of it. Our video store was a two-minute drive away, and Rich and I had already called ahead to reserve the machine and a half-dozen movies we were dying to watch. We were stoked! As the clerk, who was *maybe* seventeen, loaded up all the gear on the counter, my brother and I double-checked all the movies were in the right cases.

"All right, Mr. Weston, you're all set," the clerk chirped as my dad leaned on the counter checking out all the cables and power cords. "That'll be fifty-six-fifty for the two-day rental of the machine, twenty-four dollars for the movies."

As my dad pulled out his wallet and started flipping lose bills all hell broke loose.

"We *juuuuust* need a credit card for the deposit of the machine."

Oh. Fuck, I thought.

"What do you need my credit card number for? I'm paying cash." My old man stared a hole through this poor clerk's head.

"Well, it's just a security deposit in case anything happens to the machine. It's a standard deposit. We don't charge your card unless anything happens." This kid was nervous as hell, and Rich and I were mortified.

"What does that mean? 'In case anything happens'?"

"Well, like we won't charge you unless it breaks or if you . . ."

"No. Keep your machine. We're out of here. I know how this works. You send me home with a lemon, I plug it in and it doesn't work, then I buy *you* a new VCR. No thanks."

Here we go again.

"Come on, boys. This is a scam. I'm not getting dinged for six hundred bucks."

My dad didn't get us that VHS machine that day because he thought it was a scam, but he did eventually get us one by *running* a scam.

My mom's brother worked in insurance and had pulled this particular scam a few times in the past. It wasn't illegal, and nobody got hurt, but a scam it was. My uncle called my Pops one afternoon and told him the plan. He laid it all out, and said he needed my brother and me too.

"It's a fire damage claim. Smoke damage. No big deal," he explained to my dad over the phone. This whole thing wasn't so much a scam as it was a scam-on-a-scam, and it was brilliant. My uncle got a call to go check out the damage on a client's house fire to be able to put through the paperwork and get the family, the ones who had the fire, all the money they need to buy all new shit. When my uncle arrived, he walked into a normal-looking house, with normal-looking things. None of it was burned. "Smoke damage," he said again. "How do you prove that? It was a small kitchen fire that was put out right away, but the family is claiming smoke damage on all their old things so they can buy all *new* things. Nothing is ruined, everything is like new, and it all has to go."

"What do you need?" Dad asked.

"I need a moving company," he answered. "If someone puts through a claim like this, we have to make sure they're not going to keep all their old stuff and just double-dip when we send the cheque, so I have to hire a company—you, Rich, and Roz—and we load everything up and get rid of it."

So that's what we did. My old man rented a U-Haul and drove my brother and me two hours away to unpack a stranger's house.

The whole time we were there we had to pretend to not know my uncle. My dad named his made-up company Ralph & Sons Hauling and told us to "use that if anyone asks." I was maybe twelve but looked big enough to pull off my part in all of this. This was one of the best days of my life.

Instead of dropping everything off at the dump like we were *supposed* to, we drove that truck back to our place, unloaded everything onto our front lawn, and my dad and my uncle divided it all up between them. My uncle took most of the furniture, my mom got a fur coat, my Pops grabbed up all the speakers and stereo gear, and my brother and I went straight for the VHS machines. *Three* VHS machines! We grabbed them off the lawn, stacked them on top of each other, and Rich ran them into the house while I followed behind with that glorious family's home movies in two huge open-topped boxes. The collection turned out to be 40 percent vacation and Christmas videos, and 60 percent porno.

Rich couldn't rip our old Beta machine out fast enough. He yanked it and it came out of its little compartment in the TV unit with all its cords and cables still attached. Ninety seconds later, we were officially a *multiple* VHS family.

"You guys get what you needed?" Pops shouted from the top of the stairs as Rich and I tried to figure out what the hell to do with it all. What do you even do with *that* much porn?

"Yeah, Pops. We're good!" we yelled back up. "Everything works. Machines are great."

Anybody can be a father, but taking your two sons along for the ride of their lives to pull off an insurance scam for free VCRs is what makes you a *dad*. That much I know.

My dad's dreams weren't huge, and besides winning the lotto, most of them were totally attainable. I don't know if I ever saw him set a goal that he didn't crush. But that house in the country, though. The one with no neighbours, that he built with his boys. The solitude, privacy, and freedom. The kind of house you could die in and not mind one bit. He never got to build the place of his dreams. So *I* did.

I've had my foot to the floor for most of my adult life. For my first eighteen years, all I wanted to do was get away. Escape that small town, leave it all behind, and never look back. I was drawn to the action, opportunity, and anonymity of cities, so I fought like hell and clawed my way there. But I was always so preoccupied with escaping, I never bothered to take a look around and truly appreciate what that small town gave me. I made my life, career, and my home in a city of nearly six million people. I set that goal, and I crushed it. But now I needed a change. Roxy was getting older, I'd reduced my time with *ET Canada* down to four days a week with Fridays off, and I found myself being pulled back. I needed space and stars and sunsets, a place to recharge, slow down, and detach from the hive. A place where I could let go and disappear.

When Roxy was five, Katherine and I spent ten weekends driving out to the country to look at cottages and vacant land. After a few failed offers, and seeing a ton of spots that wouldn't work, we found the perfect place: a small two-bedroom up on a big hill, overlooking a lake. It was a little over an acre surrounded by hundred-acre farms, and no matter how hard you try, you can't see another house from anywhere on the property.

The agent described the place as a teardown. It was like walking onto a movie set—shag rug, wood panelling, floral wallpaper, a mint-green toilet that matched the mint-green sink and bathtub, and windows that were so old and busted you could slide a whole hand through the gaps. It looked like someone locked the door in 1976, walked away, and never came back. The whole thing was for sale for a little more than the cost of a parking space back in the city.

As the agent walked us through, trying her hardest to make the best of it, I looked out one of those old windows and saw Roxy rolling down the lawn. I don't know if she had ever played on grass before—not like that, anyway.

"The roof is garbage, there's no furnace, and that big circle on the living room floor is where the fireplace used to be. But they pulled it out because it wasn't vented properly—that's why everything in here smells like smoke."

Smoke damage, I thought.

"We'll take it," I told her.

We spent that first summer rolling through the grass and running through the sprinkler fully clothed. During every rainstorm Katherine and Roxy played ukuleles on the back deck, singing "The Show" by Lenka, while I spent two hours boiling twenty pots of water just to fill the tub enough for them to have a bath when they finally made it in.

This place wasn't perfect, but it *was* a home. It just needed love. It needed Katherine's heart and a kid who danced under rainbows in the backyard. One who stayed up way past her bedtime to catch fireflies in her pyjamas. We didn't tear it down, like the agent advised. We fixed it.

Because that's what we do.

My dad never played the lotto because he wanted to roll around in stacks of cash or buy flashy things to show off. It was emotional for him. He just wanted to know how it would *feel* to not have to worry about money for once in his life. Same thing with the dream house. It was never about the *house*; it was about *us*. It was about living wild and making our own rules. Slowing down and coming together. It was about getting a taste of freedom. Even if it was only on the weekends.

Here's the surprising thing: kids don't actually *need* much, and the thing they need the most costs the least. They just want to hang. They want to kick it with you, do fun shit and have you say yes more than you say no. They want that little taste of freedom. They want you to boost them up over a fence with a clear No Trespassing sign because that tree on the other side looks too good to *not* climb. When they're *way* too young but tell you they want to pitch a tent and sleep out alone in the backyard for the first time, they don't need a lecture, they just need you to leave the porch light on and the back door unlocked. They want you to play where *they* play, in a homemade fort, under the back deck or lying on the living room rug with boxes of Lego. They want you to break character every now and then, follow *their* lead, and just do stupid shit. Those moments become *their* stories, and just like my dad, I'm the King of Stupid Shit.

Anybody can be a father, but running fully clothed through a sprinkler on a dare from your kid when you're already twenty minutes late for work is what makes you a *dad*.

THE
HARD WAY
HOME

I've been more than a few different versions of myself, some by choice and a couple out of necessity, and I'll probably be a couple more before my time here is done. When I sat down to write this book and spent a year working through every word, paragraph, and page while Roxy worked *her* way through grade five, I knew I was going to wind up right here. The part where I have to come through on everything I promised. This is the part that scared me the most then and still does now.

I think the point to all of this is to just always believe there's something bigger out there—not necessarily better, just bigger. A bigger version of *you*. One that laughs louder and loves harder. One that's a little more patient and a whole lot smarter. Maybe even one that doesn't hurt all the time. Much like my dad I'm a dreamer, and that's just what us dreamers do. Always dreaming of something bigger.

I live my life with my feet on the ground and my head in the clouds, and I certainly don't have all the answers, but that's only because I haven't asked all my questions yet. And I question everything. *Question everything.*

How does this end? Where are you going? If you feel lost, left behind, or stuck today, what the hell makes you think you're going to feel any differently tomorrow? Or next year? Are you even the one writing your own story? If you jump, where would you land?

You should never be afraid to reinvent yourself. I'm talking a drastic and noticeable reinvention. Never think it's too late to rip it up and start again—to become the exact person you think about the most, even if you've convinced yourself it was never going to happen for you. Maybe because you don't think you deserve it. But it's never too late to fix the things that feel broken because, believe it or not, the fixing isn't the hard part. With the right tools we can dismantle just about anything, even ourselves, spread the parts all over the basement floor and do our best to figure out what went wrong or where the problem is. Identify the problem and fix the problem. That's actually easier than you think. It's the putting it all back together again that we're afraid of. That's why we throw things away, and why we're so quick to label ourselves damaged, ruined, used, and broken. But when you're lying there, in a thousand pieces, how do you even begin to put it all back together? Where do you even start? That's why we so easily give up on ourselves. Because we don't know how to rebuild.

We are not our mistakes. We are not our past, our scars, or our secrets. We are not our guilt.

It's easy to get stuck, or even paralyzed, in a specific traumatic moment or a whole series of them. Believe me, I know all too well what that feels like. I know what it's like when the only way to feel *anything* is to hurt yourself. I spent some of my best years protecting myself from failure, from vulnerability, and from ever feeling like I was too much. I was in a loop. I'd convinced myself, *If this is as good as it's ever going to get, then so be it.* I never wanted to be somebody's problem or their project. I was *fine*. But sometimes we protect ourselves so well that we don't give anyone else the opportunity to help, or even to care.

I was protecting myself from the things I actually needed the most. Purpose, love, and a shot at being a great dad.

So, how did I get out? Well, there's an easy way and a hard way. And much like my dad, I've never been afraid of the hard way. He would have been the first to tell you the hardest part about war isn't the fight—ask anyone who's served—it's the coming home. That's when you realize what you left behind. The parts you're never going to get back. I could have taken a lifetime to go *around* everything that was broken, all the pieces, and maybe I would have got where I am today eventually. But that's the easy way.

The hard way out is to go *through* it. That's how you rebuild.

You don't leave it behind. You take it with you, and you stop apologizing for it. You learn to breathe and cry and love. You stop blaming yourself and you fight for your goddamn life.

Do we deserve to be happy? Sure. But not *all the time*. Being in a constant state of happiness is not only unrealistic, it's slightly weird. Instead, find and do the things that make you happy. Nobody can do that for us.

Katherine taught me this. Katherine has built her life around those small moments of joy, and she's never once let common sense stand in her way. She'll drive fifty-five minutes with a single cupcake in the passenger seat because a friend said they had a shit day. She'll drop it off on their doorstep, ring the bell, and leave without sticking around for any sort of thanks. I've never met anyone who recognizes, better than Katherine does, when someone else needs a win. She's the brightest part of most people's day. That's *her* joy. That's her happiness.

Katherine is a great photographer, but what she's *brilliant* at is getting people to see beauty in themselves they didn't know existed. Most people don't like being faced with themselves, but Katherine is all about round edges and soft landings, creating a space where people can play, and celebrate their achievements, and be proud. She fights like hell with clients, models, and celebrities to *not* remove every wrinkle and scar, the imperfections and flaws we all obsess over. That's too easy. Katherine never sees an ad campaign or magazine cover when she's taking someone's picture. She sees a life. But as talented as she is, it's never the final product people remember. It's never about the shot. It's how she made them feel during the process. She was the best part of their day.

Katherine has turned me into a closet optimist. Seeing the results, everything that comes back to her, from living a life of kindness and compassion, is both inspiring and infectious. She puts it out there, and it always comes back. I still wouldn't exactly say I'm *nice*, but I am kind, and I lean into that as often as I can and always try to recognize the people who are out there just trying to do their best. Because that's most of us.

If you ask me what I do for a living, on the radio show, my answer is very simple and will always be the same: my job is to make someone else's day a little bit easier or a little better. That's it. That's what we do. We don't have to be all the things, and we certainly can't be everything to everyone. But when you're stuck in your car during your commute, which is probably the worst part of your day, my job is to try to make it a little bit easier or a little better.

On the show, we do foolish things and never mind looking like fools doing them, and we take the most ridiculous things very seriously, because that's the *only* way I know how. We play. But we've also shared the stories of our lives, our loves, and immeasurable and unspeakable heartbreak. We're upfront about our insecurities, tragedies, and failures. We've all cried. We've cried with the audience and with each other.

I said in the very beginning of this book that when you do morning radio right, when you're truly successful, you don't become famous, you become family. And that's exactly how I feel at the end of every show. Like family.

Every day I try to learn something new, then I figure out how I'm going to be better tomorrow without relying on the things that made me great today. Every day is an evolution. Every day is part of the rebuild. On a normal day I spend almost an hour and a half sitting in traffic going between my two jobs and home. I take Ubers everywhere, and spend over six hundred a month just getting myself to and from work. But having that time is worth way more to me than what I pay for it. I'd pay double.

That's ninety minutes a day, every day, that I dedicate to learning new shit. That's *my* joy. My YouTube and Google history is filled with everything from dealing with childhood trauma, to how to make the perfect béchamel, to changing the air filter on a two-stroke engine, to how to braid hair. I learn new shit every single day.

But I'm not just a viewer. I'm not passive about it. I learn it, then I do it. I collect new skills like summer camp merit badges sewn onto an ugly vest. Everything has purpose. I was numb for a lot of years, looking for freedom from being overwhelmed by everything while trying to manufacture a life I didn't even know I wanted. I was separated from the world *and* from my body, and I desperately needed to reconnect with both.

When people who need help and are feeling that same way call into the radio show, or send me messages on social media, I always ask the same question. These are people who are usually unhappy with their lives, relationships, their jobs, or the choices they've made. They're stuck. I always ask: *What are you good at?*

It's a simple question, but I'm amazed how hard it is for people to answer. There are rules to that question, too. You can't say your job, being a parent, working out, or Instagram. Being a good friend doesn't count, and you can't say making money or having sex, either. *What are you good at?* You need to get good at something, and you need to do something you're good at every single day. Without question. Something personal that brings you joy. Something analogue and something real.

You need to do something where your hands and your head are both working together. Video games don't count. Neither does doing your own makeup. You need to try something really damn hard and give yourself enough time to fail a few times before you see results. Build something, write something, or cook something, but keep it personal. This isn't a side hustle, and it'll never make you money. Try new shit and learn hard things. If vinyl can make a comeback, why can't pottery? Pottery is punishingly hard, and you don't have to look further than Seth Rogan's Instagram to understand the pride and pure fucking joy of making your first bowl or bong or whatever those weird and wonderful things are that he creates. Do something that makes you proud of *you*. It all starts by sitting down, that first time, and not being afraid to get a little dirty.

When you find yourself stuck in the middle of normal—jump.

Aside from every beautiful and bonkers minute when I'm with my girls, I'm my happiest and at my best when I'm in my kitchen, or out in the lawn. In a lot of ways, cooking helped save me. I cook 99 percent of the meals that my family eats and I have no problem whipping up three separate dinners, after having just worked thirteen hours, if we all want something a little different that night.

Just like when I was a kid, dinner with my family is always the best part of my day. Laughing around the table and listening to Roxy's kid stories is what makes sleeping five hours a night and getting up at 3:56 a.m. all worth it.

Every day you see me I'm the most tired I've ever been, but that right there is the reward.

When it comes to being a dad, I'm what you might call a Modern Classic. If they created a robot version of me in 1984, I'd be the D.A.D. 2000: The Future of Dadding. I can sew, cut hair, cook the perfect steak. And I cry. I also own five lawn mowers and have spent years trying to turn our backyard into that perfect, and perfectly striped, golf-course-quality lawn. A place for me to escape and a soft landing for Roxy's cartwheels.

I'm the dad who stands on the back deck, after a real good mow, with his hands on his hips and just watches that shit thrive. Other dads come over and immediately flip their shoes off and run their toes through my rye grass cut precisely to three-quarters of an inch. I'm every single retro cliché *and* modern meme out there, but I built that lawn. I grew it from nothing and I'm proud of it. It's my mediation and my church. A way for me to reconnect with the world and my body. It gets me out of the house and out of my head.

Lawn work isn't difficult work, but it is *hard* work, and you can't buy the perfect lawn. You have to nurture it with care and sweat and without fear. I've accidentally killed my entire lawn more than once, but failure is all part of the process. Being afraid to fail is just no fun.

I'm not perfect, but like most things my dad managed to fix, I don't have to be. I don't want to be. Perfect is boring.

Now, I'm *still* insecure and *do* still make a shit ton of mistakes. But on those days, the days when I feel like something has been taken away, when I've lost or have been beaten—when I've failed—I no longer run to the dark. I don't hide. When I lose something, I *add* something. Creativity, or *playing* or whatever you want to call it, that's what I do. It's about getting an idea out of my head and into the world. Turning ideas into life. I no longer chase opportunity. I chase creativity. We spend so much of our lives swiping past, sharing, double-tapping, and being in awe of *other* people's creativity that we've forgotten how to be creative ourselves. When we see something we love, something perfectly curated, flawless, and filtered, it doesn't inspire us. Instead, we want to know exactly how *they* did it so we can do it too. We're copycats and consumers and we've forgotten how to be artists.

We are *all* artists. That's how it started for every single one of us. We all have the ability to create, and the reason we don't is because we're afraid of criticism. We're afraid to do foolish things because we'll look like a fool doing them. We're afraid of being judged, or we feel we just don't have it in us.

It's much harder to put something beautiful out into the world than it is to sit and point out all the things that are ugly—that's easy, and too often we make decisions based on what's easy and not what's best. We walk around problems rather than walk through them. Force yourself to walk through them. Get creative, stop filtering the truth, and take the hard way. You're built for this.

You are the architect, artist, and author of your own life, so get up every single day and work on your goddamn masterpiece.

ONE LUCKY DAY

I usually tell stories by starting at the end. I was told this doesn't work in book form, so for the most part in this, my first book, I've tried to switch it up a bit and play by the rules. I hate rules. I always like to start with the end, or the lesson learned, the huge mistake, or the heartbreaking victory, then work my way back and tell you how I got there. That's always the most interesting part to me, the *how I got there*. I'll never save anything, hold back, or leave you hanging. I tell you exactly how the story ends as soon as I start telling it.

I start with the end of stories because that's always the hardest part to tell.

In the front of this book, right there in the dedication, is a note directing Katherine to come here first. Right to this page. This is where I want her to start. At the end.

—

The day I signed the deal to publish this book, we knew the offers were coming that morning, but I was still more nervous than I'd ever been. Even after all the contracts I've negotiated in the past, and the ones I've left on the table just because they didn't feel right, I was shitting my pants. I walked into the house to get set up, and Katherine had a cocktail and a gold party hat waiting for me on the coffee table—at 10:30 a.m. She'd already cleared her entire day. I reached for the drink, and before the glass hit my lips, she told me to put the hat on.

"Can I not?" I asked her. It felt silly and I was out-of-my-mind stressed and hadn't prepared for this. A show. "Can I just sit? Take the call?"

"No way. Not a chance," she told me. "We celebrate things in this family. This is your life, and we're going to celebrate it."

Faith is a gift that I've not yet received. That's no secret, but it's nothing I'm ashamed of. I'm not at all a spiritual or religious person, and I've never prayed to anything or anyone in any sort of serious way. Not even at my worst, my most lost, or my lowest low. I've never asked for *that* kind of help. I don't believe in fate. But I do believe in luck, and I believe that there's only so much of it to go around. I believe when I'm having a lucky day, someone else probably isn't. Then, of course, your luck changes. It *always* changes, and when it does, you don't fight to keep it, or try to take more than you can use. You let it go, and hope it makes its way to someone who needs it a little more than you do that day.

I've had more than my share of bad luck, but I've always tried to do my best, be a good person, even when things aren't going my way. The luckiest night of my life was the night I met Katherine. I didn't need any more lucky days after that one, and I'd happily hand them all over to just about anyone so they could feel what I feel when I'm with her. Even if it is just for *one lucky day*.

The best part about writing a book, telling your story, is *you* get to be the hero. But I'm not the hero of my story, Katherine is. I always thought that the goal was to find somebody who completes you, but that's just not the case. The goal, the mission, and that beautifully crushing adventurous quest is to find someone who's all the things you're not. I wish I was a person who led with compassion. I wish I was more open, less cynical, and only ever saw the best in people, but I'm not. It's still hard for me, but that's okay. Katherine is all those things. She's all the things I'm not, and everything I hope to be.

When you choose to spend your life with someone, you're also choosing the person who'll tell your story when you're gone, and if you're lucky, you find someone who only sees the best in you. Katherine is the reason for all of this. There are simply no words without her. There's no story worth telling.

Neither of us has ever felt that there was a step we were missing out on, and we've never talked about marriage. Not in any sort of serious way, anyway. We were an instant family, and with rain on our faces and luck on our side we strapped in and rode to the top of that mountain and never looked back. With our relationship, and the love and life we share, there's simply no way to level up, because where do you go from here? Anything *more* would feel greedy.

I've never felt there was anything better out there for us, and we certainly never felt pressure to prove our love to anyone else except each other. And I try to do that with every breath I have, and will continue to do so until my last.

—

If you're asking yourself right now if all this, this *entire* book, life, and story, was my way of finding the words to ask Katherine to marry me . . .

Well, you might not be right, but you sure as fuck aren't wrong.

I want to start with the end and write that next part together.

A book isn't a book and a life isn't a life until you're done. Everything up to that point is still a work in progress.

ACKNOWLEDGEMENTS

To my kid, Roxy. I've never wanted anything more than I wanted you. You're the proof that dreams come true. You get your dad back now.

My brother, Richard. When dad died, I stepped back but you stepped up. You filled his space. I love you and I appreciate you. I can't thank you enough.

To my mom, Diana Vivian Lee, who I didn't tell I was even doing this until *after* we went to print. I'm sorry I disappeared for two years, but I hope it was worth it. There's a lot of you in here, a story I know you were hoping to one day be able to tell yourself. I tried my best to get it all right. Thank you for raising us in a house full of love. And to your husband, Kevin Lee, I love the way you look at my mom. Please don't ever stop.

Carl Swanston. A great dad, and a great friend. You get your own chapter in the *next* one. Promise.

Rick Broadhead. My agent, my Ambassador of Quan. Thank you for the trust and hustle. You're the reason this happened.

Alice Kuipers. Thank you for being a brilliant writer, partner, editor, and vault. Thank you for pulling this story out of me, listening to me cry, and never judging. I cried a shit ton. You were the first person to ever call me an *author* and never once made me feel like I didn't belong in "book world."

To the authors. All of you. To every single person who has sat down to do just this. The self-published, the big-contract writers, and the dreamers who are still hammering out their story one word, scar, and secret at a time. This is for you. Every book you've ever read, even the bad ones, has been somebody else's entire world for at *least* a couple years. Often more, and sometimes a lifetime. And for nothing. When you're done with this one, do me a favour and leave it on the seat of a bus or the counter of a gas station bathroom. People love finding cool shit, and books are expensive. I leaned on a few authors at the very beginning of all this—John Meyer, Jonathan Scott, Lainey Lui, Scott McGillivray, and Ziya Tong. Thank you for answering my rookie questions and reminding me just how fucking hard this was going to be.

Thank you to anyone who has ever shared even a minute of your time with me on the radio, TV, podcast or wherever. There's no fair way to single out just *one* person, but fuck it, I will anyway. Andrew Hill. Your strength, courage, laugh, and big-ass smile deserve to be recognized. The day we met I realized why I do this, and who I do it for. I do it for you. You're my motivation on the days when I have nothing left.

Amy Black, Tim Rostron, and everyone at Doubleday Canada. When shit goes sideways, these are the people you want on your team. Thank you for the freedom and for believing in me.

Dad. We're all doing great and love each other lots. Farts are still funny and I miss you every day.

ROZ WESTON

© Katherine Holland Photography

ROZ WESTON is a multi-platform entertainer and storyteller. In 2013, *Hello!* magazine named him one of the 50 Most Beautiful Canadians. He has *not* made the list since. Growing up in a small town with above-average confidence but low self-esteem, Roz knew he wanted an audience, but didn't want to be noticed. Now, as host of *The Roz & Mocha Show*, and with his seventeen-year run on *Entertainment Tonight Canada* and *ET Canada Live*, Roz has entertained millions without ever having to see a single one of them. A college dropout, Roz is a Canadian Music and Broadcast Industry Awards winner, New York Festival of Radio winner, and Canadian Screen Awards winner. He is a former factory-line worker, Howard Stern intern, and late-night TV talk host. Roz lives in Toronto with his partner, their kid, and four cats. He still misses his dad.